ISBN 0-8373-5621-0
21 REGENTS EXTERNAL DEGREE SERIES

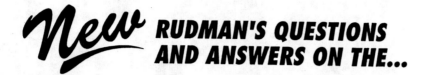

RUDMAN'S QUESTIONS
AND ANSWERS ON THE...

REDP

Regents External Degree Program
Subject Test In...

Differences in Nursing Care: Area A

Test Preparation Study Guide

Questions and Answers

NATIONAL LEARNING CORPORATION

Copyright © 1999 by

National Learning Corporation

212 Michael Drive, Syosset, New York 11791
(516) 921-8888

PRINTED IN THE UNITED STATES OF AMERICA

PASSBOOK SERIES®

THE *PASSBOOK SERIES®* has been created to prepare applicants and candidates for the ultimate academic battlefield—the examination room.

At some time in our lives, each and every one of us may be required to take an examination—for validation, matriculation, admission, qualification, registration, certification, or licensure.

Based on the assumption that every applicant or candidate has met the basic formal educational standards, has taken the required number of courses, and read the necessary texts, the *PASSBOOK SERIES®* furnishes the one special preparation which may assure passing with confidence, instead of failing with insecurity. Examination questions—together with answers—are furnished as the basic vehicle for study so that the mysteries of the examination and its compounding difficulties may be eliminated or diminished by a sure method.

This book is meant to help you pass your examination provided that you qualify and are serious in your objective.

The entire field is reviewed through the huge store of content information which is succinctly presented through a provocative and challenging approach—the question-and-answer method.

A climate of success is established by furnishing the correct answers at the end of each test.

You soon learn to recognize types of questions, forms of questions, and patterns of questioning. You may even begin to anticipate expected outcomes.

You perceive that many questions are repeated or adapted so that you gain acute insights, which may enable you to score many sure points.

You learn how to confront new questions, or types of questions, and to attack them confidently and work out the correct answers.

You note objectives and emphases, and recognize pitfalls and dangers, so that you may make positive educational adjustments.

Moreover, you are kept fully informed in relation to new concepts, methods, practices, and directions in the field.

You discover that you are actually taking the examination all the time: you are preparing for the examination by "taking" an examination, not by reading extraneous and/or supererogatory textbooks.

In short, this PASSBOOK®, used directedly, should be an important factor in helping you to pass your test.

REGENTS EXTERNAL DEGREE PROGRAM (REDP)

CONTENTS

REGENTS EXTERNAL DEGREE PROGRAM (REDP)

NEW YORK STATE COLLEGE PROFICIENCY EXAMINATIONS AND REGENTS EXTERNAL DEGREES

These may be important to you if you

1. want to get a college degree, but never had a chance to go to college. Maybe you still can't study on campus because you live too far away, have family responsibilities, or hold a full-time job.

2. want to complete a college degree you started years ago, but are uncertain about going back to college now; you would like to work at your own pace and make the most of what you have already learned.

3. have a bachelor's degree, yet need to fulfill additional requirements for teacher certification.

4. are in the military service, have taken military education courses and studied at several colleges, but have never lived in one place long enough to finish a degree.

5. have acquired a lot of college-level learning from work or other experience, and are looking for a way to earn college credit for what you know.

6. are already a college student and would like to earn some credits through independent study so you can speed up your schedule for completing college.

7. have not finished high school but think that you have the ability and motivation to work for a college degree.

These are only some of the kinds of people the Regents External Degree and College Proficiency Examination programs and the new Regents Credit Bank can help. In the following pages you will find many more reasons why one or more of these programs may be the answer to your educational needs: reasons such as wide acceptance of these credits by colleges and universities, low costs, no residence or age requirements, and having a single convenient record of your academic accomplishments.

THE REGENTS EXTERNAL DEGREE: WHAT IS IT?

REGENTS

The Regents of The University of the State of New York have broad responsibility for all educational institutions in New York State, including public and private elementary and secondary schools, colleges and universities, museums and libraries. The President of this unique University is also the Commissioner of Education for the State of New York. The Regents govern The University of the State of New York, determining educational policies, incorporating and accrediting colleges and universities, certifying teachers, and awarding college degrees.

EXTERNAL

Until recently, higher education has bypassed the many people who want a degree but cannot go -- or have not gone -- to college. Many programs are now becoming available to meet their needs' but the Regents External Degree is unique in that it is truly "external."

It has no campus, and no requirement that you do any part of your study in a particular location. It does no teaching; instead, it accepts credits from all accredited institutions of higher education. It even offers you the chance to earn a college degree without attending college, if you so desire. **The Regents External Degree is based on the idea that what you know is more important than how you learned it.**

DEGREE

Since 1972, thousands of people have earned Regents External Degrees and well over 50,000 others are working toward that goal. The Regents now offer the following External Degrees:

Associate in Arts
Associate in Science
Bachelor of Science in Business Administration
Associate in Applied Science in Nursing
Bachelor of Arts
Bachelor of Science

The requirements for each degree and the ways in which they can be met are determined by faculty and administrators from New York State colleges and universities, who serve in their capacity as faculty members of The University of the State of New York.

Some special examinations, called the Regents External Degree Examinations, have been developed in the fields of business and nursing primarily to meet the requirements for Regents External Degrees.

In addition to its accreditation by the Board of Regents, the Regents External Degree has been accepted as a candidate for accreditation by the Middle States Association of Colleges and Secondary Schools Commission on Higher Education.

NEW YORK STATE COLLEGE PROFICIENCY EXAMINATIONS: WHAT ARE THEY?

College Proficiency Examinations offer you a chance to earn college credit, an external degree, or certain other advantages without taking college classes. This program was begun in 1963 to meet the needs of people who have acquired college-level knowledge, but in unconventional ways such as through job experience, courses taken in the military, or independent reading.

There are now more than 20 examinations in college subjects in the arts and sciences, education, health, and nursing. Some 25 other tests, Regents External Degree Examinations, are available in nursing, business, and foreign languages. All of these tests are developed and graded by faculty from colleges and universities in New York State, and grading standards are set by giving the tests to groups of college students.

Some of the ways that College Proficiency Examinations can be used are: to earn college credit, to satisfy New York State teacher certification and New York City teacher licensure requirements, to meet requirements for a Regents External Degree, and to qualify for promotions, salary increases, or new jobs.

Most colleges and universities in New York State and a growing number in other states accept credits earned through College Proficiency and Regents External Degree Examinations. Over 500,000 credits have been granted for these examinations since 1963.

THE REGENTS EXTERNAL DEGREES
SOME THINGS YOU SHOULD KNOW ABOUT ALL EXTERNAL DEGREES

The Regents External Degree Program recognizes that people who want to earn college degrees have many different educational and career goals, and varying family and job responsibilities. The Regents External Degree offers a way to earn a college degree with a maximum amount of flexibility to serve the needs of many different people.

For people who have already taken a considerable number of college courses in the past but have never completed a degree, the External Degree offers a chance to combine college credits already earned, and knowledge acquired in other ways -- such as on the job, through noncredit courses or volunteer work -- to earn a degree.

For others, who may not have done college work before, the External Degree offers a chance to earn recognition on the basis of their knowledge gained from experience and independent learning. The External Degree also means having a number of different options available for earning credit that range from attending classroom courses to studying completely on your own.

Anyone can enroll in the Regents External Degree program; there are no prerequisities (such as a high school diploma), and it does not matter how old you are or where you live, in New York or around the world. You may study and meet requirements at your own pace.

In addition to the External Degree program staff who are available to answer your questions, a network of volunteer advisors has been set up throughout New York State to help people who are interested in taking College Proficiency Examinations or earning a Regents External Degree.

THE ASSOCIATE IN ARTS DEGREE

This degree is comparable in its content to a liberal arts degree offered at a two-year or community college. It is made up of 60 hours of course work or its equivalent, with at least 48 hours in the liberal arts, including a distribution of credits among these three areas: humanities; social sciences natural sciences and mathematics.

The remaining credits are electives which can be earned in any college-level subjects.

You can meet the requirements for this degree by any combination of college courses, proficiency examinations, military education courses and "special assessment." (These methods are explain in more detail in the section called "Earning Credit Toward a Degree.") The requirements can be met in any order that you wish, and you can take as long as you want to finish the degree.

THE ASSOCIATE IN SCIENCE DEGREE

This degree is very similar in content to the Associate in Arts Degree, except that one half of the 60 credit-hour total must be earned in the liberal arts, while the remaining half may be in any elective areas of college-level study. The 30 credits in the liberal arts must include a distribution among the three broad areas of the humanities, the social sciences, and the natural sciences or mathematics.

As with the other Regents External Degrees the requirements for the Associate in Science Degree can be met in a variety of ways, including proficiency examinations, college courses, military courses, special assessment, or any combination of these.

The Associate in Science Degree is designed especially for those whose interests or educational backgrounds lie in technical, professional, or occupational subjects. If you wish to develop a concentration in a specific subject area, especially one that is career-related, you can do so by planning your selection of courses within the flexible structure of the A.S. degree. The degree requirements themselves specify no "major."

There is no time limit for completing the Associate in Science Degree, and no particular order in which you must meet the requirements.

THE ASSOCIATE IN APPLIED SCIENCE IN NURSING DEGREE

This degree assesses the content comparable to that of a typical two-year nursing degree program offered by a college. Most people working toward the A.A.S. degree in nursing probably already have a background in some form of health care service, as an LPN, LVN, or RN (graduate of a hospital diploma school), a corpsman, a nursing attendant, etc.; however, this kind of background is not absolutely necessary.

In order to earn the nursing degree, you must fulfill the requirements in two components: general education and nursing.

General Education.

This requires at least 10 one-semester courses or their equivalent, including a distribution of credits among the following areas: humanities; social sciences; natural sciences and mathematics.

The rest of the credits may be in any subject except nursing.

You can also meet this requirement by passing five proficiency examinations in appropriate subjects, or by presenting appropriate military education courses.

Nursing

The knowledge which is required in this component is divided into four areas: nursing health care, commonalities in nursing care, differences in nursing care, and occupational strategy. This knowledge is comparable to what a student in a collegiate associate degree program in nursing learns, although it may be organized differently.

Seven written examinations covering these four areas have been developed. Once you have successfully completed these written tests, you must also pass a clinical performance examination in a hospital setting. This examination tests technical skills in planning, implementing, and evaluating nursing care for several different patients.

Certain combinations of college courses can be substituted for the examinations in the four nursing areas, but <u>not</u> the clinical performance test. The limitations on the use of nursing courses are:

1. They must cover material comparable to the content of the entire examination.

2. You must have earned at least a "C" grade.

3. You must have taken them within the 10-year period prior to enrolling in the External Degree, at an accredited college offering a degree in nursing.

A graduate of the External Degree program in nursing has met the educational eligibility requirement for the New York State registered nurse licensure examination. RED nursing graduates may also take the licensure examination or practice by endorsement in Vermont; other states are now considering taking similar action.

BACHELOR OF SCIENCE IN BUSINESS ADMINISTRATION DEGREE

The B.S.B.A. degree is the equivalent of a four-year degree in Business Administration on a college campus. You can choose to concentrate in accounting, finance, management of human resources, marketing or operations management. There are two parts to the degree which every candidate must complete: the general education component and the business component.

General Education

You must complete at least ten one-semester courses or their equivalent, including a distribution among the following areas: humanities; social sciences.

The rest of the ten courses can be in any liberal arts subjects that are not business related.

You can also meet this requirement by passing five proficiency examinations or by military education courses in appropriate subjects.

Business

In the business or "major" component there is a series of special Regents External Degree Examinations in each of five areas of business skills: accounting, finance, management of human resources, marketing, and operations management. You will be expected to pass three examinations on graduated levels of difficulty in the area in which you choose to concentrate. In addition, you must take some examinations in each of the other four areas. If you earn a passing grade on one of the upper level examinations in any of the subject areas, you automatically waive the lower level examination(s in that area.

College courses which cover the same content can be used in place of most of the business examinations. These business courses must have been taken within the ten years prior to the date when you enroll in the Externa Degree, and you must have earned at least a "C" grade in them.

You do not have to meet the requirements for these two components in any particular order.

Graduates of the B.S.B.A. program with a concentration in accounting are eligible to sit for the Certified Public Accountant Examination in New York State.

THE BACHELOR OF ARTS DEGREE

The newest External Degree, the Bachelor of Arts, is comparable to four-year degree programs in the arts and sciences offered on college campuses.

You may choose between two program options for the B.A. degree. The liberal studies option offers you the chance to take a broad program of study in the liberal arts without concentrating in any one subject. The second option is a B.A. degree with the designation of a major, for students who want to concentrate in one subject area.

Of the total 120 credit hours required for the Bachelor of Arts with either option, at least 90 hours must be in the arts and sciences. Included in this must be a distribution of credits among these three areas: the humanities, the social sciences, and the natural sciences or mathematics. A certain number of your credit hours must also be on the intermediate (sopho more) and advanced (junior-senior) level.

If you choose to earn a major designation in a laboratory science (physics,biology,chemistry,or geology), you will be expected to show evidence of appropriate laboratory experience.

If you already have an Associate in Arts or Associate in Science Degree, the credits which you earned toward that degree will be accepted toward the Bachelor of Arts.

The requirements for the B.A. degree can be met through college courses, recognized proficiency examinations, military education courses, or special assessment.

THE BACHELOR OF SCIENCE DEGREE

This degree is similar in content to the Regents External Bachelor of Arts Degree, except that a minimum of one half of the total 120 credit hour must be earned in the liberal arts and sciences; the remaining 60 credits may be earned in any college subjects.

In the Bachelor of Science program, as in the Bachelor of Arts, you may choose between the liberal studies option and the designation of a major field. If you choose the liberal studies option you may take. a broad progra of study in the liberal arts and sciences; the B.S. degree with a major designation is designed for those who concentrate their liberal arts courses in one subject. In both options, it is possible to concentrate up to 60 cre its in a professional or occupational field by arranging your electives in this way.

The distribution requirement for the Regents External B.S. degree is simi lar to that for the B.A.: that is, a certain number of credits in the human ties,the social sciences,and the natural sciences or mathematics. A proportion of your credits must also be earned on the intermediate (sophomore) an advanced (junior-senior) levels.

If you already have an Associate in Arts or Associate in Science degree, the credits which you earned toward that degree will be accepted toward the Bachelor of Science.

As with the B.A., the requirements for the B.S. degree can be met by college course, proficiency examinations, military education course, proficiency examinations, military education courses, or special assessment.

HOW YOU CAN EARN CREDIT TOWARD A DEGREE

There are four different approaches to earning credit for a Regents External Degree:

1. College courses, taken for credit through an accredited college or university
2. Proficiency examinations
3. Military educational programs
4. Special assessment of knowledge or performance skills which may not be tested by existing proficiency examinations.

For the associate an arts, associate in science, bachelor of arts, bachelor of science, or the general education component of the business or nursing degree, you may choose any one or more of these approaches to meet the requirements. The specially designed Regents External Degree Examinations are generally used to fulfill the requirements for the business and nursing components; however, college courses will be accepted where they are appropriate.

COLLEGE COURSES

The Regents External Degree accepts credits earned in classroom study or by correspondence from all accredited colleges and universities. You must maintain a "C" average overall for the Regents External Degree. In the general education components of the business and nursing degrees and in the A.A., A.S., B.A., and B.S. programs, grades of "D" in individual courses are accepted as long as they are balanced by "A"s or "B"s. For the business and nursing components of those degrees only courses in which you earned a "C" grade or better are acceptable.

PROFICIENCY EXAMINATIONS - College Proficiency Examination Program (CPEP) and Regents External Degree Examinations (REDE)

These examinations are offered by The University of the State of New York in more than 50 subjects. They are described in detail in the section called THE EXAMINATIONS.

These examinations are graded either Pass-Fail, on a numerical (standard score) basis, or on a letter grade basis. The minimum grades which are acceptable toward a Regents External Degree are:

Standard score: 45   Pass-Fail: P

Letter Grade: C or D, depending on the particular degree requirement being met (same grade levels as listed above under *COLLEGE COURSES*)

COLLEGE-LEVEL EXAMINATION PROGRAM (CLEP)

CLEP is a testing program of the College Entrance Examination Board. These tests are of two types: General Examinations and Subject Examinations.

The General Examinations are comprehensive tests in five basic areas of liberal arts: English Composition, Humanities, Mathematics, Natural Sciences, and Social Sciences/History. The CLEP Subject Examinations are tests of achievement in college subjects; some cover material studied in a full-year course, and others are limited to the content of a one-semester course.

The minimum acceptable total scores for the General Examinations are:

English   427 Mathematics   424* Social Sciences/History 422
Humanities 422 Natural Sciences 422

6

On the Subject Examinations you must earn a score of at least 45 to receive credit toward a Regents External Degree.

COLLEGE ENTRANCE EXAMINATION BOARD ADVANCED PLACEMENT EXAMINATIONS (AP)

These examinations are offered once a year by special arrangement through high schools in 13 different college subjects. They are graded on a five-point scale, from a low of 1 to a high of 5; in order to receive External Degree credit you must have a score of at least 3.

UNITED STATES ARMED FORCES INSTITUTE EXAMINATIONS (USAFI)

Part of a program to assist military personnel to continue their education, USAFI examinations can be used to fulfill all requirements of the A.A and A.S degrees, and certain B.A.,B.S.,business,and nursing degree requirements. The minimum acceptable scores on each type of USAFI tests are listed below:

General Education Development	Standard Scores	College-Level Examinations:	Standard Scores
Expression	55	Natural Sciences	61
Literary Materials	57	Social Sciences	60

Subject Standardized Tests: A rating of 20

End-of-Course Tests: a rating of either satisfactory(s) or with distinction (D)

Subject Examinations: a rating of satisfactory (S)

Military Service School Courses

Military courses which contain college-level work and have been evaluated by the Office of Educational Credit (formerly the Commission on Accreditation of Service Experiences) of the American Counsil on Education can be applied toward an External Degree. That office evaluates many military education programs and gives credit recommendations which are recognized by the Regents External Degree Program.

Special Assessment

Special Assessment is a way of evaluating knowledge in college subject areas where proficiency tests do not exist or are not appropriate. A faculty panel will design and conduct this individualized examination after consultation with the candidate; it may be an oral, a written or a performance examination, or may use a combination of these evaluative techniques. The amount of credit and the cost of Special Assessment will vary with the learning experience which is measured.

You cannot use Special Assessment to earn credit toward the busines or nursing components of those degrees. It does not waive any specific degree requirements, but does provide another way of meeting them.

WHAT IT COSTS

The tuition charges of the Regents External Degree Program cover evaluation of independent study by examination, analysis of student records, advisement on academic programs available, and the provision of study guides and bibliographical aids. These costs are:

Enrollment
Annual records maintenance
Graduation

These costs are paid directly to the Regents External Degree Program.

There is, of course, a charge for each proficiency examination you take, which you pay directly to the agency administering the test. Specific cost of the Regents External Degree and College Proficiency Examinations are included in the test descriptions; they are generally between 200 and 500. If you choose to meet degree requirements by taking college courses, you must also figure these tuition charges into the cost of your degree. A charge of $500-$1000 covers each Special Assessment.

If you take longer than one year to complete the degree, you will be charged   annually for maintenance of your records until your graduation.

The Regents External Degree Program has been approved for veterans' educational benefits by the State approving agency. Information on how to obtain veterans' benefits through this program is available from the REDP office.

Although the actual cost of earning a Regents External Degree varies according to the ways in which you choose to earn credits, the average cost of a degree taken entirely by examination is between $2500-$5000. If you submit college courses already taken, the cost of completing your degree may be considerably less.

THE EXAMINATIONS

College Proficiency and Regents External Degree Examinations are both tests of college-level knowledge, and may be used in similar ways. Most colleges and universities in New York State, and a growing number in other states, give credit or waive course requirements for passing scores on these examinations. However, since each institution or department within an institution sets its own credit policies, you should check with the college you are attending, or want to attend, before you taken an examination. The Regents External Degree, of course, accepts passing grades on CPEs and REDEs toward External Degree requirements.

College Proficiency Examinations test knowledge which is equivalent to the content of a one-or-more semester course in that subject on a college campus. They are available in some 20 specific subjects in the arts, the sciences, education, health, and nursing

Regents External Degree Examinations, which are given in the fields of nursing, business, and foreign languages, are designed to correspond to particular levels on a person's academic preparation, and not necessarily to the subject matter of a specific college course. Where it is necessary, the External Degree Registrar will help colleges to determine the appropriate amount of credit to give for RED examinations.

Both College Proficiency and Regents External Degree Examinations can be used to satisfy requirements for a Regents External Degree. Another frequent use of these examinations is to meet New York State teacher certification or New York City teacher licensure requirements.

Taking the Examinations -- In and Out of New York State

If you feel that you have mastered the subject matter involved, you are eligible to take College Proficiency or Regents External Degree Examinations; you do not have to meet any requirements or satisfy any prerequisites. You can also take examinations over again if you wish.

In New York State these examinations are given four times each year, in early February, May, August, and November, at about a dozen testing centers throughout the State. Exact testing dates and a list of test locations are included on the application form. The deadline for applications is about give weeks before each testing period. A fee is charged for each examination. Charges for each are listed with the examination descriptions.

Outside of New York State at the present time, College Proficiency and Regents External Degree Examinations are given at a limited number of locations in other states. Additional test administration centers will be added in the near future. Inquiries on out-of-state testing should be addressed to the Program office in Albany, New York, or, if appropriate, to a particular test administration center outside New York.

In the military, the examinations are administered to U.S. military personnel on active duty at installations around the world, under the auspices of the appropriate Base Education Officer. If you are a serviceman or woman you should request further information from the Program office.

Within 90 days of the examination you will receive a report of your grade and the amount of credit that has been granted by The University of the State of New York. An official transcript of your test results will be sent without cost to any other institution or agency, but only at your specific written request.

Using the Examinations for Teacher Certification and Licensure

You can use College Proficiency and Regents External Degree Examinations to meet certain requirements for New York State teacher certification and New York City teacher licensure. However, you should understand that a person must have at least a baccalaureate degree in order to obtain provisional New York State teacher certification. There are some requirements for which proficiency examinations cannot be used, so be sure to check with the Division of Teacher Education and Certification in the State Education Department in Albany, the Board of Examiners of the New York City Board of Education, or the teacher certification agency in the state in which you want to teach, before you take any examinations for this purpose.

—

ACT PEP: REGENTS COLLEGE EXAMINATIONS

General Information

The ACT PEP: Regents College Examinations, hereafter referred to as PEP Examinations, give you an opportunity to gain recognition for college-level learning, no matter how or where the learning took place. You may have acquired such learning in a number of ways: advanced courses in high school; evening, extension, or correspondence courses; on-the-job training; the armed forces; television courses; or reading on your own. Now you would like some official recognition of that learning—whether to apply it toward a college degree, to satisfy a professional licensing or certification requirement, to show you have skills for a better position, or perhaps simply to find out for yourself whether you are capable of college-level achievement before you apply to a college degree program.

The ACT Proficiency Examination Program can help you obtain recognition for college-level learning. PEP consists of examinations designed to let you demonstrate your proficiency in various college-level subjects. On the basis of your results on one or more examinations, colleges and universities, academic departments, and various other certifying agencies may grant you actual course or area credit, waive prerequisite course or area requirements, allow you to begin college coursework at an appropriate advanced or intermediate level in your field of knowledge, or verify skills and knowledge required for certification, licensing, or promotion.

American College Testing does **not** grant credit. **Before you register for any PEP examination, be sure to check directly with the appropriate institution, agency or company to determine whether it will grant the credit you seek on the basis of PEP examination results.** A list of institutions that grant credit for one or more PEP examinations is **a separate four-page document** in the registration packet.

The ACT Proficiency Examination Program makes available nationwide the examinations used by the University of the State of New York's Regents College Degrees. Since 1963, colleges and universities in New York and other states have granted more than one million course credits on the basis of results of these examinations, which are recommended by the American Council on Education, Office on Education Credit and Credentials for college credit. The Regents College Degrees, which awards course credit on the basis of these examinations, has been fully accredited by the New York State Education Department and the Middle States Association of Colleges and Schools, Commission on Higher Education.

The PEP examinations have been carefully designed to test your college-level proficiency. They cover undergraduate coursework in a broad range of areas, including arts and sciences, business, education, and nursing. The examinations generally cover material studied in comparable one- or two-semester courses; a few advanced examinations in business subjects deal with broader areas. All the examinations test not only how well you know facts and terminology, but also how well you can apply essential concepts and skills.

All of the ACT Proficiency Examinations are 3 hours long. Most of the examinations are objective; some are entirely essay. The list on the inside front cover indicates the kinds of questions each examination contains.

PEP examinations have been prepared by college and university faculty members who have taught comparable courses in their own schools. Each examination has been developed by a committee of teachers and scholars in the subject. This committee writes and reviews all examination items and the outlines on which they are based. Test specialists have worked with each committee to ensure that the examinations actually measure the proficiency required of students taking comparable courses. The examinations are continually reviewed and revised to ensure that they are kept up to date with current developments in each subject area.

Each examination is based on an outline that defines its scope and content. Each outline is like a syllabus for a typical course, though it may not be identical with the syllabus for the equivalent course given by the college from which you may wish to receive credit. The outline for a PEP examination is contained in the PEP Study Guide for that examination, which you can obtain by writing to ACT. The outline for an examination can be used in several ways. It will help you determine whether the test is appropriate for you and how much of the material you already know. You can identify areas with which you are not sufficiently familiar and devote more study time to them. And since each outline indicates the weight given to each area covered by the examination, you can apportion your preparation time appropriately.

American College Testing, a nonprofit educational service organization, has no affiliation with nor does it endorse or recommend any profit-making educational counseling center. Initial counseling/advising for college degrees is usually provided free by degree-granting institutions.

Study Guides/Textbooks

ACT strongly recommends that all candidates use the study guides before taking PEP examinations.

An ACT Proficiency Examination Program Study Guide is available free of charge for **each** PEP examination. Each study guide contains a course outline and a reading list. The study guide is comparable to a syllabus for a course you might take at a college or other institution. The outline indicates the scope and content of the examination, and the approximate weight given to each area covered on the examination. The reading lists suggest resources to which you may refer as you prepare for an examination. The sample questions give you an idea of the kinds of questions in each exam.

Study guides are routinely updated; therefore you should request a copy of the most recent guide within two months of the anticipated test date or call ACT PEP to check if you already have the most recent study guide copy.

To request a PEP study guide, use the order form on the back cover of this guide. Indicate the examination title and code number for each exam you plan to take. Send your order to ACT PEP Study Guides, P.O. Box 4014, Iowa City, Iowa 52243-4014, or you may call (319) 337-1363.

Selected textbooks listed in the study guides may now be ordered direct from SUNY Empire State College, External Programs Bookstore. To receive information, call or write:

SUNY Empire State College, External Programs Bookstore
5 Grande Blvd.
Saratoga Springs, NY 12866-9060
1-800-338-9179 (during business hours, EST)

ACT Proficiency Examination
Content Descriptions

ACT PEP examinations measure college-level knowledge and understanding. Most are comparable to end-of-course tests for one- or two-semester courses.

The following descriptions summarize the content of each test offered in 1994-95. Following each description is a list of the number of semester hours of credit recommended by ACE and awarded by Regents College for passing scores on PEP exams as well as the level of the examination: Upper Level=U, or Lower Level=L. Where appropriate, the specific course(s) covered by the examination is indicated. **If you requested your score report be sent to an institution other than Regents College, you should check with that institution for information about their policies and criteria for granting credit for ACT PEP exams.**

Arts and Sciences

Abnormal Psychology (459)
Corresponds to a one-semester course in abnormal psychology. Includes the historical background of abnormal psychology, the major conceptualizations, and the nature and description of abnormal disorders, as well as their definitions, classifications, etiology, and major treatments. Assumes knowledge of concepts typically learned in an introductory psychology course. 3 credits, U

The American Dream (Part I) (460)
Reflects an interdisciplinary course of study which reveals both the conflict and the consensus that resulted as groups and individuals struggled to define and shape the American dream in a variety of ways prior to the Civil War. Draws from the literature, history, and political science of the United States. 6 credits, U

Anatomy and Physiology (506)
Corresponds to an introductory, two-semester sequence of courses in anatomy and physiology. Includes an understanding of anatomical and physiological factors involved in the functioning of major body systems, with emphasis on systems that maintain, integrate, and control body functions. Assumes familiarity with basic biological terminology and with concepts such as basic cell structure and function. 6 credits, L

Foundations of Gerontology (407)
Corresponds to an introductory, one-semester course in gerontology. Includes biological, psychological, and social aspects of aging, and an understanding of issues, needs, and realities involved in the aging process. Multidisciplinary in nature and covers theories, concepts, empirical patterns and their implications for policy and practice. 3 credits, U

The History of Nazi Germany (432)
Reflects a study of the history of National Socialism. Includes the Nazis' rise to power, politics and the economy, everyday life in the Third Reich, the role of the SS in the Nazi state, the Holocaust, and the legacy of National Socialism. 3 credits, U

International Conflicts in the Twentieth Century (510)
Reflects an interdisciplinary course of study of the origins of the great international conflicts in the 20th century and their relevance to ongoing efforts to maintain international security in the post–Cold War era. 3 credits, U

Microbiology (558)
Corresponds to an introductory, one-semester course in microbiology. Tests for a knowledge and understanding of bacteria, algae, fungi, protozoa, viruses, and their relationships with humans. Includes introduction to microbiology, biology of microorganisms, control of microorganisms, disease and resistance, biology of infectious diseases, and industrial and environmental microbiology. Assumes general knowledge of chemistry, biology, and anatomy and physiology. 3 credits, L

The New Rule of Reason: Philosophy and Society in the Seventeenth Century (560)
Reflects an interdisciplinary course of study of seventeenth-century Western European philosophy viewed in the context of four major social changes: capitalism, modern science, the nation-state, and challenges to religious dogma. Based on the writings of individual philosophical thinkers of the period, as well as on selected modern critical interpretations. 3 credits, U

Religions of the World (509)
Reflects an interdisciplinary course of study of the major religions as viewed in their social and historical context. Draws content from sociology, psychology, and philosophy. Questions require student to apply an understanding of the content to an analysis and comparison of religious beliefs and practices. 3 credits, U

Statistics (408)
Corresponds to an introductory, one-semester course in statistics. Includes the fundamental concepts of descriptive and inferential statistics in a service course applicable to many majors. Assumes a basic knowledge of algebra. 3 credits, L

The War in Vietnam (1945–1975): A Global Perspective (511)
Reflects a study of the various stages of war in Vietnam from the conflict's beginnings in traditional Vietnamese culture to the aftermath of Communist victory in 1975. Throughout the chronological history of the war, the examination focuses on three major themes: the role of culture, the temporal and international context of the war, and the conflicting interpretations of the war. 3 credits, U

Business

Business Policy and Strategy (579)
Corresponds to a one-semester, upper division course in business policy and strategy. Tests for achievement typically expected of a student who has completed a capstone course at the end of an undergraduate program in business. Requires the integration of facts and concepts from core business subjects, the application of these concepts to address business problems encountered in case studies, as well as demonstrated understanding of the influence of business environments on solving business problems. 3 credits, U

Corporation Finance (581)
Corresponds to a one-semester course in corporation finance. Includes goals of financial management and introduction to strategic decisions of financial management; tools of financial analysis; management of current assets and current liabilities; intermediate and long-term financial instruments; the investment decision; the financing decision; the dividend decision; and international finance. 3 credits, L

Note: These examinations are administered in New York State by Regents College. You may register by calling (518) 464-8500.

uman Resource Management (482)
orresponds to a one-semester, upper-division course in
uman resource management. Resembles an end-of-course
st required of management majors in the junior or senior year.
cludes the role and context of human resource management,
uman resource planning and staffing, performance and the
dividual, compensation, labor-management relations, and
erformance and the organization. Tests for knowledge of facts
nd terminology, and understanding of personnel management
oncepts and principles, and particularly for the ability to apply
ese concepts to typical personnel management situations.
ssumes knowledge of the principles of management.
credits, U

Introductory Accounting (431)
orresponds to a two-semester, six-credit sequence of courses
introductory accounting designed for all majors in business.
cludes basic accounting concepts and principles; the
ccounting recording process; financial statements and analy-
is; accounting for assets, liabilities, owner's equity, revenues
nd expenses; manufacturing accounting; and analysis for
anagerial decision making. 6 credits, L

Labor Relations (535)
orresponds to a one-semester, upper-division course in labor
elations; comparable to an end-of-course test required of busi-
ess administration majors in the junior or senior year. Includes
abor relations in the United States, American labor law, collec-
ve bargaining, contract administration, and miscellaneous
elated topics. Tests for knowledge of facts and terminology, an
nderstanding of basic concepts, and particularly for the ability
apply this knowledge and understanding of typical business
ituations. 3 credits, U

Organizational Behavior (429)
orresponds to a one-semester, upper-division course in orga-
izational behavior; comparable to an end-of-course test
equired of business administration majors in the junior or
enior year. Includes individual behavior, group and interper-
onal behavior, and organizational and intergroup behavior.
ests for knowledge of facts and terminology, understanding of
asic concepts, and particularly for the ability to apply this
nowledge and understanding to typical business situations.
ssumes knowledge of the principles of management.
credits, U

Principles of Management (430)
orresponds to an introductory, one-semester course in princi-
les of management designed for all majors in business.
ncludes the evolution of management thought; planning and
ecision making; organizing, leading, influencing, and control-
ng functions; and special issues in management. 3 credits, L

Principles of Marketing (483)
orresponds to an introductory, one-semester, three-credit
ourse in principles of marketing designed for all majors in busi-
ess. Includes the role of marketing in the organization and
ociety, analysis for markets, the functional areas of marketing,
nd special topics. 3 credits, L

Production/Operations Management (582)
orresponds to a one-semester course in production/opera-
ions management. Includes definition and description of pro-
uction/operations management, design of the productive
ystem, planning the use of the productive system, and the con-
rol of the productive system. Assumes a knowledge of generally accepted production/operations management principles,
principles of economics, statistics, and basic computer science
concepts. 3 credits, L

Education

Reading Instruction in the Elementary School (555)
Corresponds to a two-semester sequence of courses in elementary school reading instruction. Includes theoretical framework, early stages of reading, word identification strategies,
comprehension, instructional strategies, and classroom
assessment and evaluation. 6 credits, L

Nursing

Fundamentals of Nursing (403)
Corresponds to a course in fundamentals of nursing. Includes
concepts basic to nursing practice; communication and inter-
personal relations; protection and promotion of safety; comfort,
rest, and activity; nutrition; elimination; oxygenation; and fluid
and electrolyte. 8 credits, L

Maternal and Child Nursing: Associate Degree Level (453)
Corresponds to one or more courses in maternal and child
nursing at the associate degree level. Includes maternity nursing and care of the well and ill child from birth through adoles-
cence. Assumes a basic knowledge of anatomy and
physiology, and growth and development. 6 credits, L

*Maternal and Child Nursing: Baccalaureate Degree Level
(457)*
Measures knowledge and understanding of material typically
taught in a sequence of courses in maternal and child nursing
at the baccalaureate degree level. The exam tests for the ability to utilize the nursing process in the nursing management of
family health and reproduction, low-risk pregnancy, the normal
neonate and family, the family with a high-risk mother or high-
risk neonate, the well child and family, and the ill child and family. 8 credits, U

Maternity Nursing (559)
Corresponds to a course in maternity nursing. Assumes a basic
knowledge and understanding of anatomy, physiology, and
developmental tasks. 3 credits, L

Adult Nursing (554)
Measures knowledge and understanding of material typically
taught in a sequence of courses in medical-surgical or adult
nursing at the baccalaureate degree level. The exam measures
knowledge and understanding of the health and nursing care of
young, middle-aged, and older adults, including the ability to
use the nursing process in the nursing management of adults
with cardiovascular, respiratory, urinary, reproductive,
endocrine, gastrointestinal, sensorimotor, musculoskeletal,
immune, or integumentary system dysfunction. 8 credits, U

Psychiatric/Mental Health Nursing (503)
Measures knowledge and understanding of material typically
taught in a sequence of courses in psychiatric/mental health
nursing at the baccalaureate degree level. The exam measures
knowledge and understanding of the theoretical/therapeutic
foundations for psychiatric mental health nursing practice, and
tests the application of this knowledge and understanding to the
nursing care of functional and dysfunctional clients using the
nursing process as an organizing framework. Within this framework, the client system is defined as the individual, the family,
the small group, or the community, with major emphasis on the
individual. 8 credits, U

Commonalities in Nursing Care: Area A (427)

Includes concepts of nursing care and nursing actions common to all patients throughout the life cycle. Assumes the technical vocabulary and knowledge of anatomy and physiology, microbiology, emotional and physical development, and nutrition generally expected of the associate degree nurse. Focuses on the nursing care of patients related to the health continuum, comfort, rest, and sleep, activity/mobility, environmental safety, biological safety, and psychological safety. 5 credits, L

Commonalities in Nursing Care: Area B (478)

Includes concepts of nursing care and nursing actions common to all patients throughout the life cycle. Assumes the technical vocabulary and knowledge of anatomy and physiology, microbiology, and emotional and physical development generally expected of the associate degree nurse. Focuses on the nursing care of patients related to nutrition, elimination, oxygenation, and fluid and electrolyte balance. 5 credits, L

Differences in Nursing Care: Area A (479)

Includes nursing care of patients experiencing problems of oxygenation or abnormal cell growth, as well as the development of the fetus and the physiological changes associated with normal pregnancy. Focuses on acute and long-term problems of medical, surgical, obstetric, and pediatric patients. Assumes knowledge of anatomy and physiology, emotional and physical development, pharmacology, and nutrition. 5 credits, L

Differences in Nursing Care: Area B (531)

Includes nursing care of patients experiencing problems with behavioral responses, metabolic mechanisms, regulatory mechanisms, and congenital anomalies, genetic disorders, and developmental problems. Focuses on both acute and long-term problems of medical, surgical, psychiatric, and pediatric patients. Assumes knowledge of anatomy and physiology, emotional and physical development, pharmacology, and nutrition. 5 credits, L

Differences in Nursing Care: Area C (578)

Includes nursing care of patients experiencing infections and communicable disease problems; tissue trauma; and neurological, sensory, and musculoskeletal dysfunctions. Focuses on both acute and long-term problems of medical, surgical, and pediatric patients. Assumes knowledge of anatomy and physiology, emotional and physical development, and nutrition. 5 credits, L

Occupational Strategies in Nursing (532)

Focuses on the roles and functions of the associate degree nurse within the occupation of nursing. Includes the health care delivery system; the health team; legal, educational, and ethical aspects of current nursing practice; and influences of nursing history, nursing organizations, and licensure on the nurse's function in the delivery of care. 3 credits, L

Professional Strategies in Nursing (426)

Measures knowledge and understanding of the professional role within the occupation of nursing. The exam focuses on trends and events that have influenced the development of the profession of nursing, accountability for professional practice, design and management of professional practice, and the health care delivery system. 4 credits, U

Health Support: Area I (530)

Measures knowledge and understanding of health promotion and prevention of illness in the nursing care of the client. While the client may be the individual, family, or community, emphasis is placed on the family and community. The exam tests the ability to apply the nursing process to support the health of the client. Emphasis is placed on health promotion and the primary and secondary aspects of health protection. The concepts of wellness tested are theoretical and philosophical; ecological and epidemiological; individual, family, and community assessment; and nursing strategies to promote and support health. The patterns of risk tested are environmental safety, nutrition, and childbearing and childrearing. 4 credits, U

Health Support: Area II (577)

Measures knowledge and understanding of nursing action related to factors which affect a client's wellness and place the client at risk for major health problems. While the client may be the individual, family, or community, emphasis is placed on the family and community. The exam tests the ability to apply the nursing process to support the health of the client. Emphasis is placed on the primary and secondary prevention aspects of health protection. The patterns of risk tested are mental health; cardiovascular and respiratory; neoplasms; infections, communicable diseases, and immune responses; neuromuscular and endocrine/regulatory; and birth defects and genetic problems. 4 credits, U

Health Restoration: Area I (425)

Measures the ability to apply the nursing process to assist clients in dealing with major health problems. While the client may be the individual, family, or community, emphasis is placed on the individual at all stages of the life cycle. The major health problems tested are cardiovascular, respiratory, neoplasms, accidents and traumatic injuries, endocrine, and autoimmune. 4 credits, U

Health Restoration: Area II (477)

Measures the ability to apply the nursing process to assist clients in dealing with major health problems. While the client may be the individual, family, or community, emphasis is placed on the individual at all stages of the life cycle. The major health problems tested are emotional and behavioral; neurological and sensory; gastrointestinal and genitourinary; infections and communicable diseases; complications of pregnancy, problems of the high-risk mother and problems of the high-risk infant; and birth defects and genetic problems. 4 credits, U

egistration materials are included in the packet with this *egistration Guide.* To register for one or more PEP exams, ou must complete the ACT PEP Registration Form according the instructions below, and mail the properly completed form ong with the correct total fee in the preaddressed return enve-pe provided.

nce your registration form has been mailed, all PEP policies oply. No changes can be made to the test date choice or xamination choices; however, you may request a test center hange (see page 6 for information).

egistration materials must be postmarked no later than the egistration deadline for the desired test date (see front cover). there is a discrepancy between the metered postmark and an fficial U.S. Postal Service postmark, the latter will be consid-red official. It is advisable not to mail registration materials too lose to the postmark deadline, because mail is sometimes ostmarked a day or two after mailing. ACT PEP will not be esponsible for registration materials lost in the mail.

Due to limited seating capacity at some PEP test centers, he sooner you send in your registration form, the more ikely it will be that you can test at your first-choice test enter.

Restrictions on Retesting

Candidates may retake an examination if 60 days have passed since they last took it.

For example, if you take an exam in October 1994, you could not retake it in November 1994 because 60 days would not have passed. You would have to wait for the next test date (February 1995) to retake the exam. **Scores for exams retaken before 60 days have passed will not be reported and fees will not be returned.**

Your ACT PEP Registration Form

Be sure you follow all the instructions in this guide and on the Registration Form carefully. Errors may delay or prevent your registration. Your ACT PEP registration will **not** be processed unless the registration form is completed fully and properly and is accompanied by a cashier's check or money order payable to ACT PEP for the correct total fee. Cash will not be accepted.

We reserve the right to return unprocessed any improperly completed forms, incomplete forms, unsigned forms, simulated forms, and forms not accompanied by correct and complete payment of the total test fee. This delay may cause you to miss the registration deadline for your test date.

Because the registration form will be processed by machine, be sure to:

• use a soft-lead (No. 2) pencil and print legibly
• blacken ONE oval under each letter or number you enter
• blacken the blank ovals below each empty box
• erase any errors completely

Do **NOT** staple your payment to the form.

Begin on Side 1 of your Registration Form.

A: Name and Mailing Address. Print your name and current mailing address on the lines provided.

B: Name. Enter your name in the sections labeled Last Name, First Name, MI (middle initial). Begin in the first box for each part of your name. If there is not enough space for your name, enter as much as possible using one box for each letter, but do not extend any part of your name beyond its designated area. Blacken the corresponding ovals.

C, D, E, and F: Mailing Address, City, State Code, and ZIP Code. The address you enter will be used for mailing your Registration Acknowledgment Form. Enter each part of the address where you are certain to receive mail from ACT PEP. If you live in an apartment, enter the apartment number after the name of the street. For example:

1420 FLDCRST #315

Leave a space between the parts of your street address. If you need to abbreviate in block C, use the abbreviations below. (Letter ovals are in the upper part and number ovals in the lower part of block C.)

Abbreviations for Street Addresses

Apartment	#	Expressway	EXPY	Route	RT
Avenue	AVE	Fort	FT	South	S
Beach	BCH	Garden	GDN	Springs	SPGS
Boulevard	BLVD	Heights	HTS	Square	SQ
Canyon	CYN	Highway	HWY	State, Street	ST
Center	CTR	Lake	LK	Terrace	TER
Circle	CIR	Mount	MT	Trail	TRL
City	CY	Mountain	MTN	Trailer	TRLR
Court	CT	North	N	Turnpike	TPKE
Crescent	CRES	Parkway	PKY	University	UNIV
Drive	DR	Place	PL	Village	VLG
East	E	Point	PT	West	W
Estates	EST	Road	RD		

For block E, State Code, see the list of state codes located adjacent to block E.

Blacken the corresponding ovals for blocks C, D, E, and F.

G: Telephone. Enter the telephone area code and numbers for both your home and work. We may need to reach you to verify information. If you do not have a telephone, indicate the number of a friend or relative with whom we can leave a message.

Turn to Side 2 of the Registration Form.

H: Social Security Number. Enter your Social Security number. If you do not have a Social Security number or do not wish to provide it, enter zeros. Canadian students should also enter zeros. ACT PEP will use your Social Security number only for positive identification of your record and will routinely include it in the score reports sent to you and reports sent at your request to agencies or institutions. Blacken the corresponding ovals.

I: Sex. Blacken the appropriate oval.

J: Date of Birth. Enter the month, day, and last two digits of the year in which you were born. Enter a zero for any blank. Blacken the corresponding ovals.

K: Test Date. **Blacken the correct oval for the test date on which you wish to take the ACT PEP examinations you mark on Side 2 of the form.** The schedule of test dates and registration deadlines is on the front cover of this guide. **Your registration will be processed for the date you indicate and must be postmarked by the deadline. An error in test date selection may cause you to miss your test date.**

L: Test Center Codes. The test center list begins on page 11 in this guide. **Note that many test centers are open only on selected test dates. It is your responsibility to check carefully that the test centers you list are open on the dates for which you are registering.** Find and print the code number for your first choice of test center; then print the code number for your second choice of test center. Blacken the corresponding ovals. If your first choice is closed or filled to capacity, you will automatically be assigned to your second choice center. If you cannot be assigned to either center because of capacity limitations, your registration form will be returned to you and your fee refunded in full. If neither of the centers you list is scheduled to be open on the test date you indicated in block K, your registration form and fee will be returned to you unprocessed.

M: Additional Registration Packet. If you plan to take additional PEP exams on a later test date and need another registration packet, blacken the appropriate oval. Packets are also available at test centers on the test dates, and you may request one at that time.

Selecting Your ACT PEP Examinations. You may register for a maximum of four PEP examinations. For test security reasons, exams may be taken **only** during the test session for which they are listed on the registration form. The **only** exception to this policy is if you wish to take two exams that are offered during the **same** session. If you wish to take two exams scheduled for the same session, blacken the oval for both exams; the ACT PEP office will reschedule one of the conflicting exams to a session during which you are not testing. **For each exam** registered, blacken the corresponding oval and write the exam fee next to the title in the space marked "Fee Enclosed."

N: Total Fee Enclosed. After you have marked the exams you wish to take, complete block N. Write the total fee for each session, then add all sessions to arrive at the total fee you must submit with the registration form. Enclose a cashier's check or money order, payable to ACT PEP, for the correct total amount. **Do *not* staple your payment to the registration form and do *not* send cash.** Your registration cannot be processed without the correct payment.

Retain your copy of your money order or cashier's check for receipt of payment. If your employer requires additional proof for reimbursement of exam fees, your copy of your ACT PEP score report is an official document and may serve as proof of payment.

O: Student's Certification. Read the statement in block O, then sign (do not print) and date the form. Your registration cannot be processed without your signature.

Mailing Your Registration Form. Carefully fold your registration form the way it was folded when you received it. Mail the completed form with the appropriate fee in the preaddressed envelope provided.

Keep this registration guide for reference. Completed registration materials, as well as all other correspondence, inquiries, requests for study guides, and requests concerning registration materials, administration, and processing, should be directed to:

ACT PEP
P.O. Box 4014
Iowa City, Iowa 52243-4014
Telephone: (319) 337-1363
TDD for hearing impaired (must call from a TDD)
   (319) 337-1701

Additional Information

Registration Acknowledgment

Normally, within 3 weeks after your PEP Registration Form and fee have been received at ACT, a Registration Acknowledgment will be sent to you. If you do not receive an acknowledgment within 3 weeks, contact ACT PEP. Note, however, that

if you submit your registration form far in advance of the test date you wish, it will take longer than 3 weeks. Registration Acknowledgments for such future registrations will be sent when processing for that date begins.

When you receive your Registration Acknowledgment, review it carefully to be sure that it lists the exams you registered for (check both code number and title) as well as the correct test center and test date. If there are any discrepancies or if you have any questions, call (319) 337-1363 immediately. TDD for hearing impaired (must call from a TDD) (319) 337-1701.

Note: Your Registration Acknowledgment Form may be used to request a reregistration or refund (see page 8); therefore **it is important for you to retain this form.** The reverse side of the Registration Acknowledgment Form gives instructions for requesting either a reregistration or refund.

Changing Your Test Center

All test center changes are subject to the availability of test materials for the exam(s) you desire and seating space.

If you cannot take a PEP examination at the test center to which you have been assigned, you may request a test center change. To initiate this change, call (319) 337-1363. Collect calls will not be accepted. Be sure that the new center you request is scheduled to be open on that test date.

There is no charge for a test center change for the same test date; however, you must pay for any last-minute communications. All changes will be made after the registration deadline but not later than 10 calendar days before the test.

Guidelines for Taking the ACT PEP Tests

Please read these guidelines carefully. They can help you do your best on the ACT PEP tests.

1. Get sufficient rest the night before taking the tests so that you are in good physical and mental shape for taking them.

2. Due to variations in room temperature at the test centers, we suggest you take a sweater or jacket to ensure your comfort.

3. Listen closely to all directions. Ask questions if you do not understand what you are to do.

4. You must complete identifying information and mark your answers on the machine-scored answer sheet. Be very precise in doing so. Be sure that you blacken the correct ovals and rectangles (see sample on page 13).

5. When taking the tests, position your answer sheet next to your test booklet so you can mark answers quickly without moving either the booklet or the answer sheet.

6. Select only one answer to each question.

7. When you are marking your answers, be sure that the number of the line of ovals on the answer sheet is the same as the number of the question you are answering. Then mark your answer in the oval that has the same number as your answer choice.

8. If you wish to change an answer, erase the unintended mark completely.

9. Read each question and the possible answers fully so that you are sure you understand them before answering.

10. **IMPORTANT: ANSWER EVERY QUESTION. THERE IS NO PENALTY FOR GUESSING.**

1. When you are unsure of the correct answer to a question, first eliminate every wrong answer you can. Then pick the best answer from those left.

2. Pace yourself throughout each test. Do not spend too much time on any one question. If a question is too hard for you, choose the answer you think is best and go on to the next question.

3. You may want to take a watch for your personal use. Each test is timed, and time remaining will not be announced. Note: Alarms may not be used during testing.

4. If you complete the test before time is called, look for any careless mistakes by rereading the questions and your answers.

Test Day Information

Important Instructions!

On the test day, you may indicate **one** institution or agency to which you wish your ACT PEP results reported for no additional fee. When completing your answer sheet, the Test Supervisor will ask you to mark the code number of the institution you wish to receive your scores. Therefore, **before the test day,** you should refer to the "List of ACT PEP Participating Institutions" (a separate 4-page list included in the registration packet) to determine the proper code number. Circle this code number for easy reference on the test day; **take this list with you to the test center. You will also receive a copy of your score report.** Because ACT maintains confidentiality of your ACT record, no other copies of your scores will be released without your permission.

Time of Examination

Morning test sessions normally begin at 8:30 a.m.; afternoon sessions normally begin at 1:30 p.m. **You are advised to report at least 15 minutes before these starting times.** No one will be admitted to the examination room after testing has begun.

NOTE: Occasionally, when a test center reporting address changes at the last minute, there is insufficient time to notify you. Be prepared to report to an address other than the one listed on your registration acknowledgment (signs should be posted). Reporting to the center 15 minutes early should allow enough time if this occurs.

Special Testing Requirements

American College Testing recognizes its obligation to make the PEP examinations equally accessible to candidates with physical or mental handicaps or disabilities. Reasonable accommodation to specific handicaps will be made whenever necessary and possible. However, it is the candidate's responsibility to advise ACT of the need for special accommodation or procedures **at the time he or she registers to take an examination.** ACT PEP reserves the right to require medical documentation of any handicap or disability and to refuse special accommodation when the applicant fails to provide adequate notice or medical justification.

Admission and Identification

The test center supervisor must positively identify each candidate before permitting admission to the testing room. The candidate's photograph, attached to the PEP Identification Card, will be used to facilitate this identification process. Candidates must provide a photograph and completed PEP ID Card **each test date,** even if they have tested on previous test dates. Attach permanently (with transparent tape or glue) a current, representative 2″ x 2″ photograph of yourself to the space indicated on the ID card. The photograph becomes the property of ACT PEP and will NOT be returned to you. Please note that formal portraits are not necessary; recent, representative snapshots are sufficient.

Each candidate must have signed the PEP ID Card. The supervisor may request additional identification and may, if necessary, inspect such documents to ascertain that they have not been altered and that they belong to the person displaying them. Each candidate's right thumbprint will be taken at the test center.

If you are taking more than one test on a test date, you need only to present one ID card at the first test session. Example: If you are scheduled to test Thursday morning and Friday afternoon, you need only to present the ID card on Thursday morning. The Test Supervisor will pull your card Friday afternoon to reverify your identification.

To avoid potential embarrassment or inconvenience in the identification process, candidates are advised to provide a recent, representative photograph of sufficient quality to make positive identification a routine procedure.

Test Center Regulations

The following regulations will be observed at all test centers in order to ensure uniform testing procedures:

1. Each candidate must bring his or her PEP Identification Card, properly completed and signed. Each candidate's right thumbprint will be taken at the test center. **No candidate will be admitted without being thumbprinted, and no candidate will receive scores without a properly completed and signed PEP ID Card for that test date.**

2. Candidates must bring at least three soft lead (No. 2) pencils and a good eraser for the objective multiple-choice examinations.

3. For examinations that are essay, candidates must bring a **black**-ink ballpoint pen.

4. Candidates are not permitted to take books, notes, slide rules, calculators, dictionaries, tables, electronic devices (pagers or similar communication devices), or aids of any kind into the examination room. Candidates also are not permitted to duplicate or record, by copying, photographing, or any other means, any part of the PEP examinations. All test materials must be returned to the test administrator; no portion of such materials may be retained by the candidate.

5. Candidates are not permitted to smoke, eat, or drink while actually testing.

6. No candidate will be admitted to the examination room after testing has started.

7. For security reasons, examinees are not allowed to receive or place telephone calls during testing.

8. Access to the examination room will be restricted to test center personnel and candidates.

9. Once the seal of the test booklet has been broken, the candidate is considered to have tested (i.e., ineligible for refund or reregistration). An exception may be made if a candidate becomes ill or ceases to test because of an emergency situation during the first 15 minutes of the examination. That candidate should return the test booklet and answer document(s) to the test supervisor, who will mark the answer document(s) VOID and indicate on the Irregularity Report that the document(s) should not be scored. No special testing arrangements can be made for a candidate in this situation. The candidate may request reregistration for a later test date or refund according to the established procedures explained below.

10. Answer documents may be voided at the request of the candidate. If a candidate discontinues testing during the first 15 minutes because of an emergency situation or illness, that candidate must request that the answer sheet not be scored in order to be eligible for refund or reregistration. In addition, a candidate who continues testing after the first 15 minutes and/or completes an examination but does not wish his or her answer documents scored must personally ask the test center supervisor to void the answer documents at the test center. The supervisor will mark the answer documents VOID and will note on the Irregularity Report the reason for voiding and that the answer document(s) are not to be scored. Such candidates are not eligible for refund or reregistration.

11. An examinee receiving or giving assistance of any kind may be required to surrender his or her test booklet(s) and answer document(s) to the supervisor and may be dismissed from the examination room. Such answer documents will be marked VOID and will not be scored; the test supervisor will attach an explanation to the Irregularity Report. Irregularities in the administration of the PEP exams can result in the cancellation of scores by ACT PEP.

12. If any question of authenticity or other irregularity in the testing process is discovered by or reported to ACT PEP, and a review confirms its significance, the candidate will be notified and given the opportunity to provide an explanation. If a significant question of authenticity or other irregularity remains, the candidate's PEP scores in question may be cancelled.

13. If you feel your performance on an examination may have been affected by an unusual situation at the test center, you may request a special review by writing to ACT PEP within ONE WEEK of the test date.

Reregistration and Refunds

Attention!

If you **cannot** test on the date assigned, reregistration for a later test date is possible; however, certain restrictions apply (see **Reregistration for a Later Test Date**).

If you originally register for one or more examinations and then do not take all of those examinations, you may request one of the following options:

1. Reregistration for **all** of the examinations that you did not take on the original test date form **to one** of the remaining valid 1994-95 test dates for an additional total fee of $10.

2. Refund of test fees for **all** of the examinations that you did not take on the original test date form minus a total fee of $15.

Note: The deadline for refund requests for the 1994-95 testing year is August 31, 1995.

You MUST make your request for a refund or reregistration for **all** exams you did not take by completing Side 2 of the Registration Acknowledgment Form which lists those exams.

The instructions outlined on Side 2 of your Registration Acknowledgment Form must be followed carefully to assure proper handling of your request. If you do not follow these procedures exactly, your request will be delayed and you may miss the registration deadline for the test date you requested.

Reregistration for a Later Test Date

Important!

All reregistration requests must be postmarked on or before the published registration deadline date for the new test date desired.

You may **not** request both reregistration and a refund for the same examination.

If you *cannot* test on the date assigned, reregistration for a later test date is possible; however, you may **not** reregister for the next month's test date. For example, if you originally registered for the October test date, you may **not** reregister for the November test date; likewise, you may **not** change your test date from February to March or from May to June.

The last test date for 1994-95 is June 1-2, 1995. If you miss that test date, you may apply for a refund but **not** for reregistration. If you wish to register for a test date during the next testing year, you must follow the steps for regular registration and submit a completed Registration Form and full fee.

If you cannot or choose not to take any particular PEP examination(s) on the requested test date, you may reregister for the **same** examination(s) for one of the remaining valid test dates in the current testing year (September 1–August 31). To register, you must send the following to ACT PEP:

1. Your PEP Registration Acknowledgment Form with Side 2 properly completed.

2. A cashier's check or money order for $10, payable to ACT PEP. Cash will not be accepted.

If you no longer have your Registration Acknowledgment Form, you must make your request for reregistration in writing. The request also must account for ALL OF THE EXAMINATIONS FOR WHICH YOU ORIGINALLY REGISTERED. That is, for each examination originally requested on your PEP Registration Form, you must state that you took the exam or that you wish to reregister to take that exam on one of the remaining test dates in the current testing year.

If you wish to register for any **different** examination(s), you must fully complete a new Registration Form and submit it along with full test fee payment. You may apply for a refund appropriate.

The reregistration policy applies as soon as you have mailed your Registration Form to ACT PEP.

Refund of Examination Fee

The deadline for refund requests for the 1994-95 testing year is August 31, 1995.

If you cannot or choose not to take any particular PEP examination(s) on the test date for which you were originally registered, **and** you cannot or do not wish to reregister, you may apply for a refund. To receive a refund, you MUST complete Side 2 of the Registration Acknowledgment Form that lists those examinations for which you are requesting a refund. The request should be made within two weeks after the original test date.

If you no longer have your Registration Acknowledgment Form, you must make your request in writing and state the original test date, test center, and the titles of the examinations.

The test fee(s) will be refunded minus a $15 service charge for processing, administrative, materials, and handling costs incurred. The maximum refund is the total test fee minus $15 even if the request is made before the test date for which you initially registered. **Refunds are not issued until after the test date** and may take 4-6 weeks to process.

Score Reports

In order to keep your scores confidential, they will not be given to anyone by telephone.

PEP results for examinations that include any essay questions are generally mailed 60 to 90 days after a test date. PEP results for entirely objective examinations are generally mailed 3 to 6 weeks after a test date.

On the test day, you may indicate one institution or agency to which you wish your ACT PEP results reported. Take the white 4-page "List of ACT PEP Participating Institutions" (included in the registration packet) with you to the test center to enter on your answer sheet the correct code for the institution of your choice. **You will also receive a copy of your score report.** These two reports are provided at no additional charge.

If you lose your score report, you will have to request and pay for an Additional Score Report (see next section).

Examinations that include essay questions will normally be graded by the appropriate faculty committee from the University of the State of New York, which develops the exams. However, the faculty at other institutions may review the essays themselves. If you indicate one of these institutions on your answer sheet, a copy of your answer documents will be sent to them also for evaluation.

ACT will retain your original PEP answer sheet for one year after the test date; score report data will be retained indefinitely. Your score report data, which include individually identifiable student information, may be used by the test developer (Regents College) to conduct research related to the test. In order to preserve the confidentiality of your PEP records, no report of your scores will be released to any institution or agency without your written authorization.

Stringent quality control procedures ensure the validity of scoring keys for objective PEP examinations each test date. However, if you question your scores because they are incon-

sistent with your previous performance on standardized tests or your level of prior learning, you may request that your scores be reverified. Your request must be in writing and must list by test code and title the PEP exams that you wish hand-scored, the test date(s) on which you took each exam, the test center where the tests were administered, and your full name, address, and date of birth. You must request this service **within six months** of the test date(s) in question. Requests after that time will **not** be honored. Results of hand-scoring are normally issued within 10 working days of receipt of the request. If you are dissatisfied with the hand score results, you may travel to Iowa City (at your expense) and witness the hand score of your answer sheet (objective tests only). However, neither your answer sheet nor test booklet will be released to you for review.

Additional Score Reports

If you wish, you may wait until you receive your copy of your score report before having your results reported to an institution or agency. All reports requested after the test date will require an additional fee.

The fee for regular Additional Score Reports (ASRs) is $4.00 per exam. A separate request form must be filed for each different institutional address. Regular ASRs are normally issued within 10 working days of receipt of the request and are mailed first-class. An ACT PEP Additional Score Request Form will be mailed to you with your score report.

In unusual situations, rush mailgram ASRs may be issued for $10.00 per exam; however do NOT request this service until you have received your score report copy. Before you request this service, we suggest that you check with the appropriate individual in the Admissions and Records department at your institution to ensure that they will accept scores listed on a mailgram from ACT PEP. Mailgram ASRs are normally issued within 48 hours after receipt of the request. If your situation requires mailgram ASR service, mark the Additional Score Request Form "RUSH" and include the fee payment of $10.00 per exam.

Diagnostic Reports

Diagnostic reports will be sent to those examinees who take objective examinations and receive a score of 44 or less. These reports are designed to assist you in evaluating your performance on the examination(s) and to provide information that may be useful in preparing to retake the exam(s).

Cancellation of Test Scores by ACT

ACT reserves the right to cancel test scores when there is reason to believe the scores are invalid. Cases of irregularities in the test administration process—for example, falsifying one's identity, impersonating another examinee (surrogate testing), unusual similarities in the answers of examinees at the same test center, or other indicators, including but not limited to student misconduct—may result in ACT's canceling the test scores. When ACT plans to cancel an examinee's test scores, the examinee is always notified prior to ACT taking that action. This notification includes information about the options available regarding the planned score cancellation, including procedures for appealing that decision. In all instances, the final and exclusive remedy available to examinees who want to appeal or otherwise challenge a decision by ACT to cancel their test scores shall be binding arbitration through written submissions to the American Arbitration Association.

Sample ACT PEP Answer Sheet

STUDY THE SAMPLES ON THIS PAGE TO BECOME FAMILIAR WITH THE FRONT SIDE OF THE ANSWER SHEET YOU WILL BE COMPLETING AT THE TEST CENTER.

BLOCK B: *NAME:* Print your Last Name, First Name, and MI (Middle Initial) in the boxes for each. Begin in the first box in each case and print only one letter per box. If your last or first name has more than one part, **leave one empty box between the parts.** If there are more letters in your last or first name than the number of boxes, print as many letters as possible, one letter per box. If you use the initial from your first name along with your middle name, print the initial in the first box for first name, leave one empty box, and print as many letters as possible of your middle name. Leave the box for middle initial blank. In the column directly below each box, blacken the oval (only one) containing the same letter as the box or the blank rectangle below each empty box.

BLOCK C: *MAILING ADDRESS.* Print your street mailing address, one letter or number per box. Begin in the first box and **leave one empty box between the parts.** Use numbers instead of words in street names that include numbers. Abbreviate when possible. In the column directly below each box, blacken the corresponding oval (only one) or the blank rectangle.

BLOCK D: *CITY.* Begin in the first box and print your city mailing address, one letter per box. If the city name has more than one part, **leave one empty box between the parts.** If the name requires more than the 14 boxes, abbreviate when possible and print as many letters as possible, one letter per box. Blacken either the appropriate oval (only one) or the blank rectangle in every column.

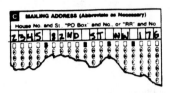

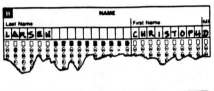

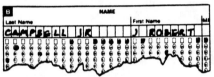

SUGGESTED ABBREVIATIONS

Beach	BCH	Highway	HWY
Boulevard	BLVD	Mile	MLE
Canyon	CYN	Parkway	PKY
Center	CTR	Place	PL
Circle	CIR	Santa, Santo	SN
City	CY	Springs	SPGS
Court	CT	Square	SQ
Crescent	CRES	State, Street	ST
Estates	EST	Terrace	TER
Expressway	EXPY	Turnpike	TPKE
Freeway	FWY	University	UNIV
Heights	HTS	Village	VLG

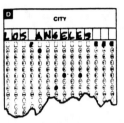

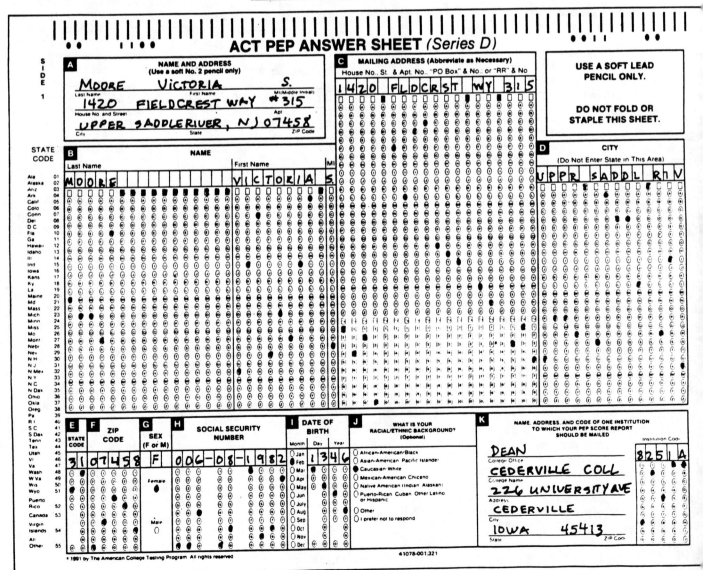

41078-001.321

ACT PEP Test Centers

Enter the correct four digit test center code for your **first and second choice** test centers in block L of your PEP Registration Form. It is your responsibility to **be sure that the test centers you indicate are open on the test date for which you are registering.** If the test center you wish is not open on a particular date, you must choose an alternate center that is open, or wait to register for the next date your desired center is open. If neither of the test centers you list is open on the test date you check in block K of your registration form, your registration form and fee will be returned to you unprocessed with an explanation that you did not indicate an open test center for the test date you selected.

X = Test center is OPEN for that test date.

City	Code	Test Center	Oct. 6-7, 1994	Nov. 3-4, 1994	Feb. 2-3, 1995	Mar. 2-3, 1995	May 4-5, 1995	June 1-2, 1995
ALABAMA								
Birmingham	0078	Lawson State Comm. Coll.	X	X	X	X	X	
Mobile	0009	Bishop State Comm. Coll.	X	X	X	X	X	X
Montgomery	0008	Alabama State Univ.	X	X	X		X	X
ARIZONA								
Flagstaff	0086	Northern Arizona Univ.	X	X		X	X	
Phoenix	0103	Rio Salado Comm. Coll.		X	X	X	X	X
Tempe	0088	Arizona State Univ.	X	X	X	X	X	X
ARKANSAS								
Blytheville	0129	Mississippi County Comm. Coll.	X	X	X	X		
Fort Smith	0122	Westark Comm. Coll.		X	X			X
Little Rock	0132	Univ. Conference Center	X	X	X	X	X	X
State Univ.	0116	Arkansas State Univ.		X		X	X	X
CALIFORNIA								
Berkeley	0162	Armstrong Univ.	X	X	X	X	X	
Carmichael	9343	San Juan Unified School District	X		X	X		
Chico	0212	California State Univ., Chico						X
El Cajon	0279	Grossmont Coll. (testing at LaMesa)	X	X	X	X	X	X
Fresno	0489	California State Univ.–Fresno	X	X	X	X	X	X
Imperial	0292	Imperial Valley Coll.	X	X	X	X	X	X
Long Beach	0300	Long Beach City Coll.	X	X	X	X	X	X
Los Angeles	0448	Moseley Salvatori Conference Ctr.	X	X	X	X	X	X
Monterey	0336	Monterey Peninsula Coll.	X	X	X	X	X	X
Montrose	0274	Montrose Campus–Glendale Comm. Coll.	X	X	X	X	X	X
Oakland	9341	HEC–Samuel Merritt College	X	X	X	X	X	X
Orange	0210	Chapman Univ.	X	X	X	X	X	X
Sacramento	0158	American River College	X	X	X	X	X	X
San Diego	0394	Univ. of San Diego			X	X		X
Whittier	0379	Rio Hondo Coll.				X	X	X
COLORADO								
Colorado Springs	0509	Pikes Peak Comm. Coll.		X	X			X
Ft. Morgan	0544	Morgan Comm. Coll.	X			X		
Grand Junction	0518	Mesa State Coll.	X	X	X	X	X	X
Greeley	0502	Univ. of Northern Colorado	X		X			
Littleton	0497	Arapahoe Comm. Coll.	X			X		
Westminster	0507	Front Range Comm. Coll.	X	X	X	X	X	X
CONNECTICUT								
Danbury	0558	Western Connecticut State Univ.	X	X	X	X	X	X
Fairfield	0560	Fairfield Univ.	X				X	X
Newington	0627	Charter Oak State Coll.		X			X	X
West Hartford	0606	Univ. of Hartford		X	X		X	X
FLORIDA								
Boca Raton	0729	Florida Atlantic Univ.	X	X	X	X	X	X
Daytona Beach	0720	Bethune-Cookman Coll.	X	X	X	X	X	X
Ft. Myers	9271	St. Cecilia's Church	X	X	X	X	X	X
Jacksonville	0717	Florida Comm. Coll. at Jacksonville			X	X	X	X
Lakeland	0732	Florida Southern Coll.	X	X	X	X	X	X
Miami	0770	Miami-Dade Comm. Coll.	X	X	X	X	X	X
Miami Shores	0718	Barry Univ.		X	X	X	X	
N. Miami	9233	Florida Int'l. Univ.			X		X	X
Panama City	0738	Gulf Coast Comm. Coll.		X	X			X
Tallahassee	0734	Florida State Univ.			X			X
Tampa	6394	Hillsborough Comm. Coll.	X	X	X	X	X	X
Tampa	0762	Univ. of Tampa	X	X	X	X	X	X
GEORGIA								
Atlanta	5571	Atlanta Area Technical Inst.		X	X		X	X
Atlanta	0810	Emory Univ.	X	X	X	X	X	X
Atlanta	0826	Georgia State Univ.	X	X	X		X	X
Augusta	0756	Augusta Coll.	X			X		X
Dahlonega	0848	North Georgia Coll.		X	X		X	
Savannah	0786	Armstrong State Coll.		X				X

City	Code	Test Center	Oct. 6-7, 1994	Nov. 3-4, 1994	Feb. 2-3, 1995	Mar. 2-3, 1995	May 4-5, 1995	June 1-2, 1995
HAWAII								
Hilo	0904	Univ. of Hawaii–Hilo	X		X	X		X
Honolulu	0902	Univ. of Hawaii–Manoa		X	X		X	
IDAHO								
Boise	0914	Boise State Univ.		X	X		X	
Pocatello	0918	Idaho State Univ.	X		X		X	
ILLINOIS								
Champaign	1015	Parkland Coll.		X			X	
Chicago	0934	City Colleges of Chicago–Harold Washington Coll.		X	X		X	X
De Kalb	1102	Northern Illinois Univ.		X	X		X	X
Dixon	1127	Sauk Valley Comm. Coll.		X	X			X
East Peoria	1035	Illinois Central Coll.			X			X
Lisle	1132	Illinois Benedictine Coll.	X	X	X	X		X
Quincy	0956	Blessing Rieman Coll. of Nrsg.	X					X
Rockford	1122	Rockford Coll.	X		X	X		X
University Park	1028	Governors State Univ.	X	X	X	X		X
INDIANA								
Evansville	1188	Univ. of Evansville			X			X
Fort Wayne	1238	Saint Francis Coll.	X		X			X
Indianapolis	1214	Indiana Univ.–Purdue Univ.	X	X	X	X	X	X
Mishawaka	1178	College Park Missionary Church	X			X	X	
IOWA								
Cedar Falls	1322	Univ. of Northern Iowa	X		X			X
Cedar Rapids	1275	Kirkwood Comm. Coll.		X	X	X		X
Des Moines	1302	Drake Univ.	X		X	X		X
Mason City	1336	No. Iowa Area Comm. Coll.		X	X	X		
Ottumwa	1269	Indian Hills Comm. Coll.	X					X
Sioux City	1276	Briar Cliff Coll.	X		X		X	X
West Burlington	1280	Southeastern Comm. Coll.	X	X	X	X	X	X
KANSAS								
Wichita	1472	Wichita State Univ.		X			X	
KENTUCKY								
Hopkinsville	1569	Hopkinsville Comm. Coll.	X					X
Lexington	1554	Univ. of Kentucky	X	X	X	X	X	X
Louisville	1556	Univ. of Louisville	X	X	X	X	X	X
LOUISIANA								
Hammond	1608	Southeastern Louisiana Univ.	X	X	X	X	X	X
Lake Charles	1594	McNeese State Univ.		X			X	X
New Orleans	1611	Southern Univ. at New Orleans	X	X	X	X	X	X
Shreveport	1613	Southern Univ.	X	X	X	X	X	X
MAINE								
South Portland	9342	Southern Maine Tech. Coll.	X			X	X	
Wiscasset	1667	Lincoln County Court House		X	X		X	X
MARYLAND								
Baltimore	1727	College of Notre Dame	X	X	X	X	X	X
Catonsville	1684	Catonsville Comm. Coll.	X	X		X	X	X
College Park	1746	Univ. of Maryland	X	X	X	X	X	X
Cumberland	1679	Allegany Comm. Coll.			X			X
Largo	1731	Prince George's Comm. Coll.	X	X	X	X	X	X
MASSACHUSETTS								
Chestnut Hill	1788	Boston Coll.	X	X	X	X	X	X
Holyoke	1844	Holyoke Comm. Coll.		X		X		X
Lynn	1875	North Shore Comm. Coll.	X	X	X	X	X	X
Newton	1911	Aquinas College at Newton	X	X	X	X	X	X
No. Dartmouth	1906	Univ. of Massachusetts–Dartmouth						X
Wellesley Hills	1861	Massachusetts Bay Comm. Coll.	X	X	X	X	X	X

11

City	Code	Test Center	Oct 6-7, 1994	Nov 3-4, 1994	Feb 2-3, 1995	Mar 2-3, 1995	May 4-5, 1995	June 1-2, 1995
MICHIGAN								
Ann Arbor	1977	Concordia Coll.	X	X	X	X	X	X
Detroit	2024	Marygrove Coll.	X	X	X	X	X	X
Detroit	2060	Univ. of Detroit Mercy	X	X	X		X	X
Grand Rapids	2004	Grand Rapids Comm. Coll.		X	X	X	X	X
Kalamazoo	2066	Western Michigan Univ.	X			X		
Traverse City	2040	Northwestern Michigan Coll.	X		X			X
University Center	2057	Saginaw Valley State Univ.	X	X	X	X	X	X
MINNESOTA								
Duluth	2157	Univ. of Minnesota–Duluth		X		X	X	
Inver Grove Hts.	2103	Inver Hills Comm. Coll.				X		
Minneapolis	2156	Univ. of Minnesota	X	X	X		X	X
White Bear Lake	2125	Lakewood Comm. Coll.						X
MISSISSIPPI								
Cleveland	2190	Delta State University	X			X	X	X
Jackson	2204	Jackson State Univ.		X	X		X	
Mississippi St.	2220	Mississippi State Univ.	X	X	X	X	X	X
MISSOURI								
Kansas City	2380	Univ. of Missouri–Kansas City	X	X	X	X	X	X
Springfield	2370	Southwest Missouri State Univ.		X	X		X	
St. Louis	2352	St. Louis Univ.–Frost Campus		X	X		X	X
St. Louis	2383	Univ. of Missouri–St. Louis	X	X	X	X	X	X
MONTANA								
Bozeman	2420	Montana State Univ.		X		X		
NEBRASKA								
Kearney	2468	Univ. of Nebraska–Kearney		X		X		
Lincoln	2482	Univ. of Nebraska–Lincoln		X		X	X	
McCook	2460	McCook Comm. Coll.	X		X	X		X
Omaha	2464	Univ. of Nebraska at Omaha		X	X			X
NEVADA								
N. Las Vegas	2498	Comm. Coll. of Southern Nevada		X	X		X	
Reno	2499	Truckee Meadows Comm. Coll.	X	X	X	X	X	X
Reno	2494	Univ. of Nevada–Reno	X	X	X	X	X	X
NEW HAMPSHIRE								
Keene	2510	Keene State Coll.	X	X	X	X	X	X
Manchester	2522	St. Anselm Coll.	X	X	X	X	X	X
NEW JERSEY								
Camden	2598	Rutgers Univ.	X	X	X	X	X	X
Lodi	2559	Felician Coll.	X	X	X	X	X	X
Morristown	2546	College of St. Elizabeth	X	X	X	X	X	X
Pemberton	2543	Burlington County Coll.	X		X		X	X
Trenton	2568	Mercer County Comm. Coll.	X	X	X	X	X	X
Trenton	2612	Thomas Edison State Coll.	X			X		
NEW MEXICO								
Albuquerque	2650	Univ. of New Mexico	X	X	X	X	X	X
Clovis	2631	Clovis Comm. Coll.	X	X	X	X	X	
Silver City	2646	Western New Mexico Univ.		X		X		

NEW YORK

These examinations are administered in New York State by Regents College. You may register with Regents College by calling (518) 464-8500.

City	Code	Test Center	Oct 6-7, 1994	Nov 3-4, 1994	Feb 2-3, 1995	Mar 2-3, 1995	May 4-5, 1995	June 1-2, 1995
NORTH CAROLINA								
Belmont	3070	Belmont Abbey Coll.	X	X	X	X	X	X
Chapel Hill	3162	Univ. of North Carolina	X		X		X	
High Point	3108	High Point Univ.	X	X	X	X		X
Raleigh	3177	Wake Technical Coll.	X		X			X
OHIO								
Cincinnati	3340	Univ. of Cincinnati	X	X	X	X	X	X
Columbus	3275	Franklin Univ.	X	X	X	X	X	X
Dayton	3295	Wright State Univ.	X	X	X	X	X	X
Elyria	3287	Lorain County Comm. Coll.	X		X		X	
St. Clairsville	3317	Ohio Univ.–Eastern Campus	X			X		
Steubenville	3258	Franciscan Univ. of Steubenville		X	X	X		
Westerville	3318	Otterbein Coll.		X	X	X	X	
Youngstown	3368	Youngstown State Univ.		X	X	X	X	X
OKLAHOMA								
Midwest City	3403	Rose State Coll.		X		X		
Norman	3442	Univ. of Oklahoma		X		X		
Oklahoma City	3423	Oklahoma State Univ.	X	X				X
Stillwater	3424	Oklahoma State Univ.	X	X				X
Tulsa	5340	Langston Univ./UCT		X		X	X	

City	Code	Test Center	Oct 6-7, 1994	Nov 3-4, 1994	Feb 2-3, 1995	Mar 2-3, 1995	May 4-5, 1995	June 1-2, 1995
OREGON								
Eugene	3498	Univ. of Oregon	X			X		X
Klamath Falls	3484	Oregon Institute of Technology		X			X	
Portland	3491	Oregon Polytechnic Institute	X	X	X	X	X	X
PENNSYLVANIA								
Bethlehem	3645	Northampton Comm. Coll.	X			X	X	
Blue Bell	3641	Montgomery County Comm. Coll.	X	X	X	X	X	X
Harrisburg	3589	Harrisburg Area Comm. Coll.	X	X	X	X	X	X
Indiana	3704	Indiana Univ. of Pennsylvania		X				X
Johnstown	3735	Univ. of Pittsburgh–Johnstown		X	X		X	X
Kutztown	3706	Kutztown Univ. of Pennsylvania		X		X		X
Philadelphia	3608	La Salle Univ.	X	X	X	X	X	X
Philadelphia	3724	Temple Univ.		X	X	X	X	
Philadelphia	9237	Thomas Jefferson Univ.	X	X	X	X	X	X
Pittsburgh	3560	Duquesne Univ.	X			X		X
Pittsburgh	3734	Univ. of Pittsburgh	X	X	X	X	X	X
Radnor	3532	Cabrini Coll.	X	X	X	X	X	X
Reading	3718	Reading Area Comm. Coll.		X		X		
Wilkes-Barre	3604	King's Coll.		X	X		X	X
RHODE ISLAND								
Providence	3810	Rhode Island Coll.	X	X	X	X	X	X
SOUTH CAROLINA								
Charleston	6465	Medical Univ. of South Carolina	X	X	X		X	X
Florence	3856	Francis Marion Univ.	X	X	X	X	X	X
Orangeburg	3876	South Carolina State Coll.	X	X	X	X	X	X
Spartanburg	3889	Univ. of South Carolina–Spartanburg	X	X	X	X	X	X
TENNESSEE								
Chattanooga	4022	Univ. of Tennessee–Chattanooga		X			X	X
Clarksville	3944	Austin Peay State Univ.	X	X	X	X	X	X
Jackson	4020	Union Univ.		X			X	X
Johnson City	3958	East Tennessee State Univ.	X	X	X	X	X	X
Knoxville	4026	Univ. of Tennessee	X	X	X	X	X	X
Murfreesboro	3994	Middle Tennessee State Univ.	X	X	X	X	X	X
Nashville	3946	Belmont Univ.			X	X	X	
TEXAS								
College Station	4198	Texas A&M Univ.	X	X	X	X	X	X
Dallas	9344	The Bill J. Priest Inst. for Economic Dev.	X	X	X	X	X	X
El Paso	4090	El Paso Comm. Coll.	X	X	X	X	X	X
Fort Worth	4222	Texas Wesleyan Univ.	X			X	X	
Houston	4236	Univ. of Houston	X	X	X	X	X	X
Houston	4170	Univ. of Houston–Downtown	X	X	X	X	X	X
Killeen	4081	Central Texas Coll.	X	X	X		X	X
Midland	4127	Midland Coll.	X			X		
Odessa	4138	Odessa Coll.		X	X			X
Plano	4046	Collin Co. Comm. Coll.	X	X	X	X		
Prairie View	4202	Prairie View A&M Univ.	X	X	X	X		X
Richardson	4243	Univ. of Texas–Dallas					X	
San Antonio	4158	St. Marys Univ.	X	X	X	X	X	X
Wharton	4252	Wharton County Jr. Coll.	X	X	X	X	X	X
UTAH								
Orem	4278	Utah Valley Comm. Coll.	X	X	X	X	X	X
Salt Lake City	4274	Univ. of Utah	X	X	X	X	X	X
VERMONT								
Johnson	4316	Johnson State Coll.		X		X	X	
VIRGINIA								
Hampton	4358	Hampton Univ.	X		X	X		
Norfolk	4425	Norfolk State Univ.	X	X	X	X	X	X
Petersburg	4424	Virginia State Univ.			X	X	X	X
Roanoke	4351	Virginia Western Comm. Coll.	X	X	X	X	X	X
WASHINGTON								
Bellingham	4490	Western Washington Univ.	X	X	X		X	X
Bothell	4497	Univ. of Washington Bothell		X	X			
Seattle	4484	Univ. of Washington	X	X	X	X	X	X
Spokane	4458	Gonzaga Univ.		X	X		X	
WEST VIRGINIA								
Beckley	4510	The Coll. of West Virginia	X	X	X	X		X
Parkersburg	4542	West Virginia Univ. at Parkersburg		X	X		X	
WISCONSIN								
Madison	4582	Edgewood Coll.		X	X		X	
Menomonie	4652	Univ. of Wisconsin–Stout	X	X	X		X	
Milwaukee	4558	Alverno Coll.		X	X		X	
Oshkosh	4674	Univ. of Wisconsin–Oshkosh	X	X	X	X	X	X
Stevens Point	4680	Univ. of Wisconsin–Stevens Point	X		X			X

ACT PEP Test Center Addendum

STATE, City	CODE	TEST CENTER	OCT	NOV	FEB	MAR	MAY	JUN
IOWA, Clinton	1292	Clinton Community Coll (at Best Western Frontier Motor Inn)	X	X		X		X

List of ACT PEP Participating Institutions

Note: This is **NOT** a list of PEP test centers. The test center list can be found on pages 11-12 of the PEP *Candidate Registration Guide*.

IMPORTANT INSTRUCTIONS!
Take this list with you to the test center on the test day. You will need it to complete your answer sheet.

The institutions listed below grant credit for successful completion of one or more ACT PEP examinations or use them to facilitate transfer to other institutions. If you have questions about which examinations are used, amount of credit awarded, minimum scores required, or deadlines, contact the institution directly. Because the number of institutions participating in ACT PEP continues to grow, the list may not be complete. If the institution of your choice is not listed, check directly with the appropriate department office or the registrar at that institution to determine whether it will grant the credit you seek on the basis of PEP examination results.

On the test date you will be asked to indicate on each of your answer sheets the name, address, and code number (four numbers and one letter) for one institution to which your PEP scores should be reported. To be sure that you list the correct code number. **It is crucial that you take this list with your to the test center on the test day to use in completing your answer sheet. The institution code number is essential for proper reporting of your PEP results. Note:** This is **NOT** a list of PEP test centers. The test center list can be found on pages 11-12 of the PEP *Candidate Registration Guide*.

ALABAMA
0009A Bishop State Comm. Coll. (Mobile)
4256A Comm. Coll. of the Air Force (Maxwell AFB)
0003A Faulkner Univ. (Montgomery)
0039A Jefferson Davis State Jr. Coll. (Brewton)
0047A Jefferson State Jr. Coll. (Birmingham)
0078A Lawson State Comm. Coll. (Birmingham)
0029A Mobile Coll. (Mobile)
0030A Oakwood Coll. (Huntsville)
0038A Southeastern Bible Coll. (Birmingham)
0133A Troy State Univ. in Montgomery (Montgomery)
0052A Univ. of Alabama–The New Coll. (University)
0059A Univ. of South Alabama Sch. of Nrsg. (Mobile)
0054A Walker Coll. (Jasper)

ALASKA
0137A Univ. of Alaska (Anchorage)
4828A Wayland Baptist Univ. (Anchorage)

ARIZONA
0088A Arizona State Univ. (Tempe)
0092A Grand Canyon Univ. (Phoenix)
0104A Navajo Comm. Coll. (Tsaile)
0086A Northern Arizona Univ. (Flagstaff)
9222A Ottawa Univ.–Phoenix Ctr.
0103A Rio Salado Comm. Coll. (Phoenix)
9255A Univ. of Phoenix (Mesa)
9203A Univ. of Phoenix (Phoenix)
9254A Univ. of Phoenix (Tucson)
0179A Western International Univ. (Phoenix)

ARKANSAS
0116A Arkansas State Univ. (State University)
0114A Arkansas Tech. Univ. (Russellville)
0131A Baptist System Sch. of Nrsg. (Little Rock)
0109A East Arkansas Comm. Coll. (Forrest City)
0115A Garland County Comm. Coll. (Hot Springs Nat. Pk.)
0126A Henderson State Univ. (Arkadelphia)
0161A Jefferson Sch. of Nrsg. (Pine Bluff)
0129A Mississippi County Comm. Coll. (Blytheville)
0134A Ouchita Baptist Univ. (Arkadelphia)
0142A Southern Arkansas Univ. (Magnolia)
0132A Univ. of Arkansas (Little Rock)
0110A Univ. of Arkansas at Monticello (Monticello)
0108A Univ. of Arkansas at Pine Bluff (Pine Bluff)
6869A Univ. of Arkansas Med. Sci. Campus (Little Rock)
0118A Univ. of Central Arkansas (Conway)
0122A Westark Comm. Coll. (Fort Smith)

CALIFORNIA
9271A American Coll. of Nrsg. (San Francisco)
0158A American River Coll. (Sacramento)
0166A Azusa Pacific Univ. (Azusa)
0165A Butte Coll. (Oroville)
9213A CA Dept. of Consumer Afrs., Bd. of Accountancy (Sacramento)
0173A Cabrillo Coll. (Aptos)
0175A Calif. Baptist Coll. (Riverside)
0489A Calif. Statewide Nrsg. Program (Carson)
0228A Cogswell Coll. (San Francisco)
0232A Coll. of Marin, Reg. Nrsg. Pro. (Kentfield)
0473A Columbia Pacific Univ. (San Rafael)
0256A Dominican Coll. of San Rafael (San Rafael)
9221A Empire Coll. (Santa Rosa)
0274A Glendale Comm. Coll. (Glendale)
0278A Golden Gate Univ. (San Francisco)
0288A Humphreys Coll. (Stockton)
0292A Imperial Valley Coll. (Imperial)
9245A Kensington Univ. (Glendale)
0294A La Sierra Univ. (Riverside)
0333A Merced Coll. (Merced)
0348A Merritt Coll. (Oakland)
0336A Monterey Peninsula Coll. (Monterey)
0439A National Univ. (San Diego)
0353A New Coll. of California (San Francisco)
0346A Northrop Univ. (Los Angeles)
0265A Ohlone Coll. (Fremont)
0356A Pacific Christian Coll. (Fullerton)
0360A Pacific Western Univ. (Encino)
0370A Point Loma Coll., Div. of Nrsg. (San Diego)
0380A Sacramento City Coll. (Sacramento)
0386A St. Mary's Coll. (Moraga)
0412A Samuel Merritt Coll. (Oakland)
0186A San Francisco Art Inst. (San Francisco)
0436A San Joaquin Delta Coll. (Stockton)
0410A San Jose State Univ. (San Jose)
0450A Univ. of Calif.–San Francisco, Sch. of Nrsg. (San Francisco)
0295A Univ. of La Verne (La Verne)
9253A Univ. of Phoenix (Fountain Valley)
9248A Univ. of Phoenix (San Diego)
9252A Univ. of Phoenix (San Jose)
0371A Univ. of San Diego–Philip Y. Hahn Sch. of Nrsg. (San Diego)
0470A Univ. of So. California, Dept. of Nrsg. (Los Angeles)
0481A Woodbury Univ. (Burbank)

COLORADO
0497A Arapahoe Comm. Coll. (Littleton)
9258A Columbia Coll. (Aurora)
0511A Comm. Coll. of Denver (Denver)
0539A Front Range Comm. Coll. (Ft. Collins)
0507A Front Range Comm. Coll. (Westminster)
0518A Mesa Coll. (Grand Junction)
0519A Metropolitan State Coll. (Denver)
0544A Morgan Comm. Coll. (Ft. Morgan)
0509A Pikes Peak Comm. Coll. (Colorado Springs)
0526A Regis Univ. (Denver)
6057A Univ. of CO Health Sci. Cen. (Denver)
0502A Univ. of Northern Colorado (Greeley)
9251A Univ. of Phoenix (Aurora)
0524A Univ. of Southern Colorado (Pueblo)

CONNECTICUT
0551A Asnuntuck Comm. Coll. (Enfield)
9228A Bridgeport Hosp. Sch. of Nrsg. (Bridgeport)
0627A Charter Oak Coll./Bd. St. Acd. Awds. (Farmington)
0616A Eastern Connecticut State Univ. (Willimantic)
0560A Fairfield Univ. (Fairfield)
0564A Holy Apostles Coll. (Cromwell)
0569A Manchester Comm. Coll. (Manchester)
0573A Mohegan Comm. Coll. (Norwich)
0577A Norwalk Comm. Coll. (Norwalk)
0589A Sacred Heart Univ. (Bridgeport)
9217D St. Francis Hospital Sch. of Nrsg. (Hartford)
9214A St. Mary's Hospital Sch. of Nrsg. (Waterbury)
0592A St. Vincent's Coll. of Nrsg. (Bridgeport)
0593A Southern Connecticut State Univ. (New Haven)
0602A Univ. of Bridgeport (Bridgeport)
0604A Univ. of Connecticut (Storrs)
0606A Univ. of Hartford (West Hartford)
0558A Western Connecticut State Univ. (Danbury)

DELAWARE
0635A Wilmington Coll. (New Castle)

WASHINGTON, D.C.
0654A Catholic Univ. of America
9220A District of Columbia Bd. of Accountancy
0674A Howard Univ. (Washngton, D.C.)
0695A Univ. of District of Columbia (Washington, D.C.)

FLORIDA
0718A Barry Univ. Sch. of Nrsg. (Miami Shores)
0720A Bethune Cookman Coll. (Daytona Beach)
0769A Brevard Comm. Coll. (Cocoa)
0722A Chipola Jr. Coll. (Marianna)
0723A Daytona Beach Comm. Coll. (Daytona Beach)
0727A Edison Comm. Coll. (Ft. Myers)
0725A Embry-Riddle Aeronautical Univ. (Bunnell)
0726A Florida A&M Univ. (Tallahassee)
0729A Florida Atlantic Univ. (Boca Raton)
0717A Florida Comm. Coll. (Jacksonville)
0776A Florida Int'l. Univ. (Miami)
9233A Florida Int'l. Univ.–Sch. of Nrsg. (No. Miami Beach)
0747A Florida Keys Comm. Coll. (Key West)
0734A Florida State Univ. (Tallahassee)
0738A Gulf Coast Comm. Coll. (Panama City)
6394A Hillsborough Comm. Coll. (Tampa)
0774A Indian River Comm. Coll. (Fort Pierce)
0766A Lake City Comm. Coll. (Lake City)
0737A Lake-Sumter Comm. Coll. (Leesburg)
9216D Martin Memorial Hospital (Stuart)
0770A Miami-Dade Comm. Coll. (Miami)
0714A Nova Univ. (Fort Lauderdale)
0744A Palm Beach Jr. Coll. (Lake Worth)
0757A Polk Comm. Coll. (Winter Haven)
0755A Saint Leo Coll. (Saint Leo)
0778A Santa Fe Comm. Coll. (Gainesville)
0779A Seminole Comm. Coll. (Sanford)
0711A Univ. of North Florida (Jacksonville)
5472A Univ. of Sarasota (Sarasota)
5828A Univ. of South Florida (Ft. Myers)
0761A Univ. of South Florida (Tampa)
0762A Univ. of Tampa (Tampa)
0771A Univ. of West Florida (Pensacola)

GEORGIA
0786A Armstrong State Coll. (Savannah)
1110A Atlanta Bible Coll. (Morrow)
0796A Augusta Coll. (Augusta)
0800A Brenau Coll. (Gainesville)
0810A Emory Univ.–Nell Hodgson Woodruff Sch. of Nrsg. (Atlanta)
9217A Floyd Jr. Coll. (Rome)
0819A Georgia Baptist Coll. of Nrsg. (Atlanta)
0836A Medical Coll. of Georgia Sch. of Nrsg. (Augusta)
0848A North Georgia Coll. (Dahlonega)

HAWAII
0903A Hawaii Loa Coll. (Kaneohe)
0900A Hawaii Pacific Univ. (Honolulu)
0904A Univ. of Hawaii–Hilo (Hilo)

IDAHO
0914A Boise State Univ. (Boise)
0924A Northwest Nazarene Coll. (Nampa)

ILLINOIS
0941A Aero-Space Inst. (Chicago)
0950A Aurora Univ. (Aurora)
0952A Barat Coll. (Lake Forest)
0954A Belleville Area Coll. (Belleville)
0956A Blessing Rieman Coll. of Nrsg. (Quincy)
4965A Board of Governors Bach. of Arts Deg. Prog. (Springfield)
1170A Carl Sandburg Coll. (Galesburg)
0992A Chicago State Univ.–BOG (Chicago)
City Colleges of Chicago:
0934A   City Wide Coll.
9267A   European Office (APO New York)
0978A   Kennedy-King Coll.
0975A   Harold Washington Coll. (Loop)
0972A   Malcolm X Coll.
0974A   Olive-Harvey Coll.
0971A   Richard J. Daley Coll.
0970A   Truman Coll.
0980A   Wright Coll.
1004A Concordia Univ. (River Forest)
5032A Concordia Coll.–WSCN (Oak Park)
1012A De Paul Univ. (Chicago)
1016A Eastern Illinois Univ.–BOG (Charleston)
1020A Elmhurst Coll. (Elmhurst)
1028A Governors State Univ.–BOG (Univ. Park)
1029A Highland Comm. Coll. (Freeport)
0995A IECC-Frontier Comm. Coll. (Fairfield)
1067A IECC-Lincoln Trail Coll. (Robinson)
1113A IECC-Olney Central Coll. (Olney)
1162A IECC-Wabash Valley Coll. (Mt. Carmel)
1132A Illinois Benedictine Coll. (Lisle)
1035A Illinois Central Coll. (East Peoria)
1044A Illinois Wesleyan Univ. Sch. of Nrsg. (Bloomington)
1017A John A. Logan Coll.–Carterville (Carterville)
1019A John Wood Comm. Coll. (Quincy)
1048A Joliet Jr. Coll. (Joliet)
0964A Kaskaskia Coll. (Centralia)
1050A Kendall Coll. (Evanston)
1051A Kishwaukee Coll. (Malta)
1057A Lakeview Med. Ctr. Sch. of Nrsg. (Danville)
1058A Lewis Univ. (Romeoville)
1038A Lewis and Clark Comm. Coll. (Godfrey)
1068A MacMurray Coll. (Jacksonville)
1076A McKendree Coll. (Lebanon)

1081A Mennonite Coll. of Nrsg. (Bloomington)
1087A Moraine Valley Comm. Coll (Palos Hills)
1090A Morton Coll. (Cicero)
1094A National-Louis Univ. (Lombard)
0993A Northeastern Illinois Univ.-BOG (Chicago)
1102A Northern Illinos Univ. (De Kalb)
1098A North Park Coll. (Chicago)
1112A Olivet Nazarene Coll. (Kankakee)
1120A Quincy Coll. (Quincy)
1091A Rend Lake Coll. (Ina)
1121A Robert Morris Coll. (Carthage)
1122A Rockford Coll. (Rockford)
1124A Roosevelt Univ. (Chicago)
1117A Rush Univ. (Chicago)
6432A St. Anthony Coll. of Nrsg. (Rockford)
1138A St. Francis Medical Center (Peoria)
1135A St. Joseph Coll. of Nrsg. (Joliet)
1134A Saint Xavier Coll. (Chicago)
1127A Sauk Valley Coll. (Dixon)
1173A Shawnee Coll. (Ullin)
1148A South Suburban Coll. (S. Holland)
1161A Southeastern Illinois Coll. (Harrisburg)
1165A Trinity Christian Coll. (Palos Heights)
1159A Waubonsee Comm. Coll. (Sugar Grove)
1158A Western Illinois Univ.-BOG (Macomb)

INDIANA

1176A Ball State Univ. (Muncie)
1178A Bethel Coll. (Mishawaka)
1180A Butler Univ. (Indianapolis)
1203A Holy Cross Jr. Coll. (Notre Dame)
1204A .v. of Indianapolis (Indianapolis)
1216A 'iana Univ. East (Richmond)
1218A .ana Univ. Northwest (Gary)
1225A .diana Univ.-South Bend (South Bend)
1235A Indiana Voc. Tech. Coll. (Madison)
1257A Ivy Tech. Coll. (Bloomington)
9247A Lutheran Coll. of Health Professions (Fort Wayne)
1233A Purdue Univ.-Calumet (Hammond)
1238A St. Francis Coll. of Fort Wayne (Fort Wayne)
1188A Univ. of Evansville (Evansville)
1258A Vincennes Univ. (Vincennes)

IOWA

1273A Allen Memorial Hosp. Sch. of Nrsg. (Waterloo)
1276A Briar Cliff Coll. (Sioux City)
1290A Clarke Coll. (Dubuque)
1294A Coe Coll. (Cedar Rapids)
1302A Drake Univ. (Des Moines)
1314A Graceland Coll. (Lamoni)
1316A Grand View Coll. (Des Moines)
1312A Iowa Central Comm. Coll. (Ft. Dodge)
1310A Iowa Lakes Comm. Coll. (Estherville)
1334A Marycrest Coll. (Davenport)
1340A Mt. Mercy Coll. (Cedar Rapids)
1280A Southeastern Comm. Coll. (West Burlington)
6260A Spencer Sch. of Business (Spencer)
1377A St. Luke's Sch. of Nrsg. (Sioux City)
1370A Teikyo Westmar Univ. (LeMars)
1356A Univ. of Iowa Coll. of Nrsg. (Iowa City)
1358A Univ. of Dubuque (Dubuque)
1360A Upper Iowa Univ. (Fayette)

KANSAS

1467A Baker Univ.-Stormont/Vail Campus (Topeka)
1399A Colby Comm. Coll. (Colby)
1408A Fort Hays State Univ. (Hays)
1412A Friends Univ. (Wichita)
1418A Highland Comm. Jr. Coll. (Highland)
1420A Hutchinson Comm. Coll. (Hutchinson)
1425A Johnson County Comm. Coll. (Overland Park)
1428A Kansas State Univ. (Manhattan)
1434A Kansas Wesleyan Univ. (Salina)
1440A McPherson Coll. (McPherson)
1445A Mid-America Nazarene Coll. (Olathe)
1446A Ottawa Univ. (Overland Park)
1464A Southwestern Coll. (Winfield)
1472A Wichita State Univ. (Wichita)

KENTUCKY

1486A Asbury Coll. (Wilmore)
1564A Ashland Comm. Coll. (Ashland)
1490A Bellarmine Coll. (Louisville)
1512A Eastern Kentucky Univ. (Richmond)
1513A Elizabethtown Comm. Coll. (Elizabethtown)
1572A Hazard Comm. Coll. (Hazard)
1557A Henderson Comm. Coll. (Henderson)
1569A Hopkinsville Comm. Coll. (Hopkinsville)
1571A Jefferson Comm. Coll. (Louisville)
1518A Kentucky Wesleyan Coll. (Owensboro)
1531A Lexington Comm. Coll. (Lexington)
1533A Madisonville Comm. Coll. (Madisonville)
1527A Maysville Comm. Coll. (Maysville)
1530A Morehead State Univ. (Morehead)
1538A Paducah Comm. Coll. (Paducah)
1541A Prestonsburg Comm. Coll. (Prestonsburg)
1570A Somerset Comm. Coll. (Somerset)
1555A Southeast Comm. Coll. (Cumberland)
1534A Spaulding Coll. (Louisville)
5535A Sullivan Jr. Coll. (Louisville)
1560A Thomas More Coll. (Crestview Hills)
1554A Univ. of Kentucky, Coll. of Nrsg. (Lexington)
1568A Univ. of Kentucky-Elizabethtown Campus (Elizabethtown)

LOUISIANA

1578A Dillard Univ. (New Orleans)
1582A Grambling State Univ. (Grambling)
1658A La Salle Univ. (Slidell)
1592A Loyola Univ.-City Coll. (New Orleans)
1594A McNeese State Univ. (Lake Charles)
1580A Nicholls State Univ. (Thibodaux)
1574A Our Lady of Holy Cross Coll. (New Orleans)
1621A Our Lady of the Lake Coll. of Nrsg. & Allied Health (Baton Rouge)
1608A Southeastern Louisiana Univ. (Hammond)
1611A Southern Univ. of New Orleans (New Orleans)
1613A Southern Univ.-Shreveport (Shreveport)

MAINE

1639A Central Maine Medical Center Sch. of Nrsg. (Lewiston)
9218A Kennebec Valley Tech. Coll. (Fairfield)
1659A Saint Joseph's Coll. (No. Windham)
9342A S. Maine Voc. Tech. Inst. (So. Portland)
1642A Univ. of Maine at Fort Kent (Fort Kent)

MARYLAND

1679A Allegany Comm. Coll. (Cumberland)
1693A Antietam Bible Coll. (Hagerstown)
1712A Bowie State Coll. (Bowie)
1681A Cecil Comm. Coll. (North East)
1727A Coll. of Notre Dame (Baltimore)
1688A Coppin State Coll. (Baltimore)
1700A Harford Comm. Coll. (Bel Air)
1704A Johns Hopkins Univ. Sch. of Nrsg. (Baltimore)
1722A Morgan State Univ. (Baltimore)
1716A Salisbury State Coll. (Salisbury)
1718A Towson State Univ. (Towson)
9264A Traditional Acupuncture Inst. (Columbia)
1749A Union Memorial Hosp. Sch. of Nrsg. (Baltimore)
1746A Univ. of Maryland (College Park)
1758A Univ. of Maryland-Sch. of Nrsg. (Baltimore)
9202J Univ. of Maryland-Asian Div. (APO San Francisco)
9201J Univ. of Maryland-European Div. (APO New York)
1753A Villa Julie Coll. (Stevenson)

MASSACHUSETTS

1772A American International Coll. (Springfield)
1784A Atlantic Union Coll. (South Lancaster)
1849A Becker Coll. (Worcester)
1788A Boston Coll. Sch. of Nrsg. (Chestnut Hill)
1803A Bristol Comm. Coll. (Fall River)
1799A Bunker Hill Comm. Coll. (Charlestown)
1807A Cape Code Comm. Coll. (W. Barnstable)
1814A Curry Coll. (Milton)
1822A Emmanuel Coll. (Boston)
9221D Framingham Union Hosp. Sch. of Nrsg. (Framingham)
1839A Greenfield Comm. Coll. (Greenfield)
1844A Holyoke Comm. Coll. (Holyoke)
1848A Lasell Jr. Coll. (Newton)
9240A Lawrence Memorial Hosp. Sch. of Nrsg. (Medford)
1861A Massachusetts Bay Comm. Coll. (Wellesley Hills)
1862A Massasoit Comm. Coll. (Brockton)
1865A Middlesex Comm. Coll. (Bedford)
9214D New England Baptist Hosp. Sch. of Nrsg. (Boston)
9256A New England Deaconess Hosp. Sch. of Nrsg. (Boston)
1878A Nichols Coll. (Dudley)
1875A North Shore Comm. Coll. (Lynn)
1880A Northeastern Univ. (Boston)
1877A Northern Essex Comm. Coll. (Haverhill)
1888A Quincy Jr. Coll. (Quincy)
1885A Quinsigamond Comm Coll. (Worcester)
1886A Regis Coll. (Weston)
9206D St. Elizabeth Hosp. Sch. of Nrsg (Brighton)
1910A Salem State Coll. (Salem)
1892A Simmons Coll. (Boston)
1918A Stonehill Coll. (North Easton)
1925A Univ. of Massachusetts, Boston (Boston)
1906A Univ. of Massachusetts, Dartmough (N. Dartmouth)

MICHIGAN

1954A Adrian Coll. (Adrian)
1992A Andrews Univ. (Berrien Springs)
1972A Central Michigan Univ. (Mt. Pleasant)
1977A Concordia Coll. (Ann Arbor)
1990A Eastern Michigan Univ. (Ypsilanti)
2004A Grand Rapids Comm. Coll. (Grand Rapids)
2005A Grand Valley State Colleges (Allendale)
2013A Hurley Medical Center Sch. of Nrsg. (Flint)
2014A Jackson Comm. Coll. (Jackson)
2011A Jordon Coll. (Cedar Springs)
1964A Kellogg Comm. Coll. (Battle Creek)
2020A Lawrence Inst. of Technology (Southfield)
2022A Madonna Coll. (Livonia)
2030A Michigan Technological Univ. (Houghton)
2045A Northeastern Sch. of Commerce (Bay City)
2041A Northwood Inst. (Midland)
2033A Oakland Univ. (Rochester)
2057A Saginaw Valley State Coll. (University Center)
2055A Southwestern Michigan Coll. (Dowagiac)
2060A Univ. of Detroit-Mercy (Detroit)
9231A Univ. of Michigan Dept. of Geol. Sci. (Ann Arbor)

MINNESOTA

2090A Brainerd Comm. Coll. (Brainerd)
2088A Bethel Coll. (St. Paul)
2094A Coll. of St. Benedict (St. Joseph)
2149A Coll. of St. Catherine-St. Mary's Campus (Minneapolis)
2098A Coll. of St. Scholastica (Duluth)
2116A Hibbing Comm. Coll.-Arrowhead (Hibbing)
2103A Inver Hills Comm. Coll. (Inver Grove Heights)
2125A Lakewood Comm. Coll. (White Bear Lake)
2126A Mankato State Univ. (Mankato)
9260A Metropolitan State Univ. (St. Paul)
2148A St. Mary's Coll. (Winona)
2102A Univ. of St. Thomas (St. Paul)

MISSISSIPPI

2190A Delta State Univ. (Cleveland)
2202A Itawamba Jr. Coll. (Fulton)
2212A Millsaps Coll. (Jackson)
2251A Univ. of Mississippi Med. Ctr. Sch. of Nrsg. (Jackson)
2253A Wesley Coll. (Florence)

MISSOURI

2287A Berean Coll. of the Assemblies of God (Springfield)
2276A Columbia Coll. (Columbia)
2280A Conception Seminary Coll. (Conception)
2293A Deaconess Coll. of Nrsg. (St. Louis)
1314A Graceland Coll. (Independence)
2320A Hannibal-LaGrange Coll. (Hannibal)
2313A Jefferson Coll. (Hillsboro)
2305A Jewish Hosp. Sch. of Nrsg. (St. Louis)
2316A Kemper Military Sch. and Coll. (Bonneville)
2330A Missouri Valley Coll. (Marshall)
2340A Park Coll. (Parkville)
2347A Research Coll. of Nrsg. (Kansas City)
2281A St. Charles County Comm. Coll. (O'Fallon)
2297A St. Louis Comm. Coll. at Florissant Valley (St. Louis)
2352A St. Louis Univ. Sch. of Nrsg. (St. Louis)
2357A St. Luke's Coll. (Kansas City)
2368A Southwest Baptist Univ. (Bolivar)
2380A Univ. of Missouri-Kansas City (Kansas City)
2383A Univ. of Missouri-St. Louis (St. Louis)
2388A Webster Univ. (Kansas City)
2388A Webster Univ. (St. Louis)
2394A William Jewell Coll. (Liberty)

MONTANA

2417A Flathead Valley Comm. Coll. (Kalispell)
2418A Montana Coll. of Mineral Sc. & Tech (Butte)
2426A Rocky Mountain Coll. (Billings)
2428A Western Montana Coll. (Dillon)

NEBRASKA

2437A Bellevue Coll. (Bellevue)
2436A Bishop Clarkson Coll. (Omaha)
2440A Coll. of St. Mary (Omaha)
2444A Creighton Univ. Sch. of Nrsg. (Omaha)
2454A Grace Coll. of the Bible (Omaha)
2468A Kearney State Coll. (Kearney)
2460A McCook Comm. Coll. (McCook)
9227A Methodist Sch. of Nrsg. (Omaha)
2491A Mid Plains Comm. Coll. (North Platte)
2462A Midland Lutheran Coll. (Fremont)
5572A Nebraska Coll. of Business (Omaha)
2474A Nebraska Wesleyan Univ. (Lincoln)

NEVADA

2498A Comm. Coll. of Southern Nevada (N. Las Vegas)
2500A Morrison Coll.-Reno (Reno)
2496A Univ. of Nevada-Las Vegas (LasVegas)
2494A Univ. of Nevada (Reno)

NEW HAMPSHIRE

2506A Colby-Sawyer Coll. (New London)
2503A Hesser Coll. (Manchester)
2510A Keene State Coll. (Keene)
2514A New Hampshire Coll. (Manchester)
2517A New Hampshire Tech. Coll. (Berlin)
2507A New Hampshire Tech. Coll. (Manchester)
2530A New Hampshire Tech. Coll.-Stratham (Stratham)
2520A Rivier Coll.-St. Joseph Hosp. Sch. of Nrsg. (Nashua)
2522A St. Anselm Coll. (Manchester)
2524A Univ. of New Hampshire (Durham)
2519A Univ. of New Hampshire (Manchester)

NEW JERSEY

2541A Bergen Comm.Coll. (Paramus)
2540A Bloomfield Coll. (Bloomfield)
2553A Brookdale Comm. Coll. (Lincroft)
2543A Burlington County Coll. (Pemberton)
2544A Centenary Coll. (Hackettsotwn)
2546A Coll. of Saint Elizabeth (Morristown)
9236A Cumberland County Coll. (Vineland)
9223A Elizabeth Gen. Med. Ctr. Sch. of Nrsg. (Elizabeth)
9216A Englewood Hosp. Sch. of Nrsg. (Englewood)
2552A Fairleigh Dickinson Univ. (Rutherford)
2559A Felician Coll. (Lodi)
2562A Georgian Court Coll. (Lakewood)
2575A Helene Fuld Sch. of Nrsg. in Camden Co. (Camden)
9270A Helene Fuld Sch. of Nrsg. (Trenton)
2570A Jersey City State Coll. (Jersey City)
2582A Kean Coll. of New Jersey (Union)
2568A Mercer County Comm. Coll. (Trenton)
2571A Monmouth Coll. (West Long Branch)
9249A Mountainside Hosp. Sch. of Nrsg. (Montclair)
2585A Ocean County Coll. (Toms River)
2586A Our Lady of Lourdes Sch. of Nrsg. (Camden)
2583A Passaic County Comm. Coll. (Paterson)
2591A Ramapo Coll. of New Jersey (Mahwah)
2609A Raritan Valley Comm. Coll. (Somerville)
2598A Rutgers, The State Univ. of NJ (Camden)
9265A St. Francis Med. Ctr. (Trenton)
9242A St. Peter's Coll. (Englewood Cliffs)
2604A St. Peter's Coll. (Jersey City)
2606A Seton Hall Univ. (South Orange)
2589A Stockton State Coll. (Pomona)
2612A Thomas Edison Coll. of New Jersey (Trenton)
9223D Winifred B. Baldwin Sch. of Nrsg. (Orange)

NEW MEXICO

2631A Eastern New Mexico Univ. (Clovis)
9241A Navajo Comm. Coll. (Shiprock)
2650A Univ. of New Mexico Coll. of Nrsg. (Albuquerque)
2646A Western New Mexico Univ. (Silver City)

EW YORK

62A Academy of Aeronautics (Flushing)
64A Adelphi Univ. (Garden City)
67A Adirondack Comm. Coll. (Glens Falls)
61A Albany Business Coll. (Albany)
66A Alfred Univ. (Alfred)
69A American Acad. McAllister Inst. (New York City)
74A Bard Coll. (Annandale on Hudson)
86A Berkeley Claremont Sch., Hicksville (Hicksville)
88A Berkeley Claremont Sch., New York City (New York City)
50J Bernard M. Baruch Coll. (New York City)
08A Borough of Manhattan Comm. Coll. (New York City)
50J Bronx Comm. Coll. (Bronx)
50J Brooklyn Coll. (Brooklyn)
84A Broome Comm. Coll. (Binghamton)
76A Bryant and Stratton Bus. Inst., Buffalo (Buffalo)
90A Canisius Coll. (Buffalo)
68A Cayahuga County Comm. Coll. (Auburn)
96A Cazenovia Coll. (Cazenovia)
01A Central City Bus. Inst. (Syracuse)
50J City Coll. (New York City)
94A Clinton Comm. Coll. (Plattsburgh)
72A Colgate Univ. (Hamilton)
76A Coll. of Insurance, The (New York City)
23A Coll. of Mt. St. Vincent (Riverdale)
12A Coll. of New Rochelle (New Rochelle)
14A Coll. of St. Rose (Albany)
15A Columbia Greene Comm. Coll. (Hudson)
04A Comm. Coll. of the Finger Lakes (Canandaigua)
22A Concordia Coll. (Bronxville)
24A Cooper Union for the Advanc. of Sci. and Art (New York City)
27A Corning Comm. Coll. (Corning)
74A Daemen Coll. (Amherst)
30A Dominican Coll. of Blauvelt (Blauvelt)
65A Dowling Coll. (Oakdale)
32A D'Youville Coll. (Buffalo)
29A Edna McConnell Clark Sch. of Nrsg. (New York City)
36A Elmira Coll. (Elmira)
37A Empire State Coll. (Saratoga Springs)
42A Erie Comm. Coll. (Buffalo)
47A Friends World Coll. (Lloyd Harbor)
49A Fulton-Montgomery Comm. Coll. (Johnstown)
51A Genesse Comm. Coll. (Batavia)
56A Hartwick Coll. (Oneonta)
09A Herbet H. Lehman Coll. (Bronx)
65A Herkimer County Comm. Coll. (Herkimer)
59A Hilbert Coll. (Hamburg)
58A Hobart and William Smith Coll. (Geneva)
60A Hofstra Univ. (Hempstead)
66A Houghton Coll. (Houghton)
50J Hunter Coll. (New York City)
72A Ithaca Coll. (Ithaca)
74A Jamestown Comm. Coll. (Jamestown)
75A Jefferson Comm. Coll. (Watertown)
10A John Jay Coll. of Crim. Just.-CUNY (New York City)
78A Juilliard Sch. (New York City)
87A Katharine Gibbs Sch., Melville (Melville)
00A Katharine Gibbs Sch., New York City (New York City)
82A Keuka Coll. (Keuka Park)
84A Kings Coll. (Briarcliff Manor)
11A Kingsborough Comm. Coll. (Brooklyn)
50J Laguardia Comm. Coll. (Long Island City)
90A LeMoyne Coll. (Syracuse)
92A Long Island Univ. Brooklyn Ctr. (Long Island)
87A Long Island Univ. C. W. Post Ctr. (Greenvale)
07A Long Island Univ., Southampton Coll. (Southampton)
96A Manhattan Coll. (Riverdale)
09A Manhattan Sch. of Music (New York City)
00A Manhattanville Coll. (Purchase)
03A Maria Coll. of Albany (Albany)
04A Marist Coll. (Poughkeepsie)
10A Marymount Coll. (Tarrytown)
11A Marymount Manhattan Coll. (New York City)
799A Mater Dei Coll. (Ogdensburg)
822A Medaille Coll. (Buffalo)
814A Mercy Coll. (Dobbs Ferry)
818A Mohawk Valley Comm. Coll. (Utica)
820A Molloy Coll. (Rockville Centre)
821A Monroe Comm. Coll. (Rochester)
819A Mount St. Mary Coll. (Newburgh)
825A Nassau Comm. Coll. (Garden City)
826A Nazareth Coll. (Rochester)
828A New Sch. for Soc. Res. (New York City)
2950J New York City Tech. Coll. (New York City)
2832A New York Inst. of Tech. (Old Westbury)
2829A New York Sch. of Int. Design (New York City)
2838A New York Univ. (New York City)
2843A Niagra County Comm. Coll. (Sanborn)
2842A Niagra Univ. (Niagra University)
2864A North Country Comm. Coll. (Saranac Lake)
2846A Nyack Coll. (Nyack)
2847A Onondaga Comm. Coll. (Syracuse)
2848A Orange County Comm. Coll. (Middletown)
2852A Pace Univ. (Pleasantville)
2862A Pratt Inst. (Brooklyn)
2950J Queens Coll. (Flushing)
2950J Queensborough Comm. Coll. (Bayside)
2868A Roberts Wesleyan Coll. (Rochester)
2870A Rochester Inst. of Tech. (Rochester)
2873A Rockland Comm. Coll. (Suffern)
2882A St. Bonaventure Univ. (St. Bonaventure)
2886A St. John Fisher Coll. (Rochester)
2888A St. John's Univ. (Jamaica)
2890A St. Joseph's Coll. (Brooklyn)
2896A St. Lawrence Univ. (Canton)
2897A St. Thomas Aquinas Coll. (Sparkill)
2892A Schenectady County Comm. Coll. (Schenectady)
2895A Sch. of Vis. Arts (New York City)
2878A Siena Coll. (Loudonville)
2906A Skidmore Coll. (Saratoga Springs)
2910A SUNY-Ag. and Tech. Coll. at Alfred (Alfred)
2912A SUNY-Ag. and Tech. Coll. at Canton (Canton)
2914A SUNY-Ag. and Tech. Coll. at Cobleskill (Cobleskill)
2916A SUNY-Coll. of Technology at Delhi (Delhi)
2918A SUNY-Ag. and Tech. Coll. at Farmingdale (Farmingdale)
2920A SUNY-Ag. and Tech. Coll. at Morrisville (Morrisville)
2978A SUNY at Buffalo (Buffalo)
2952A SUNY at Stony Brook (Stony Brook)
2981A SUNY Upstate Med. Str. (Syracuse)
2930A SUNY-Coll. at Buffalo (Buffalo)
2932A SUNY-Coll. at Cortland (Cortland)
2934A SUNY-Coll. at Fredonia (Fredonia)
2938A SUNY-Coll. at New Paltz (New Paltz)
2940A SUNY-Coll. at Oneonta (Oneonta)
2942A SUNY-Coll. at Oswego (Oswego)
2944A SUNY-Coll. at Plattsburgh (Plattsburgh)
2946A SUNY-Coll. at Potsdam (Potsdam)
2931A SUNY-Coll. at Purchase (Purchase)
2936A SUNY-Coll. of Arts and Sci. at Geneseo (Geneseo)
2948A SUNY-Coll. of Envir. Sci. and Forest. at Syracuse (Syracuse)
2953A SUNY-Coll. of Tech. at Utica-Rome (Utica)
2954A SUNY-Maritime Coll. at Fort Schuyler (Bronx)
2965A Suffolk County Comm. Coll. (Selden)
2967A Sullivan County Comm. Coll. (Loch Sheldrake)
2968A Syracuse Univ. (Syracuse)
2963A Tompkins Cortland Comm. Coll. (Dryden)
2961A Touro Coll. (New York City)
2964A Trocaire Coll. (Buffalo)
2971A Ulster County Comm. Coll. (Stone Ridge)
2980A Univ. of Rochester, Sch. of Nrsg. (Rochester)
2834A Univ. of State of New York/ Regents College Degrees (Albany)
2973A Utica Coll. of Syracuse Univ. (Utica)
6361A Utica Sch. of Commerce, The (Utica)
2984A Wagner Coll. (Staten Island)
2988A Wells Coll. (Aurora)
4972A Westchester Bus. Inst., The (White Plains)
2990A Westchester Comm. Coll. (Valhalla)
2992A Yeshiva Univ. (New York City)

NORTH CAROLINA

3070A Belmont Abbey (Belmont)
3076A Campbell Coll. (Buies Creek)
3096A Elon Coll. (Elon College)
3102A Gardner-Webb Coll. (Statesville)
3031A Montreat-Anderson Coll. (Montreat)
3060A North Carolina A & T St. Univ. (Greensboro)
3135A North Carolina Wesleyan Coll. (Rocky Mount)
3064A Univ. of North Carolina (Asheville)

NORTH DAKOTA

3210A Dickinson State Coll. (Dickinson)
3200A Jamestown Coll. (Jamestown)
3214A Minot State Coll. (Minot)
3206A North Dakota State Sch. of Science (Wahpeton)
3202A North Dakota State Univ. (Fargo)
3201A Univ. of Mary (Bismarck)
3196A UND Graduate Center–Bismarck State Coll. (Bismarck)

OHIO

3238A Bluffton Coll. (Bluffton)
3245A Cedarville Coll. (Cedarville)
9257A Christian Union Sch. of the Bible (Greenfield)
3247A Clark Tech. Coll. (Springfield)
3268A Dyke Coll. (Cleveland)
3377A Edison St. Comm. Coll. (Piqua)
3271A Fairview General Hosp. Sch. of Nrsg (Cleveland)
3258A Franciscan Univ. of Steubenville (Steubenville)
3275A Franklin Univ. (Columbus)
3278A Heidelberg Coll. (Tiffin)
3279A Kettering Coll. of Medical Arts (Kettering)
3287A Lorain County Comm. Coll. (Elyria)
3598A Lourdes Coll. (Sylvania)
3351A Marion Tech. Coll. (Marion)
3296A Miami-Jacobs Jr. Coll. (Dayton)
3294A Miami Univ. (Hamilton)
3299A Miami Univ.–Middletown (Middletown)
3305A Muskingum Area Tech. Coll. (Zanesville)
3300A Muskigum Coll. (New Concord)
3312A Ohio State Univ. Coll. of Nrsg. (Columbus)
3314A Ohio Univ. (Athens)
3322A Ohio Univ. (Zanesville)
3318A Otterbein Coll. (Westerville)
3308A Raymond Walters Coll. of the Univ. of Cincinnati (Cincinnati)
3324A Rio Grande Coll. & Comm. Coll. (Rio Grande)
3336A Shawnee State Univ. (Portsmouth)
3276A Southern State Comm. Coll. (Hillsboro)
3349A Walsh Coll. (Canton)
3295A Wright State Univ. (Dayton)
3320A Xavier Coll. (Cincinnati)
3368A Youngstown State Univ. (Youngstown)

OKLAHOMA

3380A Bacone Coll. (Muskogee)
3386A Cameron Univ. (Lawton)
3430A Carl Albert Jr. Coll. (Poteau)
3390A Central State Univ. (Edmond)
3400A Langston Univ. (Langston)
3408A Northeastern Oklahoma State Univ. (Tahlequah)
3410A Northern Oklahoma Coll. (Tonkawa)
3406A Northeastern Oklahoma A & M (Miami)
3414A Oklahoma Baptist Univ. (Shawnee)
3435A OCU/St. Anthony Sch. of Nrsg. (Oklahoma City)
3416A Oklahoma City Univ. CBDP (Oklahoma City)
3423A Oklahoma State Univ.–Oklahoma City (Oklahoma City)
3424A Oklahoma State Univ. (Stillwater)
3398A Redlands Comm. Coll. (El Reno)
3420A Rogers State Coll. (Claremore)
3403A Rose State Coll. (Midwest City)
3436A Deminole Jr. Coll. (Seminole)
3441A Tulsa Jr. Coll. (Tulsa)
3442A Univ. of Oklahoma, The (Norman)
3418A Univ. of Science & Arts of Oklahoma (Chickasha)
3378A Western Oklahoma State Coll. (Altus)

OREGON

3461A Clatsop Comm. Coll. (Astoria)
3468A Marylhurst Coll. (Marylhurst)
3484A Oregon Inst. of Tech. (Klamath Falls)
3500A Univ. of Portland (Portland)

PENNSYLVANIA

9219D Abington Memorial Hosp. Sch. of Nrsg (Abington)
3521A Alvernia Coll. (Reading)
3524A Beaver Coll. (Glenside)
3532A Cabrini Coll. (Radnor)
3694A Calif. Univ. of Pennsylvania (California)
9220D Chester County Hosp. Sch. of Nrsg. (West Chester)
3698A Clarion Univ. (Clarion)
3543A Comm. Coll. of Philadelphia (Philadelphia)
9250A Comm. Med. Ctr. Sch. of Nrsg. (Scranton)
3560A Duquesne Univ. Sch. of Nrsg (Pittsburgh)
3562A Eastern Coll. (St. David's)
3702A Edinboro Univ. of Pennsylvania (Edinboro)
9208D Frankford Hosp. Sch. of Nrsg (Philadelphia)
9266A Geisinger Med. Ctr. (Danville)
3578A Geneva Coll. (Beaver Falls)
3583A Gwynedd Mercy Coll. (Gwynedd)
3586A Hahnemann Medical Coll. & Hosp. (Philadelphia)
3589A Harrisburg Area Comm. Coll. (Harrisburg)
3596A Immaculata Coll. (Immaculata)
3704A Indiana Univ. of Pennsylvania (Indiana)
3604A Kings Coll. (Wilkes-Barre)
3706A Kutztown Univ. (Kutztown)
3605A Lackawana Jr. Coll. (Scranton)
9207D Lancaster Gen. Hosp. Sch. of Nrsg (Lancaster)
3607A LaRoche Coll. (Pittsburgh)
3608A LaSalle Coll. (Philadelphia)
3611A Lehigh County Comm. Coll. (Schnecksville)
9324A Memorial Hosp. Sch. of Nrsg.–Roxborough (Philadelphia)
3630A Messiah Coll. (Grantham)
3712A Millersville Univ. (Millersville)
3641A Montgomery County Comm. Coll. (Blue Bell)
3635A Mount Aloysius Coll. (Cresson)
3645A Northampton Comm. Coll. (Bethlehem)
3659A Peirce Jr. Coll. (Philadelphia)
3658A Philadelphia Coll. of the Bible (Langhorne)
3530A Point Park Coll. (Pittsburgh)
3718A Reading Area Comm. Coll. (Reading)
3674A Robert Morris Coll.–Moon Campus (Coraopolis)
3675A Robert Morris Coll. (Pittsburgh)
3682A St. Francis Coll. (Loretto)
3684A St. Joseph's Univ.–Univ. Coll. (Philadelphia)
9218D Sharon Regional Health System Sch. of Nrsg. (Sharon)
3716A Slippery Rock State Coll. (Slippery Rock)
9237A Thomas Jefferson Univ. (Philadelphia)
3724A Temple Univ. (Philadelphia)
3735A Univ. of Pittsburgh at Johnstown (Johnstown)
3734A Univ. of Pittsburgh Sch. of Nrsg. (Pittsburgh)
3736A Univ. of Scranton (Scranton)
3740A Valley Forge Military Jr. Coll. (Wayne)
3742A Villa Maria Coll. (Erie)
3744A Villanova Univ. (Coll. of Nrsg.) (Villanova)
3752A Westminster Coll. (New Wilmington)
3762A York Coll. of Pennsylvania (York)

RHODE ISLAND

3811A Comm. Coll. of Rhode Island (Warwick)
3804A Johnson and Wales Univ. (Providence)
3810A Rhode Island Coll. (Providence)
3818A Univ. of Rhode Island Coll. of Nrsg (Kingston)

SOUTH CAROLINA

3832A Anderson Coll. (Anderson)
3848A Columbia Bible Coll. (Columbia)
3856A Francis Marion Univ. (Florence)
3860A Lander Coll. (Greenwood)
3862A Limestone Coll. (Gaffney)
6465A Medical Univ. of South Carolina (Charleston)
3829A Piedmont Tech. Coll. (Greenwood)
3876A South Carolina St. Coll. (Orangeburg)
3889A Univ. of South Carolina–Spartanburg (Spartanburg)

SOUTH DAKOTA

3902A Augustana Coll. (Sioux Falls)
3906A Dakota Wesleyan Univ. (Mitchell)
3912A Huron Coll. Regional Med. Ctr. Sch. of Nrsg. (Huron)
3914A Mount Marty Coll. (Yankton)
3924A South Dakota State Univ. (Brookings)

TENNESSEE

3944A Austin Peay State Univ. (Clarksville)
3946A Belmont Coll. (Nashville)
4009A Bristol Coll. (Bristol)
3950A Carson-Newman Coll. (Jefferson City)
3957A Cooper Institute, Inc. (Knoxville)
3956A David Lipscomb Univ. (Nashville)
3958A East Tennessee State Univ. (Johnson City)

3963A Ft. Sanders Presby. Hosp. Sch. of Nrsg.
(Knoxville)
3974A Lambuth Coll. (Jackson)
3988A Maryville Coll. (Maryville)
3994A Middle Tennessee State Univ.
(Murfreesboro)
4006A Southern Coll. of Seventh-Day Adventist
(Collegedale)
4014A Tennessee Wesleyan Coll. (Athens)
4017A Tomlinson Coll. (Cleveland)
4022A Univ. of Tennessee at Chattanooga
(Chattanooga)

TEXAS

4073A Amber Univ. (Garland)
1499A Calvary Coll. (Lewisville)
4081A Central Texas Coll. (Killeen)
9212A Central Texas Coll.–Overseas Europe
(APO New York)
9261A Corpus Christi State Univ.
(Corpus Christi)
4090A El Paso Comm. Coll. (El Paso)
4103A Galveston Coll. (Galveston)
4100A Howard Coll. at Big Spring (Big Spring)
4260A Kingwood Coll. (Kingwood)
4123A Lubbock Christian Univ. (Lubbock)
4139A North Harris Coll. (Houston)
4202A Prairie View A&M Unv. (Prairie View)
4158A St. Mary's Univ. (San Antonio)
4160A St. Philip's Coll. (San Antonio)
4178A Southwest Texas State Univ.
(San Marcos)
4198A Texas A & M (College Station)
4222A Texas Wesleyan Coll. (Fort Worth)
4261A Tomball Coll. (Tomball)
4055A Univ. of Central Texas (Killeen)
4241A Univ. of Texas Medical Branch at
Galveston (Galveston)
4239A Univ. of Texas at San Antonio
(San Antonio)
4246A Wayland Baptist Coll. (Plainview)
4254A Wiley Coll. (Marshall)

UTAH

9259A Hawthorne Univ. (Salt Lake City)
9269A Univ. of Phoenix (Salt Lake City)

VERMONT

4329A Burlington Coll. (Burlington)
4314A Castleton State Coll. (Castleton)
4298A Champlain Coll. (Burlington)
4316A Johnson State Coll. (Johnson)
4308A Norwich Univ. (Northfield)
4322A Univ. of Vermont (Burlington)
4328A Vermont Coll. (Montpelier)

VIRGINIA

4338A Averett Coll. (Danville)
4354A Central Virginia Comm. Coll.
(Lynchburg)
4336A Embry-Riddle Aero Univ. (NAS Norfolk)
4357A George Mason Univ. (Fairfax)
4358A Hampton Univ. (Hampton)
4364A Liberty Baptist Coll. (Lynchburg)
4374A Mary Baldwin Coll. (Staunton)
4378A Marymount Univ. (Arlington)
4376A Mountain Empire Comm. Coll.
(Big Stone Gap)
4425A Norfolk State Univ. (Norfolk)
4384A Piedmont Virginia Comm. Coll.
(Charlottesville)
4422A Radford Univ. (Radford)
4396A Shenandoah Coll. & Conservatory of
Music (Winchester)
4401A Southwest Virginia Comm. Coll.
(Richlands)
4407A Thomas Nelson Comm. Coll. (Hampton)
4353A Tidewater Comm. Coll. (Portsmouth)
4435A Upper Iowa Univ. Extension Division
(Roanoke)
4379A Virginia Commonwealth Univ.
(Richmond)
4351A Virginia Western Comm. Coll.
(Roanoke)

WASHINGTON

4442A Big Bend Comm. Coll. (Moses Lake)
4505A City Univ. (Bellevue)
4457A Evergreen State Coll., The (Olympia)
4458A Gonzaga Univ. (Spokane)
4470A Pacific Lutheran Univ. (Tacoma)
4476A Seattle Pacific Univ. (Seattle)
9226A State Bd. of Accountancy (Olympia)

4497A Univ. of Washington–Bothell (Bothell)
9244A Univ. of Washington Grd. Sch. Nrsg.
(Seattle)
4484A Univ. of Washington, Sch. of Nrsg.
(Seattle)
4493A Univ. of Washington–Tacoma (Tacoma)
4491A Whatcom Comm. Coll. (Bellingham)

WEST VIRGINIA

4508A Alderson-Broaddus Coll. (Philippi)
4512A Bethany Coll. (Bethany)
4525A Southern W. V. Comm. Coll. (Logan)
4528A Univ. of Charleston (Charleston)
4534A West Liberty State Coll. (West Liberty)

WISCONSIN

4558A Alverno Coll. (Milwaukee)
4563A Bellin Coll. of Nrsg. (Green Bay)
4568A Cardinal Stritch Coll. (Milwaukee)
4574A Concordia Coll. (Milwaukee)
4582A Edgewood Coll. (Madison)
4556A Fox Valley Tech. Inst. (Appleton)
4615A Madison Area Tech.Coll. (Madison)
4620A Mt. Mary Coll. (Milwaukee)
4585A Northeast Wisconsin Tech. Inst.
(Green Bay)
4644A St. Norbert Coll. (Depere)
4586A Silver Lake Coll. (Manitowoc)
4688A Univ. of Wisconsin–Green Bay
(Green Bay)
4656A Univ. of Wisconsin–Madison (Madison)
4658A Univ. of Wisconsin–Milwaukee, Sch. of
Nrsc. (Milwaukee)
4674A Univ. of Wisconsin–Oshkosh (Oshkosh)
4692A Univ. of Wisconsin Center–Manitowoc
(Manitowoc)
4652A Univ. of Wisconsin–Stout (Menomonie)
4671A Waukesha County Tech. Inst.
(Pewaukee)

WYOMING

5004A Northwest Comm. Coll. (Powell)
5006A Univ. of Wyoming (Laramie)
5005A Western Wyoming Comm. Coll.
(Rock Springs)

FOREIGN

ANTILLES
5296A Universidat Di Aruba (Netherlands)

CANADA
9201A Canadian Sch. of Management
(Toronto)

ENGLAND
9215A Centre for Business Studies (London)

FRANCE
5295A American Univ. of Paris (Paris)

GERMANY
5248A Schiller International Univ. (Heidelberg)

HAITI
9202A Haitian-American Institute
(Port-Au-Prince)

SWITZERLAND
9268A Business School Lausanne (Lausanne)

THAILAND
5238A American Coll. of Thailand (Bangkok)

VIRGIN ISLANDS
5288A Coll. of the Virgin Islands (St. Thomas)

Note: If the institution you wish to receive a copy of your score report is not included in this list, print the institution's name and address in the space provided on your answer sheet. Your scores will be reported to that address.

Differences in Nursing Care: Area A
(Associate Degree Level)

General Description of the Examination

The Differences in Nursing Care: Area A examination measures knowledge and understanding of the various health care problems encountered by the associate degree nurse. Questions are based on the common and specific manifestations of these problems and the nursing care actions properly associated with them. Questions pertain to patients of various age groups in the proportion that members of these groups use health care services. Questions concern both acute and long-term problems of medical, surgical, obstetric, and pediatric patients.

The examination requires you to possess the technical vocabulary and have the knowledge of anatomy and physiology, emotional and physical development, pharmacology, and nutrition generally expected of the associate degree nurse. The examination requires students to demonstrate knowledge of the theoretical framework for each content area as well as the ability to apply this knowledge to nursing practice using the nursing process.

The major content areas tested on the examination and the percent of the examination devoted to each content area are listed below. A detailed outline of the content begins on page 3.

Content Area	Percent of Examination
I. Cardiovascular/Pulmonary Problems	50%
II. Cellular Growth (Pregnancy)	25%
III. Abnormal Cellular Growth	25%
	100%

Examination Objectives

You will be expected to demonstrate the ability to:

1. identify the typical patterns of deviation from wellness associated with each content area;
2. identify the differences in nursing care that result from:
   a. manifestations of the specific health problems;
   b. the influence of culture on the patient's perception of illness and health care;
   c. the individualized response of the patient to illness;
3. apply knowledge of the theoretical framework for each content area when using the nursing process to provide direct care to patients.

Uses for the Examination

Regents College of the University of the State of New York, the test developer, recommends the granting of five semester hours of undergraduate credit to students who receive a standard score of 45 or higher on the Differences in Nursing Care: Area A examination, and the examination satisfies part of the nursing component of the Regents College Associate Degrees in Nursing. Other colleges and universities also recognize the Differences in Nursing Care: Area A examination as a basis for granting credit or advanced standing. Individual institutions set their own policies for the amount of credit awarded and the minimum acceptable score. Before taking the examination, you should check with the institution from which you wish to receive credit to determine whether credit will be granted.

Examination Length and Scoring

The examination consists of approximately 145–180 four-option multiple-choice questions. A testing time of three hours is allowed. Your score will be reported as a standard score, ranging from 20 to 80. Standard scores are based on the performance of a norm group of college and university students. The American Council on Education recommends a minimum passing score of 45, and this minimum passing score is accepted by Regents College. Other colleges and universities may establish different minimum passing scores. Your score will be mailed to you within approximately one month of the date of your examination.

Note Concerning Wording of Nursing Diagnoses

The North American Nursing Diagnosis Association (NANDA) continuously revises and updates its listing of diagnostic categories, defining characteristics, and etiological factors. For example, between 1989 and 1991 the term "potential" was revised to "high risk." Questions on the examination that include nursing diagnoses are not intended to test your knowledge of current wording or phrasing. The questions are intended to test your ability to recognize nursing diagnoses that result from nursing assessments. For the purposes of the examination, all diagnoses should be considered correctly worded, even if a newer version of the diagnosis is being used by NANDA.

Preparing for the Examination

ACT PEP examinations are a means of validating and documenting that you have mastered material comparable to the content of a college-level course. Therefore, to prepare successfully for this examination, you should undertake a process of study and review just as you would if you were taking a college course. Study the examination content as you would study topics assigned by a teacher. Remember, as an independent student, you are acting as your own teacher.

The content of the examination is summarized in the content outline on pages 3 to 9. It is important that you structure your study using this content outline, rather than working your way systematically through any one textbook. You may find that textbooks vary in their presentation of material. The Content/Reference Chart on page 11 may help you to locate the material for each content area.

In preparing for the examination, be certain to allow sufficient time for both study and review. Study is an in-depth activity, involving careful reading and reflection. Most of the learning and growth that you will experience as you prepare for this examination results from the time you invest in study.

When planning how much time to spend, think about the considerable amount of time that is needed both to attend class and study at home for a five-credit college course. As a guideline, most college instructors expect that students enrolled in a five-credit course will spend a total of 75 hours in class and 150 hours of preparation time during a 15-week semester. You may need to spend at least that much time preparing for this examination. For example, you might plan to spend 15 hours a week for a 15-week period.

You may find it helpful to study with a partner or a small group. Even if you cannot locate another person or group for study, you may be able to find a good listener who will help you reflect on the content you have studied.

When you feel confident that you have learned a content area, review what you have learned. Review means taking a second look at the content to evaluate how well you have learned it. Some students find it helpful to review notes that they have written on cards or recorded on audiotape. If you have a study partner, you can review by explaining the content to your partner. If you are studying alone, you may find useful review questions at the end of the chapters in your textbooks. In addition, some publishers sell workbooks to accompany certain textbooks.

Students who would like additional suggestions on how to undertake and successfully complete an independent study project may order at no charge the ACT PEP publication "Preparing to Do Your Best on the ACT PEP Examinations" by writing American College Testing, ACT PEP Study Guides (85), P.O. Box 4014, Iowa City, Iowa, 52243. A similar document, "How to Study Independently," can be obtained at no cost by writing or calling Regents College, 1450 Western Avenue, Albany, NY 12203-3524; telephone (518) 474-3703.

Content Outline

Cardiovascular/Pulmonary Problems

This area focuses on the nursing care of patients with problems affecting the cardiovascular and pulmonary systems. These problems include respiratory failure, croup, asthma, smoke inhalation, chronic obstructive pulmonary disease (COPD), atelectasis, pneumonia, pulmonary edema, peripheral vascular disease, hypertension, myocardial infarction (MI), congestive heart failure (CHF), shock, and anemias.

A. Theoretical framework—basis for care

1. Types of cardiovascular/pulmonary problems

   a. Problems of intake and supply

      1) Depression of respiratory center (for example: drugs, pH imbalances, respiratory failure)
      2) Blocked airway (for example: croup, foreign body, laryngeal edema, mucoid secretions, asthma)
      3) Altered expansion (for example: fractured rib, paralysis of diaphragm, aging process, surgery)
      4) Alteration in supply of oxygen (for example: smoke inhalation)

   b. Problems of absorption

      1) Blocked alveoli (for example: COPD, atelectasis)
      2) Decreased absorbing surface (for example: pneumonia, pneumothorax, lung surgery, pulmonary edema, adult respiratory distress syndrome [ARDS])

   c. Problems of transportation

      1) Impairment of blood vessels (for example: hypertension, peripheral vascular disease, pulmonary embolus, arteriosclerotic heart disease, angina pectoris, gangrene, abdominal aortic aneurysm)
      2) Pump problems (for example: dysrhythmia, MI, CHF, valvular disease, cardiac infections)
      3) Disturbance in volume (for example: hemorrhagic diseases, shock)
      4) Alteration in oxygen-carrying factors (for example: iron deficiency anemia, Mediterranean anemia, polycythemia)
      5) Alteration in coagulation (for example: disseminated intravascular coagulation, thrombocytopenia purpura)

2. Clinical manifestations of cardiovascular/pulmonary problems

   a. Altered vital signs
   b. Altered breathing patterns
   c. Altered breath sounds
   d. Altered skin and body temperature
   e. Altered skin color
   f. Altered physical appearance (for example: clubbing of the fingers, barrel chest, jugular vein distention, chest retraction, flaring nostrils, trophic changes)
   g. Alterations in behavior (for example: restlessness, confusion, lethargy, altered mentation)
   h. Alteration in comfort (for example: pain, fatigue)

3. Factors influencing the patient's susceptibility and response to cardiovascular/pulmonary problems

   a. Age and physiological factors
   b. Psychological factors (for example: stress)
   c. Socioeconomic and cultural factors (for example: dietary patterns, smoking, occupation, sedentary lifestyle, health practices)
   d. Nutritional status
   e. Presence of other illnesses
   f. Site of problem (for example: CHF, peripheral vascular disease)
   g. Degree of involvement (for example: acute v. chronic, pneumonia/COPD, MI/CHF)

4. Theoretical basis for interventions related to cardiovascular/pulmonary problems

   a. Medications (for example: coronary and peripheral vasodilator, anticoagulants, diuretics, antihypertensives, drugs used to treat anemias and hyperlipidemia; antihistamines, decongestants, expectorants, antitussive drugs, bronchodilators, mucolytic agents, cardiac glycosides, antiarrhythmics)
   b. Dietary modifications (for example: sodium, fat, cholesterol, calorie and fluid restriction)
   c. Therapeutic devices (for example: chest tubes, mechanical ventilators, pulse oximeters, central venous pressure monitors, cardiac monitors, cardiac pacemakers)
   d. Preoperative and postoperative care (for example: thoracic surgery, peripheral vascular surgery)
   e. Health instruction (for example: rationale for breathing exercises, stress management, preventive measures)

B. Nursing care related to theoretical framework

1. Assessment—gather and synthesize data about the patient's health status in relation to the patient's functional health patterns

   a. Gather assessment data

      1) Obtain the patient's health history (for example: subjective symptoms, diet, medications, past illnesses, health habits, family history, allergies, occupation)
      2) Assess factors influencing the patient's response to cardiovascular/pulmonary problems (for example: stress in patient's daily life, dietary patterns, [see IA3])
      3) Obtain objective data related to the patient's cardiovascular/pulmonary problems (for example: determine clinical manifestation, altered vital signs, peripheral pulses, breath sounds)
      4) Review laboratory and other diagnostic data (for example: blood gases, complete blood count, cardiac enzymes, pulmonary function test, bronchoscopy, thoracentesis, cardiac catheterization, electrocardiogram, theophylline levels)

   b. Synthesize assessment data (see IB1a [1-4] above)

2. Analysis—identify the nursing diagnosis (patient problem) and determine the expected outcomes (goals) of patient care

   a. Identify actual or high-risk nursing diagnoses (for example: pain [chest] related to coronary spasm; noncompliance related to negative side effects of antihypertensive drug therapy; ineffective airway clearance related to swelling of bronchial tubes)
   b. Set priorities and establish expected outcomes (patient-centered goals) for care (for example: patient will state that discomfort is relieved, patient's blood pressure will be within designated limits, patient will verbalize that respirations are less labored)

3. Planning—formulate specific strategies to achieve the expected outcomes

   a. Incorporate factors influencing the patient's response to cardiovascular/pulmonary problems in planning patient care [see IA3] (for example: plan care of patient post-MI to include ethnic dietary patterns, plan to discuss resumption of patient's sexual activities)
   b. Plan nursing measures on the basis of established priorities to help the patient achieve the expected outcomes (for example: monitor breath sounds, encourage fluid intake to loosen secretions, provide rest to decrease myocardial oxygen demand)

4. Implementation—carry out nursing plans designed to move the patient toward the expected outcomes

   a. Use nursing measures to maintain a patent airway (for example: provide suctioning, provide tracheotomy care, encourage coughing and deep breathing)
   b. Use nursing measures to increase oxygen supply (for example: positioning, administration of oxygen, instruction in breathing exercises and use of an inhaler, administration of blood, management of mechanical ventilation, management of chest drainage apparatus, position for postural drainage, provide a humidified croupette for a child with croup)
   c. Use nursing measures to reduce cell demand for oxygen (for example: promote rest and comfort, manipulate the environment to reduce anxiety)
   d. Use nursing measures to prevent complications of cardiovascular/pulmonary problems (for example: encourage coughing and deep breathing, apply antiembolic stockings, administer humidified oxygen, position chest drainage tubes)
   e. Use nursing measures specific to prescribed medications (see IA4a) (for example: take blood pressure prior to the administration of an antihypertensive agent, check prothrombin times prior to the administration of a long-acting anticoagulant, administer intramuscular iron preparations via Z-track, determine the pulse rate prior to the administration of cardiac glycosides)
   f. Use measures to assist the patient and/or family to cope with the health problem (for example: refer the patient to a local support group, discuss lifestyle changes to reduce stress)
   g. Provide information and instruction (for example: instruct the patient regarding breathing techniques, instruct the patient about the use and side effects of medications, instruct the patient about risk factors for cardiovascular/pulmonary problems, discuss the avoidance of allergens for a child with asthma)

5. Evaluation—appraise the effectiveness of the nursing interventions relative to the nursing diagnosis and the expected outcomes

   a. Record and report the patient's response to nursing actions (for example: chart changes in color and amount of sputum, chart changes in breath sounds, chart absence of redness and swelling in a patient with thrombophlebitis, report that patient verbalizes lack of pain relief following the administration of nitroglycerin)

b. Reassess and revise the patient's plan of care as necessary (for example: encourage additional fluid intake to increase production of sputum, provide diversional activity for the patient with an MI who is experiencing boredom and restlessness)

I. Cellular Growth (Pregnancy)

This area focuses on the nursing care of the neonate and of the patient who is pregnant.

A. Theoretical framework—basis for care

1. The pregnant woman

   a. Antepartal period

      1) Signs and symptoms of pregnancy
      2) Physiological changes (for example: uterine growth, cardiovascular changes, lungs, gastrointestinal/genitourinary [GI/GU] system, hormonal alterations)
      3) Psychosocial changes in the expectant family (for example: emotional responses, role transition, alterations in sexuality, differences based on age and culture)
      4) Health maintenance (for example: calculation of date of conception; obstetrical history; lab tests such as serology for syphilis, smear for gonorrhea, Pap smear; patient education regarding nutrition, childbirth exercises, activities of daily living [ADLs], and symptoms to be reported)
      5) Minor discomforts of pregnancy
      6) Complications of pregnancy

         a) Pregnancy-specific complications (for example: spontaneous abortion, ectopic pregnancy, pregnancy-induced hypertension [PIH], incompetent cervix, placenta previa)
         b) Co-existing medical conditions (for example: infection, anemia, cardiac disease)
         c) Co-existing psychosocial problems (for example: substance abuse, adolescent pregnancy, advanced maternal age, low socioeconomic status)

      7) Medications (for example: magnesium sulfate, ritodrine)

   b. Intrapartal period

      1) Process of labor (for example: stages and phases of labor, fetal presentation and positions)
      2) Complications of labor (for example: fetal malposition, primary and secondary inertia, premature rupture of membranes, prolapsed cord)
      3) Medical interventions (for example: amniotomy, episiotomy, induction of labor, forceps, cesarean section)
      4) Medications (for example: oxytocics, prostaglandins, anesthesia, analgesics)

   c. Postpartal period

      1) Anatomical and physiological changes (for example: uterine involution, breast changes, body system changes)
      2) Psychosocial adaptation
      3) Family planning
      4) Postpartal complications (for example: hemorrhage, puerperal infections, lacerations, mastitis)
      5) Medications (for example: $Rh_o(D)$ Immune Globulin [RhoGAM], lactation suppressants)

2. The fetus/neonate

   a. Conception and ovum development
   b. Functions of the placenta (for example: waste elimination, oxygen exchange, endocrine)
   c. Embryonic—fetal development

      1) Patterns of development (for example: cephalocaudal, proximal-distal)
      2) Fetal circulation patterns

   d. Factors influencing fetal growth and well-being (for example: genetic makeup, nutrition, oxygen supply, drugs, teratogens)
   e. Physiology of the neonate—normal transition to extrauterine life (for example: respiratory changes, circulatory changes, temperature regulation, newborn reflexes, GI/GU function)
   f. Nutritional needs of the neonate
   g. Complications of the neonate (for example: prematurity, postmaturity, large or small for gestation, respiratory distress syndrome, hemolytic disease, infection)

B. Nursing care related to theoretical framework—the pregnant woman

1. Assessment—gather and synthesize data about the patient's health status in relation to the patient's functional health patterns

   a. Gather assessment data

      1) Obtain the patient's health history (for example: obstetric-gynecologic history; history of this pregnancy—expected date of delivery, history of bleeding, use of drugs and alcohol)

2) Assess factors influencing the patient's response to childbearing (for example: preparation for childbirth, cultural factors, socioeconomic status, patient age, lifestyle, psychological factors, nutrition)

3) Obtain objective data (for example: fetal heart rate, weight gain, amount and color of lochia, color of amniotic fluid, location and contraction of the fundus)

4) Review laboratory and other diagnostic data (for example: sonogram, fetal heart monitor, amniocentesis, estriol levels, alpha-fetoprotein level, nonstress test, stress test)

b. Synthesize assessment data (see IIB1a [1-4] above)

2. Analysis—identify the nursing diagnosis (patient problem) and determine the expected outcomes (goals) of patient care

a. Identify actual or high-risk nursing diagnoses (for example: fluid volume deficit related to inadequate fluid intake during labor; impaired tissue integrity related to episiotomy; urinary retention related to urethral trauma; knowledge deficit: care of the perineum)

b. Set priorities and establish expected outcomes (patient-centered goals) for care (for example: patient will correctly demonstrate childbearing exercises, patient will perform care of perineum correctly)

3. Planning—formulate specific strategies to achieve the expected outcomes

a. Incorporate factors influencing the patient's response to childbearing (see IIB1a[2]) and involve the patient's family in planning patient care (for example: plan sibling visits, consider low socioeconomic status, consider ethnicity, consider patient age)

b. Plan nursing measures on the basis of established priorities to help the patient achieve the expected outcomes (for example: provide feedback on the progress of labor to reduce anxiety, monitor the patient for urinary retention)

4. Implementation—carry out nursing plans designed to move the patient toward the expected outcomes

a. Use nursing measures to enhance normal cellular development (for example: provide instruction regarding the effects of nutrition, lifestyle, drugs, medications, and infections; manipulate the environment to foster rest, nutrition, and reduction of stress)

b. Use nursing measures to promote optimal feto-placental blood flow (for example: position to prevent vena caval syndrome, monitor fetal heart rate during labor and delivery)

c. Use nursing measures to ensure a safe environment (for example: safety measur the patient with preeclampsia, maintain b rest prior to fetal engagement)

d. Use nursing measures to facilitate the pro of labor (for example: positioning, coachi encourage ambulation)

e. Use nursing measures to facilitate involu and healing (for example: episiotomy car nipple care, fundal massage)

f. Use nursing measures to provide emotior support (for example: assist with role transition, foster bonding)

g. Use nursing measures to ensure optimal nutrition (for example: provide instructio regarding antepartal weight gain, provide postpartal dietary instruction)

h. Use nursing measures to relieve patient discomfort (for example: instruction in breathing patterns, application of heat an cold)

i. Use nursing measures specific to prescrib medications during the childbearing cycl example: monitor uterine contractions for patient receiving oxytocin [Pitocin]; keep calcium gluconate at the bedside of a pat receiving magnesium sulfate; check the b pressure of a patient receiving ergonovin maleate; monitor the blood pressure of a patient receiving anesthesia)

j. Use nursing measures to assist the patien making educated choices throughout the childbearing cycle (for example: birthing options, family planning)

k. Provide information and instruction (for example: home health care, signs and symptoms of impaired involution, self-ca needs, infant care, referrals)

5. Evaluation—appraise the effectiveness of the nursing interventions relative to the nursing diagnosis and the expected outcomes

a. Record and report the patient's response nursing actions (for example: chart color amount of lochia, condition of nipples, condition of episiotomy; report tetanic contractions)

b. Reassess and revise the plan of care (for example: coach the patient in progressive levels of breathing during labor, monitor signs with increased frequency as labor progresses)

C. Nursing care related to theoretical framework—th fetus/neonate

1. Assessment—gather and synthesize data abou patient's health status in relation to the patie functional health patterns

a. Gather assessment data

   1) Obtain the patient's health history (for example: length of labor, type of delivery, exposure to teratogens, mother's use of drugs or alcohol)
   2) Obtain objective data related to the patient's health status (for example: vital signs, Apgar score, reflexes, condition of umbilical cord stump, hyperexcitability, high-pitched cry)
   3) Review laboratory and other diagnostic data (for example: tests for fetal maturity, bilirubin, Coombs' test, screening for phenylketonuria [PKU], galactosemia, and hypothyroidism)

b. Synthesize assessment data (see IIC1a [1-3])

2. Analysis—identify the nursing diagnosis (patient problem) and determine the expected outcomes (goals) of patient care

   a. Identify actual or high-risk nursing diagnoses (for example: ineffective breast-feeding related to poor sucking reflex; ineffective thermoregulation related to newborn transition to the extrauterine environment)
   b. Set priorities and establish expected outcomes (patient-centered goals) for care (for example: axillary temperature will be stable, mother will use the rooting mechanism to initiate feeding, circumcision will show no signs of infection)

3. Planning—formulate specific strategies to achieve the expected outcomes

   a. Plan for anticipated needs of the patient on the basis of established priorities (for example: plan to facilitate bonding)
   b. Plan nursing measures on the basis of established priorities to help the patient achieve the expected outcomes (for example: swaddle the neonate to promote security and maintain body temperature, provide a dark, quiet environment for a neonate with drug addiction, increase fluid volume for a neonate who is undergoing phototherapy)

4. Implementation—carry out nursing plans designed to move the patient toward the expected outcomes

   a. Use nursing measures to ensure a safe environment (for example: provide warmth for the neonate, encourage rest, cover the eyes of a neonate undergoing phototherapy)
   b. Use nursing measures to increase the patient's oxygen supply (for example: suction the neonate's airway, handle the neonate gently, administer oxygen at no more than 60%)
   c. Use nursing measures to ensure optimal nutrition (for example: assist with neonate feeding)
   d. Use nursing measures to relieve patient discomfort (for example: provide a quiet environment for the neonate with drug addiction)
   e. Use nursing measures to provide emotional support (for example: foster bonding)
   f. Use nursing measures specific to prescribed medications (for example: administer prophylactic eye drops, administer vitamin K)
   g. Use nursing measures to facilitate healing (for example: cord care, circumcision care)
   h. Use nursing measures to maintain physiological stability (for example: care during phototherapy, positioning, maintain cord clamp)

5. Evaluation—appraise the effectiveness of the nursing interventions relative to the nursing diagnosis and the expected outcomes

   a. Record and report the patient's response to nursing actions (for example: chart daily weight, chart color and consistency of stool, chart response to feeding and bonding, report elevated bilirubin levels)
   b. Reassess and revise the plan of care (for example: provide water in response to temperature elevation, refer mother to a home health care agency if the neonate's weight gain is poor)

III. Abnormal Cellular Growth

This area focuses on the nursing care of patients with problems such as fibroids; pyloric stenosis; cancer of the liver, prostate, and uterus; Wilms' tumor, leukemias, sarcomas, and lymphomas.

A. Theoretical framework—basis for care

   1. Types of abnormal cellular growth

      a. Problems resulting from benign abnormal cellular growth (for example: fibroids, hydatidiform mole, fibrocystic disease of the breast)
      b. Problems resulting from hypertrophy (for example: pyloric stenosis, prostatic hypertrophy)
      c. Problems resulting from malignant abnormal cellular growth (for example: cancer of the skin, stomach, intestines, liver, prostate, breast, uterus, lungs, bladder; Wilms' tumor; neuroblastoma; leukemia; sarcomas; lymphomas)

   2. Clinical manifestations of abnormal cellular growth

      a. Alteration in size
      b. Alteration in rate of growth

c. Altered function of involved cells
d. Local and systemic effects resulting from altered size, altered rate of growth, and altered function of involved cells (for example: metastasis, pressure on vital organs, pain)
e. Behavioral changes (for example: confusion, slurred speech, altered mentation)

3. Factors influencing the patient's response to abnormal cellular growth

   a. Age and physiological factors
   b. Psychological factors
   c. Socioeconomic and cultural factors (for example: lifestyle, occupation, health practices)
   d. Nutritional status
   e. Presence of other illness
   f. Site of abnormal cell growth (for example: local v. systemic)
   g. Degree of involvement (for example: benign v. malignant, acute v. chronic)

4. Theoretical basis for interventions related to abnormal cellular growth

   a. Medications (for example: antineoplastic agents, steroids, analgesics, hormonal therapy)
   b. Other treatment modalities (for example: chemotherapy, radiation therapy, surgical intervention, immunotherapy, bone marrow transplant)
   c. Preoperative and postoperative care (for example: laryngectomy, mastectomy, prostatectomy, colostomy, ileal conduit)
   d. Health instruction (for example: risk factors, warning signs, prevention)

B. Nursing care related to theoretical framework

1. Assessment—gather and synthesize data about the patient's health status in relation to the patient's functional health patterns

   a. Gather assessment data

      1) Obtain the patient's health history (for example: subjective symptoms, diet, medications, health habits, family history, allergies, occupation)
      2) Assess factors influencing the patient's response to abnormal cell growth (for example: weight loss, occupation, [see IIIA3])
      3) Obtain objective data related to the patient's abnormal cellular growth (for example: determine clinical manifestations, weight changes, presence of mass, abdominal distention)

      4) Review laboratory and other diagnost data (for example: biopsy, scan, bloo studies, vital signs, complete blood c [CBC], uric acid, calcium, acid phosphatase, magnetic resonance ima [MRI])

   b. Synthesize assessment data (see IIIB1a [1-

2. Analysis—identify the nursing diagnosis (pati problem) and determine the expected outcom (goals) of patient care

   a. Identify the psychological and physiologi ramifications of treatment modalities on patient and family (for example: consider effects of alopecia, stomatitis, osteoporosi erythema, bone marrow depression, naus and vomiting, bone marrow transplant, depressed mood, body image)
   b. Identify actual or high-risk nursing diagr (for example: impaired oral mucous membranes related to immunosuppressio secondary to chemotherapy; altered nutri less than body requirements related to difficulty swallowing; ineffective individ coping related to diagnosis of cancer)
   c. Set priorities and establish expected outc (patient-centered goals) of nursing care (f example: patient will state coping mechan to be utilized, patient's mouth will be fre ulcers)

3. Planning—formulate specific strategies to ach the expected outcomes

   a. Incorporate factors influencing the patien response to abnormal cell growth and inv the patient's family in planning individu patient care (for example: consider role changes, sexuality, changes in body imag changes in lifestyle)
   b. Plan nursing measures on the basis of established priorities to help the patient achieve the expected outcomes (for exam provide a low-residue diet for a patient receiving radiation therapy, provide a mechanically soft diet for the patient wit stomatitis, provide play therapy for a chi with leukemia)

4. Implementation—carry out nursing plans des to move the patient toward the expected outc

   a. Provide instruction in the prevention an detection of abnormal cellular growth (fo example: instruct the patient concerning self-examination [BSE], the seven danger signals of cancer, teratogenic influences, screening and diagnostic testing)

b. Use nursing measures to provide patient comfort (for example: cutaneous stimulation, imaging, meditation, medications, patient-controlled analgesia [PCA], positioning, mouth care, skin care)

c. Use nursing measures to promote optimal nutrition (for example: offer small frequent feedings, continuous enteral feedings, total parenteral nutrition [TPN])

d. Use nursing measures to promote elimination (for example: manage altered elimination routes such as ileo-conduit or colostomy, instruct the patient regarding self-care, monitor urinary drainage in a patient following a transurethral prostatectomy)

e. Use nursing measures to promote safety (for example: prevention of infection and hemorrhage; minimize side effects of treatment modalities by providing skin care, mouth care, and protective isolation)

f. Use nursing measures to provide spiritual and emotional support

g. Use nursing measures specific to prescribed medications (for example: monitor platelet count with antineoplastic agents, monitor fluid balance for a patient receiving steroids, monitor for side effects of medications)

h. Use nursing measures to provide information and instruction (for example: provide referrals to self-help groups, reinforce patient's knowledge about prosthetic devices, emphasize conception control for a patient following removal of a hydatidiform mole)

5. Evaluation—appraise the effectiveness of the nursing interventions relative to the nursing diagnosis and the expected outcomes

a. Record and report the patient's response to nursing actions (for example: record daily weight for a patient on total parenteral nutrition, report skin breakdown for a patient undergoing radiation therapy, chart intake and output for an infant with pyloric stenosis)

b. Reassess and revise the plan of care (for example: increase fluid intake when hematuria is noted in a patient on chemotherapy)

Reference Materials

The following reference materials can help you prepare for the examination. Because most textbooks are revised regularly, you may find more recent editions than the ones listed. A more current edition will meet your study needs.

If you are planning to take several of the associate degree nursing examinations, you will need to begin building a library of nursing textbooks. You should purchase one textbook from each of the following nursing practice areas: fundamentals, maternity, pediatrics, pharmacology, and medical-surgical. Textbooks in nutrition, microbiology, anatomy and physiology, and nursing diagnosis will also supplement your study. You might want to arrange to have access to textbooks in these areas.

You may purchase textbooks in college bookstores, through the textbook service of Empire State College, or by contacting the publishers directly. Publishers' phone numbers and addresses are listed in *Books in Print,* available in any library or bookstore. Most publishers have toll-free numbers (which can be obtained by calling the toll-free information number 1-800-555-1212) and books can be ordered by phone. Some publishers require use of a major credit card or prepayment before shipping a book. Also, you may find textbooks in college libraries, schools of nursing, medical schools, and hospitals. Public libraries may have some of them or may be able to obtain them through interlibrary loan. You should allow sufficient time to obtain textbooks and to study in preparation for taking the examination.

Major References—Textbooks

These textbooks are suggested as major references to be used in preparing for the examination.

Bobak, I. & Jensen, M. (1991). *Essentials of maternity nursing* (3rd ed.). St. Louis: Mosby-Yearbook, Inc.

Ladewig, P., et al. (1990). *Essentials of maternal-newborn nursing* (2nd ed.). Menlo Park, CA: Addison Wesley Nursing.

Phipps, W., et al. (1991). *Medical-surgical nursing: Concepts and clinical practice* (4th ed.). St. Louis: Mosby-Yearbook Inc.

Pillitteri, A. (1992). *Maternal and child health nursing: Care of the childbearing and childrearing family.* Boston: Little, Brown, and Co.

Reeder, S. & Martin, L. (1992). *Maternity nursing* (17th ed.). Philadelphia: J. B. Lippincott Co.

Smeltzer, S. & Bare, B. (1992). *Brunner and Suddarth's textbook of medical-surgical nursing* (7th ed.). New York: J. B. Lippincott Co.

Whaley, L. & Wong, D. (1993). *Essentials of pediatric nursing* (4th ed.). St. Louis: Mosby-Yearbook Inc.

Supplementary References—Textbooks

These textbooks are suggested to supplement your understanding of the material in the major references.

Carpenito, L. J. (1993). *Nursing diagnosis: Application to clinical practice* (5th ed.). Philadelphia: J. B. Lippincott Co.

Eliopoulos, C. (1987). *Gerontological nursing* (2nd ed.). Philadelphia: J. B. Lippincott Co.

Ignatavicius, D. & Bayne, M. (1991). *Medical-surgical nursing: A nursing process approach.* Philadelphia: W. B. Saunders Co.

Kozier, B. & Erb, G. (1991). *Fundamentals of nursing: Concepts and procedures* (4th ed.). Menlo Park, CA: Addison Wesley Nursing.

Potter, P. & Perry, A. (1993). *Fundamentals of nursing: Concepts, process, and practice* (3rd ed.). St. Louis: Mosby-Yearbook Inc.

Reiss, B. & Evans, M. (1990). *Pharmacological aspects of nursing care* (3rd ed.). Albany, NY: Delmar Publishers.

Robinson, C. (1989). *Basic nutrition and diet therapy* (6th ed.). New York: MacMillan Inc.

Shlafer, M. (1993). *The nurse, pharmacology and drug therapy* (2nd ed.). Menlo Park, CA: Addison Wesley Nursing.

Spencer, R., et al. (1993). *Clinical pharmacology and nursing management* (4th ed.). Philadelphia: J. B. Lippincott Co.

Williams, S. R. (1990). *Essentials of nutrition and diet therapy* (5th ed.). St. Louis: Mosby-Yearbook Inc.

Supplementary References—Articles

These articles are suggested to supplement your understanding of the material learned from the major references. The articles are grouped according to the content area to which they apply. A reference librarian can probably assist you in locating these articles.

I. Cardiovascular/Pulmonary Problems

Benner, et al. (1990). Pulmonary and acid-base assessment. *Nursing Clinics of North America, 25*(4), 761–770.

Blank, et al. (1990). Peripheral vascular disorders: Assessment and intervention. *Nursing Clinics of North America, 25*(4), 777–794.

Bone, B. (1991). Chronic obstructive pulmonary disease: Strategies for detecting disease and slowing progression. *Consultant, 31*(5), 21–27.

Bright, et al. (1992). Peripheral vascular disease—is it arterial or venous? *American Journal of Nursing, 92*(9), 34–43 and 45–47.

Ellis, P. (1990). Drugs and inhalation devices. *Professional Nurse, 6*(2), 76–78 and 80–81.

Ellstrom, K. (1990). What's causing your patient's respiratory distress? *Nursing 1990, 20*(11), 56–61.

Feury, et al. (1990). Hypertension: The nurse's role. *RN 1990, 53*(11), 54–60.

Finesilver, et al. (1991). Right ventricular infarction: The critically different MI. *American Journal of Nursing, 91*(4), 32–36 and 38–39.

Gomberg, S. (1990). Mistaken identity...is it epiglottitis or croup? *Pediatric Nurse, 16*(6), 567–570.

Kuhn, M. (1991). Myocardial infarction. *Critical Care Nurse, 11*(1), 14–19.

Leach, M. (1991). Anemia: Nursing care and intervention. *Professional Nurse, 6*(8), 454–456.

Orsi, A. (1991). Asthma—the danger is real. *RN 1991, 54*(4), 58–63.

Rice, V. (1991). Shock, a clinical syndrome: An update. (Part 1) *Critical Care Nurse, 11*(4), 20–24 and 26–27.

Rice, V. (1991). Shock, a clinical syndrome: An update. (Part 2) *Critical Care Nurse, 11*(5), 74–79.

Russell, J. (1991). Successful methods for arterial blood gas interpretation. *Critical Care Nurse, 11*(4), 14–19.

Solomon, J. (1991). Managing a failing heart. *RN 1991, 54*(8), 46–51.

Young, L. (1990). DIC: The insidious killer. *Critical Care Nurse, 10*(10), 26–30 and 32–33.

II. Cellular Growth (Pregnancy)

Albrech, et al. (1989). Anxiety levels, health behaviors, and support systems of pregnant women. *Journal of Maternal Child Nursing, 18*(1), 49–60.

Kost, et al. (1991). Comparing the health risks and benefits of contraceptive choices. *Family Planning Perspective, 23*(2), 54–61.

Matheson, et al. (1989). Diabetes and pregnancy: Need and use of intensive therapy. *Diabetes Educator, 15*(3), 242–48.

Oehler, et al. (1991). Beyond technology: Meeting developmental needs of infants in NICUS. *Maternal Child Nursing, 16*(3), 148–151.

Reeves, et al. (1991). Fatigue in early pregnancy: An exploratory study. *Journal of Nurse Midwife, 36*(5). 303–309.

III. Abnormal Cellular Growth

Arena, F. (1991). Update on acute lymphocytic leukemia. *Hospital Medicine, 27*(3), 33–44.

_____ (1990). Caring for patients with intracranial tumors. *Nursing 1990, 20*(8), 32C–32G.

Jacobs, E., et al. (1991). Lung cancer: Current knowledge. *Hospital Medicine, 27*(6), 99–108.

Knobf, M. (1990). Early stage breast cancer: The options. *American Journal of Nursing, 90*(11), 28–30 and 34–35.

Mack, E. (1990). Most breast lumps aren't cancer!...fibro-cystic breast disease. *RN 1990, 53*(12), 20–23.

Content/Reference Chart

Listed below are some of the major references that cover the material in each content area. The list may help you begin to locate the topics in the content outline. The list is not intended to be comprehensive. To cover <u>all</u> of the material in this study guide, you will need to refer to other chapters in the reference textbooks.

<u>Content Area</u>	<u>Major References</u>
I. Cardiovascular/Pulmonary Problems	Phipps, et al. (4th ed., 1991) Chapters 26 through 34 Pillitteri (1992) Chapters 38 and 39, pages 328–337 Shlafer (2nd ed., 1993) Chapters 35 and 38 Smeltzer & Bare (7th ed., 1992) Chapters 23 through 32 Whaley and Wong (4th ed., 1993) Chapters 22 and 24
II. Cellular Growth (Pregnancy)	Pillitteri (1992) Chapters 7, 8, 14, 19, and 21 Whaley & Wong (4th ed., 1993) Chapters 8 and 9
III. Abnormal Cellular Growth	Phipps, et al. (4th ed., 1991) Chapter 17 Pillitteri (1992) Chapter 57 Shlafer (2nd ed., 1993) Chapter 59 Smeltzer & Bare (7th ed., 1992) Chapter 19 Whaley and Wong (4th ed., 1993) Chapter 25

Sample Questions

The questions that follow illustrate the format and structure of those typically found on this examination. These sample questions are included to allow you to familiarize yourself with the type of questions you will find on the examination. They are not intended to determine your readiness to take the examination.

1. The six-second rhythm strip below illustrates an example of

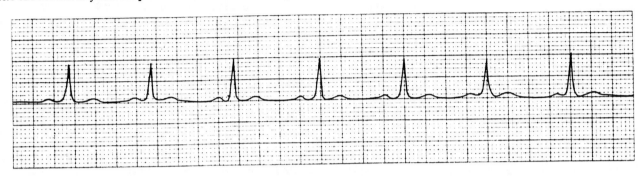

    1) normal sinus rhythm
    2) sinus arrhythmia
    3) sinus bradycardia
    4) sinus tachycardia

2. Which assessment data is indicative of pernicious anemia?

    1) spoon-shaped fingernails
    2) smooth, sore, red tongue
    3) inflamed, swollen joints
    4) petechiae on the face and neck

3. A patient with pneumonia has a nursing diagnosis of ineffective airway clearance related to increased tracheobronchial secretions. Which nursing action will help <u>decrease</u> the viscosity of the secretions?

    1) Administer humidified oxygen at 4 L/min.
    2) Encourage the liberal intake of clear liquids.
    3) Implement postural drainage.
    4) Request an order for intravenous fluids.

4. A postpartum patient whose breasts are engorged is having difficulty breast-feeding her neonate. Which nursing action should facilitate the feedings?

    1) Teach the patient to express some milk manually before each feeding.
    2) Allow the patient to substitute formula until the engorgement subsides.
    3) Provide the patient with a nipple shield and instructions for its use.
    4) Instruct the patient to roll each nipple between her thumb and forefinger.

5. Which observation is indicative of dehydration in a neonate?

    1) pink-tinged urine
    2) low urine specific gravity
    3) poor skin turgor
    4) bulging fontanelle

6. Which nursing intervention would be most helpful to a postpartum patient who experiences afterpain when she breast-feeds her neonate?

    1) Teach the patient relaxation techniques to use after breast-feeding.
    2) De-emphasize the discomfort she feels by pointing out how beneficial breast milk is for the neonate.
    3) Teach the patient to express the milk by hand until the discomfort subsides.
    4) Administer a p.r.n. analgesic to the patient 60 minutes before she nurses her neonate.

7. Which is a positive sign of pregnancy?

    1) auscultation of fetal heart tones
    2) elevation of basal body temperature
    3) maternal perception of fetal movement
    4) absence of menses for two consecutive months

8. A patient receiving chemotherapy is experiencing stomatitis. The nurse's plan of care for this patient should include which action?

    1) Encourage a regular diet and good oral hygiene.
    2) Provide snacks of liquids, hard candy, and ice chips p.r.n.
    3) Keep the patient n.p.o. and promote hygiene with sterile water mouth rinses q. 2h.
    4) Provide a soft-bristled toothbrush and normal saline mouth rinse q. 2h.

9. Which clinical manifestation indicates that a six-week-old infant has pyloric stenosis?

    1) poor sucking reflex
    2) absence of bowel movements
    3) nonprojectile vomiting containing bile
    4) visible gastric peristaltic waves

Answer Key

Question 1: 1	Question 6: 4
Question 2: 2	Question 7: 1
Question 3: 2	Question 8: 4
Question 4: 1	Question 9: 4
Question 5: 3	

HOW TO TAKE A TEST

You have studied hard, long, and conscientiously.

With your official admission card in hand, and your heart pounding, you have been admitted to the examination room.

You note that there are several hundred other applicants in the examination room waiting to take the same test.

They all appear to be equally well prepared.

You know that nothing but your best effort will suffice. The "moment of truth" is at hand: you now have to demonstrate objectively, in writing, your knowledge of content and your understanding of subject matter.

You are fighting the most important battle of your life — to pass and/or score high on an examination which will determine your career and provide the economic basis for your livelihood.

What extra, special things should you know and should you do in taking the examination?

BEFORE THE TEST

YOUR PHYSICAL CONDITION IS IMPORTANT

If you are not well, you can't do your best work on tests. If you are half asleep, you can't do your best either. Here are some tips:

1. Get about the same amount of sleep you usually get. Don't stay up all night before the test, either partying or worrying — DON'T DO IT.

2. If you wear glasses, be sure to wear them when you go to take the test. This goes for hearing aids, too.

3. If you have any physical problems that may keep you from doing your best, be sure to tell the person giving the test. If you are sick or in poor health, you really cannot do your best on any test. You can always come back and take the test some other time.

AT THE TEST

EXAMINATION TECHNIQUES

1. Read the *general* instructions carefully. These are usually printed on the first page of the examination booklet. As a rule, these instructions refer to the timing of the examination; the fact that you should not start work until the signal and must stop work at a signal, etc. If there are any *special* instructions, such as a choice of questions to be answered, make sure that you note this instruction carefully.

2. When you are ready to start work on the examination, that is as soon as the signal has been given, read the instructions to each question booklet, underline any key words or phrases, such as *least, best, outline, describe,* and the like. In this way you will tend to answer as requested rather than discover on reviewing your paper that you *listed without describing,* that you selected the *worst* choice rather than the *best* choice, etc.

3. If the examination is of the objective or so-called multiple-choice type, that is, each question will also give a series of possible answers: A, B, C, or D, and you are called upon to select the best answer and write the letter next to that answer on your answer paper, it is advisable to start answering each question in turn. There may be anywhere from 50 to 100 such questions in the three or four hours allotted and you can see how much time would be taken if you read through all the questions before beginning to answer any. Furthermore, if you come across a question or a group of questions which you know would be difficult to answer, it would undoubtedly affect your handling of all the other questions.

4. If the examination is of the essay-type and contains but a few questions, it is a moot point as to whether you should read all the questions before starting to answer any one. Of course if you are given a choice, say five out of seven and the like, then it is essential to read all the questions so you can eliminate the two which are most difficult. If, however, you are asked to answer all the questions, there may be danger in trying to answer the easiest one first because you may find that you will spend too much time on it. The best technique is to answer the first question, then proceed to the second, etc.

5. Time your answers. Before the examination begins, write down the time it started, then add the time allowed for the examination and write down the time it must be completed, then divide the time available somewhat as follows:

   a. If 3½ hours are allowed, that would be 210 minutes. If you have 80 objective-type questions, that would be an average of about 2½ minutes per question. Allow yourself no more than 2 minutes per question, or a total of 160 minutes, which will permit about 50 minutes to review.

   b. If for the time allotment of 210 minutes, there are 7 essay questions to answer, that would average about 30 minutes a question. Give yourself only 25 minutes per question so that you have about 35 minutes to review.

6. The most important instruction is *to read each question* and make sure you know what is wanted. The second most important instruction is to *time yourself properly* so that you answer every question. The third most important instruction is to *answer every question*. Guess if you have to but include something for each question, Remember that you will receive no credit for a blank and will probably receive some credit if you write something in answer to an essay question. If you guess a letter, say "B" for a multiple-choice question, you may have guessed right. If you leave a blank as the answer to a multiple-choice question, the examiners may respect your feelings but it will not add a point to your score. Some exams may penalize you for wrong answers, so in such cases *only*, you may not want to guess unless you have some basis for your answer.

7. Suggestions

   a. Objective-Type Questions

      (1) Examine the question booklet for proper sequence of pages and questions.

      (2) Read all instructions carefully.

      (3) Skip any question which seems too difficult; return to it after all other questions have been answered.

      (4) Apportion your time properly; do not spend too much time on any single question or group of questions.

      (5) Note and underline key words—*all, most, fewest, least, best, worst, same, opposite*.

      (6) Pay particular attention to negatives.

      (7) Note unusual option, e.g., unduly long, short, complex, different or similar in content to the body of the question.

      (8) Observe the use of "hedging" words—*probably, may, most likely, etc.*

      (9) Make sure that your answer is put next to the same number as the question.

     (10) Do not second guess unless you have good reason to believe the second answer is definitely more correct.

     (11) Cross out original answer if you decide another answer is more accurate; do not erase, *until* you are ready to hand your paper in.

     (12) Answer all questions; guess unless instructed otherwise.

     (13) Leave time for review.

b. Essay-Type Questions

    (1) Read each question carefully.

    (2) Determine exactly what is wanted. Underline key words or phrases.

    (3) Decide on outline or paragraph answer.

    (4) Include many different points and elements unless asked to develop any one or two points or elements.

    (5) Show impartiality by giving pros and cons unless directed to select one side only.

    (6) Make and write down any assumptions you find necessary to answer the question.

    (7) Watch your English, grammar, punctuation, choice of words.

    (8) Time your answers; don't crowd material.

8. Answering the Essay Question

Most essay questions can be answered by framing the specific response around several key words or ideas. Here are a few such key words or ideas:

    M's: manpower, materials, methods, money, management

    P's: purpose, program, policy, plan, procedure, practice, problems, pitfalls, personnel, public relations

a. Six basic steps in handling problems:

    (1) preliminary plan and background development

    (2) collect information, data and facts

    (3) analyze and interpret information, data and facts

    (4) analyze and develop solutions as well as make recommendations

    (5) prepare report and sell recommendations

    (6) install recommendations and follow up effectiveness

b. Pitfalls to Avoid

    (1) *Taking Things for Granted*
    A statement of the situation does not necessarily imply that each of the elements is necessarily true; for example, a complaint may be invalid and biased so that all that can be taken for granted is that a complaint has been registered

    (2) *Considering only one side of a situation*
    Wherever possible, indicate several alternatives and then point out the reasons you selected the best one.

    (3) *Failing to indicate follow up*
    Whenever your answer indicates action on your part, make certain that you will take proper follow-up action to see how successful your recommendations, procedures, or actions turn out to be.

    (4) *Taking too long in answering any single question*
    Remember to time your answers properly.

EXAMINATION SECTION

EXAMINATION SECTION
TEST 1

DIRECTIONS: Each question or incomplete statement is followed by several suggested answers or completions. Select the one that BEST answers the question or completes the statement. *PRINT THE LETTER OF THE CORRECT ANSWER IN THE SPACE AT THE RIGHT.*

Questions 1-6.

DIRECTIONS: Questions 1 through 6 are to be answered on the basis of the following information.

A 35 year-old black male is admitted to the ICU with intense, crushing, substernal chest pain. According to the patient, the pain started about 40 minutes earlier and is not relieved by nitroglycerin. The patient has had two bouts of vomiting, which contain the previous night's food particles. The patient is a smoker and is mildly obese.

1. Nursing interventions to decrease the patient's cardiac workload include all of the following EXCEPT to   1.___
   A. administer oxygen as needed
   B. ask the patient to perform valsalva's maneuver
   C. give diuretics as ordered to reduce circulating blood volume
   D. prevent constipation and reduce anxiety

2. Nursing interventions to keep the patient free from new blood vessel occlusion would NOT include   2.___
   A. applying anti-embolic hose
   B. vigorous massage of extremities
   C. giving anticoagulants
   D. advising the patient on ankle flexion exercises

3. The nurse should interpret all of the following ECG findings as significant EXCEPT   3.___
   A. a P-R interval from 12 to 20 seconds
   B. elevation of the S-T segment
   C. inversion of T waves
   D. the appearance of pathological Q waves

4. In developing a discharge plan for a patient with a myocardial infarction, nursing goals should include   4.___
   A. restoring the patient to his optimal physiological, psychological, social, and work levels
   B. eliminating all risk factors
   C. entering the patient in an intensive program of occupational therapy
   D. all of the above

5. Nursing interventions to provide care after a percutaneous   5.__
   transluminal coronary angioplasty do NOT include
      A. monitoring pulses distal to puncture site
      B. monitoring arterial puncture site for bleeding
      C. keeping foot of bed elevated
      D. all of the above

6. Laboratory studies helpful in the diagnosis of this   6.__
   patient include all of the following EXCEPT
      A. maximal level of CPK achieved 12-24 hours after the
         onset of symptoms
      B. decreased white blood cells
      C. LDH remains elevated for 5-7 days
      D. elevated sedimentation rate

Questions 7-10.

DIRECTIONS: Questions 7 through 10 are to be answered on the
           basis of the following information.

    A 45 year-old black male comes to the hospital with complaints
of generalized headache and palpitations. According to the patient,
headaches started about 3 days before, are severe in intensity and
are not accompanied by any chest pain, of shortness of breath,
vomiting or impairment of consciousness. Palpitations started the
previous day. On examination, his pulse is 89, blood pressure is
185/110, and respiratory rate is 23/minute.

7. Nursing roles in the education of this patient include   7.__
   advising him on all of the following EXCEPT
      A. remaining on a salt-restricted diet
      B. lying flat in bed to avoid orthostatic hypertension
      C. reducing calories and losing weight
      D. practicing moderation in the use of coffee and alcohol

8. In the differential diagnosis of this condition, all of   8.__
   the following should be included EXCEPT
      A. essential hypertension
      B. renal disease
      C. coarctation of the aorta
      D. hypothyroidism

9. In the diagnostic work-up of this patient, all of the   9.__
   following should be done EXCEPT
      A. serum cholesterol and triglycerides
      B. fasting blood glucose
      C. serum ammonium concentration
      D. urinalysis

10. Nursing implementations for a patient carrying out self-   10.__
    care activities after discharge include
       A. taking own blood pressure
       B. eliminating fats from the diet
       C. reducing weight by 20%
       D. all of the above

Questions 11-14.

DIRECTIONS: Questions 11 through 14 are to be answered on the
basis of the following information.

A 32 year-old white patient is admitted to the floor with a
diagnosis of unstable angina. In trying to reach a definitive
diagnosis, cardiac catheterization is planned.

11. Pre-catheterization nursing interventions for this   11.___
patient do NOT include
A. explaining the procedure to the patient and his family
B. administering epidural anesthetics
C. teaching relaxation techniques
D. all of the above

12. After catheterization, the patient is diaphoretic and   12.___
exhibits tachypnea, wheezing, tachycardia, and pallor.
Nursing interventions in this case include all of the
following EXCEPT
A. encouraging increased fluid intake
B. checking patient's output frequently
C. adding 35 meq. KCl in every D5 drip
D. observing for signs of hypovolemia

13. Nursing guides for self-management by the patient, after   13.___
cardiac catheterization, include all of the following
EXCEPT
A. watching for bleeding or swelling at dressing sites
B. decreasing fluid intake for 24 hours
C. observing for signs of circulatory impairment of the
extremities, such as discoloration, numbness,
tingling, or lack of warmth
D. expecting some pain at the site and taking pain
medication

14. In order to prevent stress on an incision line, nursing   14.___
advice should include
A. no bending of affected limb
B. no ambulation for 12-24 hours if femoral site is
involved
C. feeling temperature in area distal to operation site
D. all of the above

Questions 15-22.

DIRECTIONS: Questions 15 through 22 are to be answered on the
basis of the following information.

A 43 year-old male comes to the hospital with dyspnea and
orthopnea. According to the patient, symptoms started about 10
days before and gradually the dyspnea became severe. On examination, ankle edema is present and neck veins are distended. On
auscultation, pulmonary rales and third heart sounds are present.

15. This history is MOST consistent with a diagnosis of   15.__
    A. congestive heart failure
    B. coarctation of the aorta
    C. hyperthyroidism
    D. all of the above

16. Nursing interventions for the elimination of excess fluid   16.__
in this patient include
    A. giving diuretics as ordered
    B. limiting fluid intake to 500 ml per day
    C. eliminating sodium intake
    D. all of the above

17. Symptoms indicative of right side congestive cardiac   17.__
failure include all of the following EXCEPT
    A. peripheral pitting edema
    B. dyspnea
    C. hepatomegaly
    D. distended neck veins

18. Nursing interventions to establish a balance between   18.__
oxygen supply and demand include
    A. scheduling 30 minute sessions of cardiovascular
       exercise daily
    B. giving appropriate sedation to relieve nighttime
       anxiety and to provide restful sleep
    C. supplying oxygen through a nasal cannula
    D. all of the above

19. Upon discharge, the nurse should advise the patient to be   19.__
alert to all of the following signs and symptoms of
recurrence EXCEPT
    A. swelling of ankles, feet, or abdomen
    B. loss in weight
    C. persistent cough
    D. frequent urination at night

20. All of the following complications may be expected in a   20.__
patient with congestive cardiac failure EXCEPT
    A. cardiac dysrhythmias   B. digitalis toxicity
    C. restrictive myocarditis D. pulmonary infarction

21. If the same patient develops pulmonary edema, nursing   21.__
interventions to keep the patient adequately oxygenated
do NOT include
    A. placing the patient in the prone position
    B. administering oxygen as ordered
    C. preparing to assist with phlebotomy if indicated
    D. all of the above

22. Nursing interventions to keep the patient free from the   22.__
hazards of immobility include all of the following EXCEPT
    A. advising the patient to avoid deep breathing and
       coughing
    B. turning frequently

C. providing passive range of motion exercises as needed
D. providing good back care

23. A patient with cardiopulmonary arrest is brought to the   23.____
emergency room by EMS. The patient is breathless and
unresponsive.
Nursing interventions to keep the airway open so that
patient receives adequate ventilation include
    A. placing the patient in an upright sitting position
    B. performing an emergency tracheotomy
    C. opening the airway by head tilt-chin lift maneuver
    D. all of the above

24. Shock is a state in which tissue perfusion is not suffi-   24.____
cient to sustain life.
Precipitating factors for shock include all of the
following EXCEPT
    A. myocardial infarction   B. spinal anesthesia
    C. pneumonia   D. burns

25. The body's responses to shock include all of the follow-   25.____
ing EXCEPT stimulation of
    A. the adrenal medualla by sympathetic nervous system
    B. the pancreas and secretion of insulin
    C. the renin-angiotensin-aldosterone system and anti-
       diuretic hormone
    D. cortisol and growth hormone secretions

26. Nursing interventions in a patient with shock, to ensure   26.____
adequate perfusion, include
    A. monitoring blood pressure, pulse, respiration, and
       CVP
    B. maintaining urine output of at least 30 ml/hour and
       equal to intake
    C. administering blood, colloid fluids or electrolyte
       solution as necessary
    D. all of the above

27. In a patient with shock, nursing interventions to keep   27.____
him protected from injury and complications do NOT include
    A. turning frequently to prevent decubitus ulcers and
       pulmonary problems
    B. wrist and ankle restraints
    C. using sterile techniques with all procedures, since
       patient has decreased resistance to infection
    D. keeping bed's side rails up; if patient is confused,
       watch carefully and avoid restraints

Questions 28-33.

DIRECTIONS: Questions 28 through 33 are to be answered on the
               basis of the following information.

A 28 year-old smoker is admitted with chronic cough and
expectoration, episodic dyspnea, and weight gain. Physical
examination shows hyperinflation, poor diaphragmatic movement,
use of accessory muscles of respiration, decreased breath sounds
and wheezing on auscultation. X-ray shows loss of vascularity,
a flattened diaphragm, and a small heart.

28. Nursing evaluation of the predisposing factors for the   28.___
     above condition include
        A. smoking
        B. poor diet
        C. an adolescent case of pneumonia
        D. all of the above

29. Nursing interventions to maintain a PO_2 of at least 60   29.___
     mmHg, a clear airway, and thin and clear sputum include
     all of the following EXCEPT
        A. administering bronchodilators and expectorants as
           ordered
        B. teaching relaxation techniques and breathing exercises
        C. administering high concentrations of humidified oxygen
        D. encouraging activity to tolerance

30. The nurse should advise the patient to avoid bed rest, if   30.___
     at all possible, to prevent all of the following EXCEPT
        A. stasis of secretions
        B. weakened respiratory muscles
        C. hyperventilation
        D. decreased cough reflex

31. Nursing interventions to protect this patient from injury   31.___
     include all of the following EXCEPT
        A. avoiding restraints, sedatives or tranquilizers
        B. keeping bed high above the floor
        C. maintaining a quiet environment
        D. speaking in low, calm, soothing tone

32. Which of the following are symptoms of oxygen narcosis?   32.___
        A. Decreased respiratory rate and depth
        B. Flushing of skin
        C. Headache and confusion progressing to coma
        D. All of the above

33. Education of the patient so that he can live as actively   33.___
     as possible within the limitations of the disease includes
        A. cough suppression techniques
        B. stressing the need for intense daily exercise
        C. postural drainage
        D. all of the above

Questions 34-35.

DIRECTIONS: Questions 34 and 35 are to be answered on the basis of the following information.

An 18 year-old boy has nasal discharge, sneezing, fever, and watery eyes for the last four days. A common cold is diagnosed.

34. Nursing interventions to educate the patient for self-management include all of the following EXCEPT   34.___
    A. resting to conserve energy for the body to use in fighting the infection
    B. decreasing fluid intake to help liquefy secretions
    C. using a vaporizer to soothe mucous membranes and liquefy secretions
    D. blowing nose by opening the mouth slightly and blowing through both nostrils to equalize pressure

35. Nursing instructions to the above patient for the control   35.___
    of spread of the disease include
    A. covering mouth when sneezing or coughing
    B. properly disposing of used tissues
    C. avoiding crowded areas
    D. all of the above

———

KEY (CORRECT ANSWERS)

1. B	11. B	21. A	31. B
2. B	12. C	22. A	32. D
3. A	13. B	23. C	33. C
4. A	14. D	24. C	34. B
5. C	15. A	25. B	35. D
6. B	16. A	26. D	
7. B	17. B	27. B	
8. D	18. B	28. A	
9. C	19. B	29. C	
10. A	20. C	30. C	

———

TEST 2

DIRECTIONS: Each question or incomplete statement is followed by several suggested answers or completions. Select the one that BEST answers the question or completes the statement. *PRINT THE LETTER OF THE CORRECT ANSWER IN THE SPACE AT THE RIGHT.*

1. A 55 year-old patient is admitted with impaired peripheral arterial circulation.
   The nurse should tell the patient to avoid or eliminate all of the following EXCEPT
   A. exposure to temperature extremes
   B. excessive exercise
   C. loose clothing
   D. tobacco

   1.___

2. Nursing advice for the modification of diet in the above patient includes all of the following EXCEPT
   A. high sodium
   B. low cholesterol
   C. moderate fat
   D. reduced calories if patient is obese

   2.___

3. Nursing intervention to protect a patient with thrombo-phelibitis from dislodgement of the thrombus include all of the following EXCEPT
   A. maintaining bed rest for 7-10 days
   B. performing valsalva maneuver
   C. applying warm, moist packs to involved site
   D. advising patient not to rub legs

   3.___

Questions 4-7.

DIRECTIONS: Questions 4 through 7 are to be answered on the basis of the following information.

A 30 year-old alcoholic male develops fever with cough; on auscultation rales are heard. An x-ray shows an area of consolidation

4. Organisms involved in pneumonia include all of the following EXCEPT
   A. S. pneumonia   B. H. influenza
   C. compylobacter jejuni D. moraxella catarrhalis

   4.___

5. Nursing interventions to improve pulmonary ventilation include all of the following EXCEPT
   A. decreasing fluid intake
   B. providing good oral hygiene
   C. discouraging antitussives
   D. administering analgesics for chest pain

   5.___

6. The nursing objective for keeping the patient free from   6.___
    atelactasis will be achieved by all of the following
    EXCEPT
        A. assessing patient status every 2-4 hours
        B. reducing anxiety
        C. positioning patient on affected side
        D. checking pulse rate

7. Nursing instructions for the self-care of this patient   7.___
    after discharge include
        A. 20 minutes of cardiovascular exercise 3 times per week
        B. pneumococcal vaccine if a high-risk patient
        C. oxygen therapy
        D. all of the above

Questions 8-13.

DIRECTIONS: Questions 8 through 13 are to be answered on the
              basis of the following information.

    A 50 year-old black male develops increasing cough with sputum
production, weight loss, hemoptysis, and fatigue. A chest x-ray
shows calcified intrathoracic lymph nodes and infiltrates in the
posterior segment of upper lobes.

8. The MOST likely diagnosis is   8.___
        A. bronchiatasis   B. tuberculosis
        C. asthma   D. none of the above

9. A nursing evaluation of predisposing factors for tubercu-   9.___
    losis does NOT include
        A. alcoholism
        B. overcrowded, poorly ventilated living conditions
        C. debilitating diseases
        D. immunosuppressive conditions

10. Nursing interventions to arrest active tuberculosis do   10.___
    NOT include
        A. administering antituberculous drugs as ordered
        B. surgical removal of tuberculous tissue
        C. providing adequate rest
        D. instituting a nutritionally adequate diet

11. Nursing implementations for the patient to cope with the   11.___
    disease do NOT include
        A. encouraging suppression of fears, concerns or questions
        B. advising patient of social stigma associated with
            tuberculosis
        C. spending time talking with the patient
        D. all of the above

12. Nursing interventions to ensure that the patient will   12.___
    practice health habits that prevent reactivation of
    infection include all of the following EXCEPT stressing
    the
    A. importance of follow-up care
    B. need to swallow, rather than spit up, sputum
    C. importance of physical activity
    D. use of isolation techniques if necessary

13. Certain individuals are at high risk for the development   13.___
    of significant symptomatic tuberculosis and should be
    offered chemoprophylaxis.
    High risk groups do NOT include
    A. adolescents between 13-21 years of age
    B. individuals who live in the same house or come in
       close contact with an infected or contagious patient
    C. individuals in which a -VE skin test turns +VE
    D. individuals with a positive skin test who receive
       corticosteroid therapy

14. A woman develops chills, headache, sneezing, nasal dis-   14.___
    charge, and obstruction. A common cold is diagnosed.
    Nursing instructions in this case include all of the
    following EXCEPT
    A. observing careful handwashing techniques to avoid
       person-to-person spread of virus-contaminated secre-
       tions
    B. maximizing alcohol intake
    C. employing humidity measures indoors during winter
       months
    D. avoiding irritating substances such as smoke,
       chemicals, dust, and sprays

15. A 45 year-old patient with COPD develops increasing   15.___
    dyspnea, fatigue, and peripheral edema. An x-ray shows
    right heart enlargement.
    The MOST likely diagnosis is
    A. chronic bronchitis   B. cor pulmonale
    C. tuberculosis   D. lung abscess

16. Nursing interventions to monitor the above patient and   16.___
    his response to therapy include all of the following
    EXCEPT
    A. watching for alterations in electrolyte levels,
       especially potassium
    B. employing ECG monitoring to detect dysrhythmia
    C. encouraging physical activity
    D. restricting sodium intake if there is evidence of
       fluid retention

17. Nursing interventions to improve ventilation and correct   17.___
    hypoxemia in a patient with cor pulmonale include all of
    the following EXCEPT
    A. monitoring arterial blood gas values
    B. using continuous high-flow oxygen
    C. avoiding CNS depressants
    D. combatting respiratory infections

18. To promote muscle relaxation and to slow the respiratory   18.___
    rate, breathing exercises are offered to a number of
    patients.
    The nurse's role involves all of the following EXCEPT
    A. advising the patient to breathe slowly and rhythmical-
       ly in a relaxed manner to permit complete exhalation
       and emptying of lungs
    B. advising patient to inhale through the mouth
    C. scheduling breathing exercise sessions 2-4 times
       daily
    D. discontinuing breathing exercises if shortness of
       breath occurs

19. The nurse's role in a patient undergoing postural drainage   19.___
    includes
    A. giving bronchodilator aerosol medications, if ordered,
       before the procedure
    B. instructing the patient to suppress a cough when
       position is changed
    C. suctioning the drainage tube during the procedure
    D. all of the above

20. The goal of using intermittent positive pressure breathing   20.___
    (IPPB) in a patient with respiratory failure includes
    A. delivering aerosols that mobilize secretions and
       promote coughing
    B. assisting in ventilation in order to decrease the
       work of breathing
    C. preventing atelectasis
    D. all of the above

Questions 21-25.

DIRECTIONS: Questions 21 through 25 are to be answered on the
             basis of the following information.

    A 65 year-old CVA patient aspirates fluid and develops progres-
sive tachypnea and dyspnea. Pulmonary function and blood gas studies
show increased minute ventilation, decreased lung volume, and acute
respiratory alkalosis. An x-ray shows patchy diffuse bilateral
fluffy infiltrates.

21. The MOST likely diagnosis is   21.___
    A. adult respiratory distress syndrome
    B. reactivated tuberculosis
    C. pneumonia
    D. none of the above

22. For the purpose of mechanical ventilation, a tracheotomy   22.___
    is done on this patient.
    Nursing interventions to keep a patent airway include all
    of the following EXCEPT
    A. recording respiratory rate and characteristics every
       4 hours
    B. elevating the foot end of the bed
    C. providing humidification
    D. keeping obstructive material such as sheets or cotton
       away from the stoma

23. Nursing interventions to keep this patient free from   23.___
    infection do NOT include
    A. inspecting skin around stoma for signs of inflamma-
       tion every 2-4 hours initially
    B. washing the skin around the stoma with soap and water
       every morning
    C. changing the external dressing and ties when wet or
       soiled
    D. applying povidone-iodine ointment around the stoma
       and covering with a sterile dressing

24. Nursing interventions to aid a patient in establishing   24.___
    an effective communication method do NOT usually include
    A. providing pad and pencil or erasable slate for
       writing
    B. arranging signal for bells or buzzers
    C. working out an alternative method of communication
       for common needs
    D. teaching the patient ASL (American sign language)

25. Nursing interventions to decrease patient anxiety include   25.___
    A. explaining the process to the patient and significant
       others carefully
    B. preventing the patient from seeing the procedure or
       equipment
    C. allowing the patient to read a surgical description
       of tracheotomy techniques
    D. all of the above

26. Application of nursing processes to a patient at high   26.___
    risk for aspiration during a bronchoscopy includes
    A. positioning the patient in a flat or semi-Fowler's
       side lying position
    B. instructing the patient to let saliva drain out of
       the corner of the mouth into a basin or tissue
    C. keeping patient NPO until the swallow or cough reflex
       returns
    D. all of the above

27. A 45 year-old male is on transtracheal oxygen therapy   27.___
    after severe trauma to the chest.
    The nurse educating the patient for self-management
    should advise him to immediately report all of the
    following signs or symptoms EXCEPT
       A. a cough unrelieved by cough suppressant
       B. decreased sputum production
       C. cyanosis of the lips or nail beds
       D. edema of the face or neck

28. Pneumonectomy is the surgical removal of an entire lung.   28.___
    Indications for pneumonectomy include all of the following
    EXCEPT
       A. bronchogenic carcinoma
       B. atypical pneumonia
       C. bronchiectasis
       D. extensive unilateral tuberculosis

29. Nursing guidelines to aid in educating a patient for self-   29.___
    management after a pneumonectomy include
       A. eliminating all contact with smoke
       B. performing breathing, cardiovascular, and upper body
          exercises for 45 minutes every day
       C. avoiding heavy lifting
       D. all of the above

30. A 25 year-old man has a sudden onset of a sore throat   30.___
    accompanied by chills and high grade fever. He also has
    some difficulty in swallowing. The patient is diagnosed
    with acute pharyngitis.
    Nursing instructions to this patient include all of the
    following EXCEPT:
       A. Drink 2000-3000 ml of fluid per day
       B. Drink citrus juices
       C. Consume cool, clear fluids or ice to soothe the
          throat during the acute stage of disease
       D. Adjust diet from clear liquids to full liquids to a
          pureed or soft diet, depending on individual tolerance

31. Nursing advice to a patient who has undergone a tonsillec-   31.___
    tomy for peritonsillar abscess (quincy) includes all of
    the following EXCEPT
       A. adding soft food to the diet as tolerated
       B. resting in bed or on a couch for 24 hours after the
          operation and then gradually resume full activity
       C. adding foods such as salads and orange juice to the
          diet
       D. reporting any heavy bleeding or a temperature greater
          than 100.4°F

32. A 49 year-old patient with arterial hypertension comes to   32.___
the emergency room with epistaxis.
Nursing interventions should include
    A. loosening clothing around the neck to prevent pressure
       on the carotid arteries
    B. assisting the patient to a prone position
    C. performing cardiac compressions
    D. all of the above

33. A patient with acute bronchitis is being discharged.   33.___
Nursing instructions for the prevention of recurrent
infection include
    A. maintaining a cool environment, 62-68°
    B. avoiding exposure to environmental irritants like
       smoke and air pollutants
    C. eating a high carbohydrate-high fiber diet
    D. all of the above

34. A patient with pneumonia is being discharged.   34.___
Nursing instructions to increase metabolic demands
secondary to infection and to increase respiratory rate
include all of the following EXCEPT
    A. consuming at least 1500 calories daily
    B. aiming for a positive nitrogen balance to replete
       body tissue
    C. ensuring a diet rich in fats
    D. a liquid or blenderized diet may be better tolerated
       in the beginning

35. Nursing advice to a patient with lung cancer for   35.___
decreasing risks of respiratory infection includes
    A. maintain good oral hygiene
    B. avoid crowds
    C. drink at least 10 glasses of liquid daily
    D. all of the above

─────

KEY (CORRECT ANSWERS)

1. C	11. A	21. A	31. C
2. A	12. B	22. B	32. A
3. B	13. A	23. B	33. B
4. C	14. B	24. C	34. C
5. A	15. B	25. A	35. D
6. C	16. C	26. D	
7. B	17. B	27. B	
8. B	18. B	28. B	
9. A	19. A	29. C	
10. B	20. D	30. B	

EXAMINATION SECTION
TEST 1

DIRECTIONS: Each question or incomplete statement is followed by several suggested answers or completions. Select the one that BEST answers the question or completes the statement. *PRINT THE LETTER OF THE CORRECT ANSWER IN THE SPACE AT THE RIGHT.*

1. Nursing interventions to make a patient understand the importance of periodic examinations in reproductive health maintenance include
   A. explaining the need for papanicolaou (PAP) smears
   B. explaining the importance of regular breast self-examination
   C. providing supplemental reading materials to increase patient's knowledge
   D. all of the above

1.___

2. Health education recommendations to reduce the risk of osteoporosis in adult women include all of the following EXCEPT
   A. eating a balanced diet to ensure adequate vitamin and mineral intake
   B. increasing fats and multiple phosphorus supplements
   C. increasing daily food sources of calcium
   D. exercising regularly to strengthen bones

2.___

Questions 3-5.

DIRECTIONS: Questions 3 through 5 are to be answered on the basis of the following information.

   A 28 year-old black woman presents with hypermenorrhea and mild lower abdominal pain. She also complains of urinary frequency and constipation.

3. The MOST likely diagnosis is
   A. myomata uteri   B. pelvic inflammatory disease
   C. endometriosis   D. all of the above

3.___

4. Predisposing factors for the above condition include all of the following EXCEPT
   A. infertility   B. hormone usage
   C. diabetes mellitus   D. age

4.___

5. Nursing interventions to keep the patient free from problems during conservative management of this condition include
   A. supporting the patient's decision for immediate pregnancy
   B. monitoring for increased severity of symptoms
   C. discouraging hormone usage
   D. all of the above

5.___

6. Predisposing factors for vaginal wall changes, associated   6.___
   with childbearing or aging, include all of the following
   EXCEPT
      A. hirsutism
      B. multiparity
      C. inappropriate bearing down during labor
      D. congenital weakness

7. As a result of reproduction, all of the following changes   7.___
   are expected in the uterus EXCEPT
      A. increase in length, width, and depth
      B. shape changes from oval to globular
      C. weight increases from 60-1000 g.
      D. distension out of pelvis at twelfth week

8. All of the following statements about changes in the   8.___
   vagina during pregnancy are true EXCEPT:
      A. Increased vascularity
      B. Thinning of the mucosa
      C. Loosening of connective tissue
      D. Increased vaginal discharge without signs of itching
         or burning

9. All of the following are subjective signs and symptoms   9.___
   of pregnancy EXCEPT
      A. quickening
      B. Hegar's sign
      C. Goodell's sign
      D. Braxton-Hicks contractions

10. Which of the following is NOT a function of the placenta?   10.___
      A. Hormone secretion from the early weeks of pregnancy
      B. A barrier to some substances and organisms
      C. Fluid and gas transport
      D. Cushioning the fetus inside placental membranes

11. Nursing goals of health promotion through anticipatory   11.___
   guidance can be achieved by all of the following EXCEPT
      A. telling patients to expect a decreased need for sleep
         during pregnancy
      B. advising patients to continue their usual exercise
         regimen
      C. recommending comfortable, nonrestricting maternity
         clothing, a well-fitting bra, and low-heeled suppor-
         tive shoes
      D. advising patients to stop or reduce cigarette
         consumption

12. In the health maintenance program of a pregnant woman,   12.___
   nursing interventions for relief of common discomforts
   include all of the following EXCEPT
      A. eating dry crackers or toast before slowly arising
      B. eating greasy, highly seasoned foods at one meal per
         day
      C. drinking adequate fluids between meals
      D. eating a protein snack at bedtime

13. Nursing instructions for avoiding varicose veins would   13.___
    be to
       A. elevate legs frequently when sitting or lying down
          in bed
       B. avoid sitting or standing for prolonged periods or
          crossing legs at the knees
       C. avoid tight or constricting hosiery or garters
       D. all of the above

14. Which of the following are NOT nutritional risk factors   14.___
    at the early stages of pregnancy?
       A. Mild obesity
       B. Frequent pregnancies and adolescence
       C. Vegetarian diet
       D. Smoking, drug addiction, or alcoholism

15. Predisposing factors for ectopic pregnancies include all   15.___
    of the following EXCEPT
       A. repeated pregnancies
       B. pelvic inflammatory disease (PID)
       C. puerperal and postabortal sepsis
       D. prolonged use of IUD

16. Nursing interventions for a patient with an ectopic   16.___
    pregnancy do NOT include
       A. monitoring vital signs and continually assessing for
          shock
       B. preparing client for surgery
       C. supporting the grieving process
       D. counseling patient on possible demise of fetus

17. A 37 year-old primipara is diagnosed with pregnancy-   17.___
    induced hypertension. She has no prior history of
    hypertension.
    Nursing interventions in this case include
       A. detecting preeclampsia through early and regular
          antepartal care
       B. instructing the patient to weigh herself daily
       C. monitoring IRO, blood pressure, weight, urine for
          protein, FHR for hospitalized patients
       D. all of the above

18. Nursing interventions to keep a hypertensive patient   18.___
    free from physical injury in the event of a seizure do
    NOT include
       A. maintaining a patent airway
       B. utilizing full body restraints
       C. monitoring for signs of abruptio placentae
       D. noting nature, onset, and progression of seizure

19. A 29 year-old female at the end of her first trimester   19.___
    of pregnancy is diagnosed having a valvular heart defect.
    Nursing interventions to prevent anemia and cardiac
    decompensation include
    A. encouraging early and more frequent antepartal care;
       monitoring vital signs, fetal heart rate, and weight
    B. teaching proper nutrition with adequate iron intake
       to prevent anemia
    C. emphasizing the need for additional rest and stress
       reduction
    D. all of the above

20. In the postpartum period, nursing interventions in the   20.___
    same patient consist of all of the following EXCEPT
    A. assessing for signs of hemorrhage
    B. assessing for congestive cardiac failure
    C. administering ergonovine and other oxytocins
    D. assessing for thromboembolism

21. A 17 year-old female has hyperemesis gravidarum.   21.___
    Nursing interventions should include
    A. administering parenteral fluids
    B. promoting a quiet environment
    C. providing frequent, small meals when oral feeding is
       tolerated
    D. all of the above

22. A 26 year-old black female took clomophine for the induc-   22.___
    tion of ovulation. She is now pregnant with twins.
    Nursing interventions for this patient include all of the
    following EXCEPT
    A. advising rest in the right lateral position to provide
       oxygenation for the fetal/placental unit
    B. monitoring fetal heart rate carefully for fetal
       distress
    C. promoting a balanced diet, with adequate protein,
       iron, and vitamin supplements
    D. preparing for vaginal delivery unless complications
       arise

23. All of the following signs and symptoms favor a diagnosis   23.___
    of *true* labor EXCEPT
    A. contractions increasing progressively in strength,
       duration, and frequency
    B. discomfort felt in lower abdomen and groin
    C. increasing effacement and dilatation of cervix
    D. regular pattern not relieved by walking

24. Physiological alterations occurring during labor do NOT   24.___
    include
    A. cervical dilatation up to 10 cm
    B. expulsion of the umbilical cord
    C. effacement, thinning, shortening, and obliteration
       of cervix
    D. separation of upper and lower uterine segments

25. Nursing interventions to ensure that a patient will remain   25.___
    stable during the recovery period following delivery
    include
        A. taking vital signs every 15 minutes until stable
        B. having patient ambulatory within 30 minutes of
           delivery
        C. administration of analgesics
        D. all of the above

26. Nursing interventions checking pre-term labor and allowing   26.___
    the patient to carry the fetus as close to term as
    possible include all of the following EXCEPT
        A. maintaining bed rest in the lateral recumbent posi-
           tion in a quiet environment
        B. administering a selected oxytocin agent
        C. maintaining adequate hydration through oral or
           parenteral intake
        D. providing emotional support

27. A forceps delivery is planned on a 29 year-old diabetic   27.___
    woman due to a suspected large head obstruction.
    Nursing interventions to ensure that the patient and
    fetus will experience minimal trauma despite the delivery
    would NOT include
        A. providing the physician with selected forceps
        B. padding the forceps with sterile gauze
        C. monitoring fetal heart rate continuously during the
           procedure
        D. assessing the newborn for forceps bruises and facial
           paralysis

28. All of the following are indications for a cesarean birth   28.___
    EXCEPT
        A. a diabetic mother
        B. cephalopelvic disproportion
        C. a prolapsed cord
        D. active herpes lesions

29. Nursing interventions after a cesarean birth do NOT   29.___
    include
        A. assessing for signs and symptoms of hemorrhage
        B. providing assistance as necessary during mother-
           infant interactions
        C. stressing the importance of post-cesarean delivery
           exercises
        D. monitoring maternal-fetal status

30. Nursing interventions in a case of postpartal hemorrhage   30.___
    include all of the following EXCEPT
        A. massaging boggy fundus gently but firmly
        B. administering oxytocic agents in the fourth stage of
           labor
        C. discouraging frequent voiding
        D. replacing fluid and blood as ordered

KEY (CORRECT ANSWERS)

1. D	11. A	21. D
2. B	12. B	22. A
3. A	13. D	23. B
4. C	14. A	24. B
5. D	15. A	25. A
6. A	16. D	26. B
7. B	17. D	27. B
8. B	18. B	28. A
9. A	19. D	29. C
10. D	20. C	30. C

TEST 2

DIRECTIONS: Each question or incomplete statement is followed by
several suggested answers or completions. Select the
one that BEST answers the question or completes the
statement. *PRINT THE LETTER OF THE CORRECT ANSWER IN
THE SPACE AT THE RIGHT.*

Questions 1-4.

DIRECTIONS: Questions 1 through 4 are to be answered on the
basis of the following information.

A 27 year-old black female has 101°F fever on the third day
after delivering an 8 lb. boy. She has had three other deliveries
without complications. This time she has a history of prolonged
labor after the rupture of membranes.

1. Bacterial organisms responsible for this condition include   1.___
   all of the following EXCEPT
   A. a mixed aerobic-anaerobic infection
   B. E. coli
   C. compylobacter
   D. streptococcus hemolyticus

2. Predisposing conditions for this disorder do NOT include   2.___
   A. soft tissue trauma and/or hemorrhage
   B. retention of placental fragments
   C. multiparity
   D. debilitating antepartal conditions

3. Nursing interventions in the management of this patient   3.___
   include
   A. encouraging a semi-Fowler's position to facilitate
      lochia drainage
   B. reinforcing perineal hygiene techniques
   C. providing comfort measures, i.e., sitz baths, to
      promote perineal healing
   D. all of the above

4. If the puerperal fever is due to mastitis, nursing inter-   4.___
   ventions should include all of the following EXCEPT
   A. promoting comfort by suggesting a supportive bra
   B. terminating lactation in breastfeeding mothers
   C. encouraging good handwashing and breast hygiene
   D. preparing the patient for incision and drainage of
      abscess if necessary

5. Advanced gestational age and placental insufficiency   5.___
could cause all of the following EXCEPT
    A. a thick, short newborn
    B. dry, parchment-like skin
    C. a decreased or absent vernix
    D. meconium staining of amniotic fluid

6. After the 34th week of gestation, a stress test or   6.___
contraction stress test is used to evaluate the ability
of the fetus to withstand the stress of uterine contractions as would occur during labor.
Nursing interventions in the performance   of this test
include all of the following EXCEPT
    A. placing the woman in a semi-Fowler's or side lying
       position
    B. advising the woman to hold her urine prior to the
       test
    C. obtaining a 30 minute strip of the fetal heart rate
       and uterine activity for baseline data
    D. administering a diluted oxytocin via an infusion
       pump

7. Contraindications for an oxytocin challenge or stress   7.___
test include all of the following EXCEPT
    A. a previous cesarean birth
    B. third trimester bleeding
    C. a non-reactive nonstress test
    D. all of the above

8. Metabolic screening tests should be done for all of the   8.___
following pathological conditions EXCEPT
    A. phenylketonuria   B. scurvy
    C. sickle cell anemia   D. hypothyroidism

Questions 9-10.

DIRECTIONS: Questions 9 and 10 are to be answered on the basis
              of the following information.

    A 22 year-old white female at 16 weeks of gestation comes to
the emergency room with persistent bleeding. On examination, her
uterus is large for gestational age. Hydatiform mole is diagnosed
based on laboratory results.

9. Nursing interventions to ensure adequate fluid status of   9.___
the patient would NOT include
    A. having the patient drink 1000 cc of fluid every two
       hours
    B. establishing and maintaining an IV line with a large
       needle
    C. assessing maternal vital signs and evaluating bleeding
    D. typing and screening the blood and having 2-4 units
       of whole blood available

10. In the health education plan of this patient, all of the   10.___
    following should be advised EXCEPT
    A. the need for follow-up care and the importance of
       continuing the follow-up care
    B. avoiding pregnancy for a minimum of 1 month
    C. biweekly measurement of chorionic gonadotropin levels
    D. a rise in chorionic gonadotropin levels or plateau
       requires further treatment

Questions 11-16.

DIRECTIONS: Questions 11 through 16 are to be answered on the
              basis of the following information.

    A 35 year-old white female has a hard, discharging lump on the
upper outer side of her right breast. After a thorough examination
and laboratory work-up, carcinoma of the breast is diagnosed.

11. Major predisposing factors for carcinoma of the breast   11.___
    include all of the following EXCEPT
    A. late menarche and early menopause
    B. a family history of breast cancer on the maternal
       side
    C. uterine cancer
    D. chronic irritation; fibrocystic disease

12. Nursing guidelines in preparing this patient for surgery   12.___
    do NOT include
    A. having patient sign an organ donor card
    B. exploring patient's expectations of what the surgical
       site will look like
    C. discussing the possibility of reconstructive surgery
    D. allaying anxiety and fear

13. Nursing interventions to ensure that the patient will   13.___
    regain joint and arm movement on the side of the surgery
    include
    A. positioning the arm on the operative side on a pillow
       to decrease incidence of lymphedema
    B. teaching exercises at the appropriate time to prevent
       contracture of the shoulder and to promote lymphatic
       flow
    C. having patient use arm and hand for daily activities
       (e.g., brushing hair)
    D. all of the above

14. Nursing interventions to explain incision care and the   14.___
    choice of available prostheses include all of the follow-
    ing EXCEPT
    A. encouraging the patient to look at the incision
    B. upon discharge having patient wear her own bra with
       cotton padding
    C. teaching patient not to wash the incision with soap
       and water
    D. discussing with the patient plans for obtaining a
       permanent prosthesis

15. Nursing education of the patient to describe lymphedema   15.___
and state ways to prevent it includes all of the following
EXCEPT
    A. suggesting patient elevate arm throughout the day
    B. advising patient to wear a constrictive bandage
       around her arm
    C. suggesting that the patient decrease sodium and
       fluid intake
    D. teaching the patient to sleep with arm elevated on
       a pillow

16. Of the following precautions, the one which a nurse should   16.___
NOT encourage to prevent infections in a mastectomy
patient is
    A. not to shave axilla on the affected side and attend
       to any small cut or scrape immediately
    B. using only electrolysis to depillate the axilla on
       the affected side
    C. avoiding blood pressure measurements, injections, and
       blood drawing on the affected side
    D. avoiding carrying heavy objects with affected arm

Questions 17-20.

DIRECTIONS: Questions 17 through 20 are to be answered on the
basis of the following information.

A 62 year-old black singer comes to the emergency room with
complaints of hoarseness and dyspnea. A diagnostic work-up of the
patient is done, and he is diagnosed with glottic (vocal cords)
cancer.

17. Risk factors for laryngeal cancer include all of the   17.___
following EXCEPT
    A. cocaine abuse
    B. familial predisposition
    C. excessive alcohol intake and smoking
    D. vocal abuse

18. Post-operatively, nursing interventions to maintain   18.___
adequate respiratory function include all of the following
EXCEPT
    A. frequent assessment for patency of airway and rate
       and depth of respiration
    B. promoting drainage and facilitation by having the
       patient lie flat on bed
    C. administration of humidified oxygen
    D. frequent suction of tracheostomy

19. Nursing measures to ensure that the patient will have   19.___
satisfactory post-operative communication abilities do
NOT include
    A. using communications measures decided upon pre-opera-
       tively

B. encouraging the patient to use his voice as soon as possible
C. staying with the patient as often as possible
D. explaining to the patient how to summon a nurse and responding promptly when called

20. In discharge planning for this patient, the nurse should advise him to   20.___
    A. always keep the stoma covered for hygienic manage-ment of secretions
    B. avoid cold air
    C. expect some loss of smell and impairment of taste sensation
    D. all of the above

21. A prostatectomy has been done on a 65 year-old patient   21.___
who was admitted to the floor with complaints of frequency, urgency, and some incontinence.
Nursing interventions to keep a clean, intact incision do NOT include
    A. washing the incision with soap and water twice a day
    B. no insertion of thermometers or tubes
    C. giving sitz baths after drains are removed
    D. maintaining patency of foley catheter

22. Nursing interventions to ensure that the patient will   22.___
regain perineal muscle tone and urinary continence include all of the following EXCEPT
    A. teaching pubo-coccygeal exercises
    B. instituting exercises immediately after operation
    C. encouraging the patient to perform exercises hourly
    D. reassuring the patient that some urinary control can be obtained

23. Of the following, the BEST initial means of detecting   23.___
abnormal breast masses is by
    A. annual mammography
    B. biopsy
    C. breast self-examination
    D. annual gynecologic examinations

24. In a patient receiving radiation therapy, nutritional   24.___
planning should include
    A. a low-residue diet   B. sodium restriction
    C. a high fiber diet   D. all of the above

25. Abnormal cellular growths which are generally benign do   25.___
NOT include
    A. hydatidiform mole   B. fibroid tumors
    C. epitheliomas   D. lipomas

KEY (CORRECT ANSWERS)

1. C		11. A	
2. C		12. A	
3. D		13. D	
4. B		14. C	
5. A		15. B	
6. B		16. B	
7. C		17. A	
8. B		18. B	
9. A		19. B	
10. B		20. D	

21. A
22. B
23. C
24. A
25. C

EXAMINATION SECTION
TEST 1

DIRECTIONS: Each question or incomplete statement is followed by several suggested answers or completions. Select the one that BEST answers the question or completes the statement. *PRINT THE LETTER OF THE CORRECT ANSWER IN THE SPACE AT THE RIGHT.*

1. A patient is admitted to the hospital with a diagnosis of Adams-Stokes syndrome. His symptoms will MOST likely include
   A. slurred speech and flushing
   B. vertigo and nausea
   C. low ventricular rate and syncope
   D. blurred vision

1.___

2. A client complains of frequent leg cramps after delivering twins. A nurse should suspect
   A. hypocalcemia   B. hypokalemia
   C. hypercalcemia   D. hyperkalemia

2.___

3. A client has been diagnosed with basal cell carcinoma. The nurse's questioning of the client should focus on the client's
   A. smoking history
   B. family history of cancer
   C. diet
   D. exposure to ultraviolet radiation

3.___

4. The MOST common side effect associated with the use of IUDs is
   A. ectopic pregnancy   B. missed periods
   C. uterine rupture   D. heavy menstrual flow

4.___

5. A client suffers a complete pneumothorax, and consequently a mediastinal shift. The client's MOST immediate risk is
   A. rupture of the pericardium
   B. decreased filling of the right heart
   C. infection of the subpleural lining
   D. increased volume in the unaffected lung

5.___

6. Generally, as a patient's red blood cell count *increases*, the
   A. patient's immunity *decreases*
   B. patient's hematocrit *decreases*
   C. blood viscosity *increases*
   D. blood pH *increases*

6.___

7. A client receiving anticoagulants should be observed for
   A. epistaxis   B. chest pain
   C. nausea   D. hemoptysis

7.___

8. A pregnant woman with _____ is MOST likely to experience abrupto placentae.
   A. hyperthyroidism
   B. cephalopelvic disproportion
   C. pregnancy-induced hypertension
   D. cardiac disease

8.__

9. What is the preferred treatment for malignant melanoma of the eye?
   A. Cryosurgery   B. Chemotherapy
   C. Enucleation   D. Radiation

9.__

10. While a pacemaker catheter is being inserted, a client's heart rate drops to 36. The nurse should expect the physician to order
    A. Pronestyl   B. Atropine sulfate
    C. Lanoxin   D. Lidocaine

10.__

11. In the absence of pathology, a client's respiratory system is stimulated by
    A. carbon dioxide   B. sodium ions
    C. oxygen   D. lactic acid

11.__

12. Where should a nurse place the stethoscope when taking a client's apical pulse?
    A. In the fifth intercostal space, along the left mid-clavicular line
    B. Between the sixth and seventh ribs, at the left mid-axillary line
    C. Just to the left of the midpoint of the sternum
    D. Between the third and fourth ribs, to the left of the sternum

12.__

13. A client receiving vincristine as treatment for leukemia should be placed on a diet that is
    A. high in fluids, but low in residue
    B. high in both fluids and roughage
    C. low in fluids, with increased iron
    D. low in fat

13.__

14. The MOST significant causes of puerperal or postpartal infection are hemorrhage and
    A. anemia during pregnancy
    B. preeclampsia
    C. organisms present in the birth canal
    D. trauma during labor

14.__

15. A client is admitted to the hospital with carcinoma of the descending colon, with metastases to the lymph nodes. Which procedure would be performed?
    A. Colostomy   B. Colectomy
    C. Ileostomy   D. Cecostomy

15.__

16. Which of the following conditions is the clearest contra-   16.___
    indication for the administration of Librium?
    A. Hypotension   B. Muscle twitching
    C. Extreme drowsiness   D. Blurred vision

17. A client who is receiving aminophylline intravenously   17.___
    should be observed for
    A. decreased urinary output B. hypotension
    C. auditory hallucinations   D. decreased pulse rate

18. What is the MOST common symptom of a rectrocele caused   18.___
    by overstretching of perineal supporting tissues during
    childbirth?
    A. A sensation of bearing down
    B. Recurrent urinary tract infections
    C. Urinary incontinence
    D. Sharp abdominal pain

19. Which of the following is an early manifestation of cancer   19.___
    of the cervix?
    A. A full-bladder manifestation
    B. A sensation of having a full stomach
    C. Bloody spotting after intercourse
    D. Malodorous discharge

20. A client with a long history of emphysema is now terminal-   20.___
    ly ill with cancer of the stomach. Her plan of care
    includes modified postural drainage, a soft diet, and
    nebulizer treatments twice a day. She is weak, apathetic,
    and dyspneic.
    The nursing care plan for this patient should give priority
    to
    A. posture and body mechanics
    B. intake and output
    C. comfort and hygiene
    D. diet and nutrition

21. A 60-year-old female client is admitted to the hospital   21.___
    with a diagnosis of hypertension. She is placed on a
    cardiac monitor, and her serum potassium level is low.
    She is to receive intravenously 40 mEq potassium chloride
    in 750 ml of 5% dextrose in water.
    When observing the monitor pattern in order to obtain a
    baseline for the evaluation of the client's progress, what
    would be shown by the monitor pattern?
    A. Spiking of the ST segment
    B. Increased Q wave deflection
    C. Lowering of the T wave
    D. Shortened QRS complex

22. Following a thoracentesis, it is MOST important for a   22.___
    nurse to observe a client for
    A. shallow breathing   B. blurred vision
    C. spitting blood   D. increased breath sounds

23. During what period is prenatal growth MOST rapid?   23.___
    A. Implantation   B. 1st trimester
    C. 2nd trimester   D. 3rd trimester

24. A client receiving chemotherapy for cancer of the bone   24.___
    is at risk for mouth lesions. The nurse should instruct
    the client to
    A. brush with foam-tipped applicators
    B. rinse the mouth frequently with undiluted anti-
       bacterial mouthwash
    C. brush three times a day with a toothbrush
    D. rinse the mouth frequently with hydrogen peroxide

25. A client on a cardiac monitor displays ventricular irri-   25.___
    tability. Which of the following should the nurse prepare
    to administer?
    A. Heparin   B. Levophed
    C. Lidocaine   D. Lanoxin

———

KEY (CORRECT ANSWERS)

1. C		11. A	
2. A		12. A	
3. D		13. B	
4. D		14. D	
5. B		15. A	
6. C		16. C	
7. A		17. B	
8. C		18. A	
9. C		19. C	
10. B		20. C	

21. C
22. C
23. D
24. A
25. C

———

TEST 2

DIRECTIONS: Each question or incomplete statement is followed by several suggested answers or completions. Select the one that BEST answers the question or completes the statement. *PRINT THE LETTER OF THE CORRECT ANSWER IN THE SPACE AT THE RIGHT.*

1. The reason that emphysema decreases a patient's oxygen supply is because
   A. the patient is experiencing respiratory muscle paralysis
   B. there is a loss of aerating surface
   C. there is pleural effusion
   D. there are infectious obstructions in the lung and bronchii

1.___

2. A 27-year-old pregnant client claims to have weighed 100 pounds before pregnancy, and now, during her first trimester, she weighs 104 pounds. The client is concerned about regaining her figure after delivery, and expresses a wish to diet during pregnancy.
   The nurse should inform the client that
   A. since she is so small, dieting is often recommended to ease delivery
   B. dieting is often recommended to reduce the chances of stillbirth
   C. an inadequate food intake during pregnancy can result in a low birthweight infant
   D. an inadequate food intake during pregnancy can result in hypertension

2.___

3. A client has two Jackson-Pratt portable wound drainage systems in place after a modified radical mastectomy. Which of the following would be involved in nursing care of these drains?
   A. Irrigating the drains with normal saline
   B. Leaving the drains open to the air to ensure maximum drainage
   C. Compressing the receptacles after emptying in order to maintain suction
   D. Attaching the tubes to straight drainage in order to monitor output

3.___

4. A nurse should measure a client's _____ before giving the client digoxin.
   A. radial pulse in both arms
   B. brachial pulse
   C. difference between apical and radial pulses
   D. apical pulse rate

4.___

5. When rotating tourniquets are used on a client with acute   5.__
   pulmonary edema, the tourniquets are typically rotated
   every _____ minutes.
      A. 5   B. 15   C. 40   D. 60

6. A predisposing factor that causes morning sickness during   6.__
   the first trimester of pregnancy is the mother's adaptation
   to increased levels of
      A. chorionic gonadotropin   B. progesterone
      C. estrogen   D. prolactin

7. Which of the following would MOST likely accompany   7.__
   atelectasis?
      A. Slow, deep respirations
      B. A normal oral temperature
      C. Diminished breath sounds
      D. A wheezy cough

8. A possible side effect of digitalis preparations is a   8.__
   depletion of
      A. sodium   B. phosphate   C. potassium D. calcium

9. Which of the following would MOST likely be observed in   9.__
   a client with a cerebellar tumor?
      A. Execution of jerky, imprecise movements
      B. Inability to execute voluntary movements
      C. Unconsciousness
      D. Absent knee-jerk and other reflexes

10. A pregnant client with heart disease presents anemia with   10.__
    a hemoglobin level of 7.6 g. The client is at a high risk
    for
       A. atrial fibrillation   B. cardiac compensation
       C. cardiac failure   D. heart block

11. The radioisotope cesium-137 is commonly used in brachy-   11.__
    therapy for each of the following EXCEPT _____ cancer.
       A. intracavitary uterine
       B. interstitial breast
       C. intracavitary cervical
       D. interstitial head and neck

12. A 58-year-old client is admitted to the hospital with   12.__
    severe dyspnea, and is expectorating blood. Cancer of
    the lung is suspected, and the client is scheduled for a
    bronchoscopy.
    If the client develops pleural effusion, it is MOST likely
    the result of
       A. low fluid intake
       B. shallow respiration
       C. enlargement of cancerous lesions
       D. irritation from the bronchoscopy

13. Which of the following would NOT typically be used to   13.___
    manage immune-mediated anemia that results from chronic
    lymphocytic leukemia?
    A. Allopurinol   B. Splenectomy
    C. IV gamma globulin   D. Prednisone

14. The ovum is believed to remain viable for _____ hours   14.___
    after ovulation.
    A. 1-4   B. 10-24   C. 24-36   D. 36-72

15. A client states that she experiences anginal pain after   15.___
    periods of activity. The nurse should suspect
    A. coronary thrombosis   B. arrhythmia
    C. mitral insufficiency   D. myocardial ischemia

16. Which of the following is involved in caring for a client   16.___
    following a craniotomy?
    A. Reporting yellow drainage on dressing immediately
    B. Administering sedatives at the first signs of irri-
       tability
    C. Encouraging deep coughing
    D. Taking only axillary temperatures

17. Which of the following is a precaution that must be taken   17.___
    against retrolental fibroplasia when caring for preterm
    infants?
    A. Maintain a high concentration of oxygen (above 70%)
       and high humidity
    B. Use phototherapy to prevent jaundice and retinopathy
    C. Carefully control temperature and humidity
    D. Keep oxygen at less than 40% concentration

18. The MOST common complication of chronic asthma is   18.___
    A. pneumothorax   B. atelectasis
    C. pulmonary embolism   D. emphysema

19. A nursing assessment of a client reveals pulmonary edema.   19.___
    MOST likely, this condition will be associated with
    A. pulmonary valve stenosis
    B. severe arteriosclerosis of the tricuspid valve
    C. mitral stenosis
    D. incomplete closure of the tricuspid valve

20. A physician orders that a client receive an intravenous   20.___
    digitalis preparation. Which of the following preparations
    would be given to the client?
    A. Deslanode   B. Digitalis leaf
    C. Digoxin   D. Gitalin

21. A nurse notes a prolapsed cord in a client in labor. The   46.___
    MOST effective position for this client would be
    A. Trendlenburg   B. Sims'
    C. half-Fowler's   D. prone

22. A client whose platelet count is very low should have her   22.__
    urine checked for the presence of
       A. lymphocytes   B. casts
       C. erythrocytes   D. leukocytes

23. Which of the following diagnosis categories would be   23.__
    prioritized first for treatment?
       A. Penetrating abdominal wound
       B. Fractured tibia
       C. Head injury
       D. Ventricular fibrillation

24. A laboratory report showing acid-fast rods in a client's   24.__
    sputum would indicate the presence of
       A. mycobacterium tuberculosis
       B. bordatella pertussis
       C. influenza virus
       D. diphtheria bacillus

25. When instructing a client about the use of nitroglycerin   25.__
    tablets, the client should be informed that the tablets
    have probably lost their potency when
       A. pain occurs even after taking the tablet
       B. the client experiences increased facial flushing
       C. there is no tingling sensation accompanying the place-
          ment of the tablet under the tongue
       D. the onset of relief is delayed

———

KEY (CORRECT ANSWERS)

1. B		11. B	
2. C		12. C	
3. C		13. A	
4. D		14. C	
5. B		15. D	
6. A		16. A	
7. C		17. D	
8. C		18. D	
9. A		19. C	
10. C		20. A	

21. A
22. C
23. D
24. A
25. C

———

TEST 3

DIRECTIONS: Each question or incomplete statement is followed by several suggested answers or completions. Select the one that BEST answers the question or completes the statement. *PRINT THE LETTER OF THE CORRECT ANSWER IN THE SPACE AT THE RIGHT.*

1. A client diagnosed with metastatic melanoma should be assessed for the presence of
   A. lymphadenopathy   B. sweating palms
   C. Nikolsky's sign   D. oily skin

   1.___

2. If a nurse observes asymmetrical gluteal folds on a newborn infant, what is the MOST likely cause?
   A. Tissue necrosis due to uneven pressure
   B. Damage to the peripheral nervous system
   C. A dislocated hip
   D. An inguinal hernia

   2.___

3. After being admitted to the emergency room, a client is diagnosed with a spontaneous pneumothorax. The client's assessment interview reveals that she has a history of emphysema. Later, the client becomes extremely drowsy, and her pulse and respirations increase.
   The MOST likely situation is
   A. elevated PO_2 B. hypokalemia
   C. respiratory alkalosis   D. hypercapnia

   3.___

4. What is the chief function of progesterone?
   A. Developing female reproductive organs
   B. Preparing the uterus for receiving a fertilized ovum
   C. Stimulating follicles to ovulate
   D. Establishing secondary male sex characteristics

   4.___

5. A client is diagnosed with acute lymphocytic leukemia. A nurse would commonly observe each of the following EXCEPT
   A. pallor   B. marked jaundice
   C. enlarged lymph nodes   D. multiple bruises

   5.___

6. Which of the following molecules is/are capable of passing through the capillary endothelium?
   A. Plasma proteins   B. O_2 and water
   C. Ions   D. Glucose and CO_2

   6.___

7. A client would receive isoproterenol in order to
   A. alleviate hypertension
   B. relax bronchial spasm
   C. increase bronchial secretions
   D. increase heart volume

   7.___

8. Which of the following nursing recommendations may help   8.__
   a pregnant client overcome morning sickness?
   A. Taking a prescribed antiemetic
   B. Eating nothing until the nausea subsides
   C. Eating dry toast before getting out of bed in the
      morning
   D. Taking an antacid before bedtime

9. Before a client undergoes a surgical procedure to remove   9.__
   a carcinoma of the colon, the nurse would administer
   neomycin sulfate in order to
   A. decrease the incidence of secondary infection
   B. destroy intestinal bacteria
   C. increase the production of vitamin E
   D. decrease the possibility of postoperative UTI

10. A likely effect of whole-body irradiation treatment for a   10.__
    client with Hodgkin's disease is
    A. *increased* tendency for fractures
    B. *decreased* number of erythrocytes
    C. *increased* immunity to infections
    D. *increased* blood viscosity

11. For what reason is chemotherapy delayed for a period of   11.__
    about 2 weeks following a radical mastectomy?
    A. The treatment may increase edema in areas near the
       incision by blocking lymph channels.
    B. It may cause vomiting, which would endanger the
       integrity of the incision area.
    C. It may decrease red blood cell production resulting
       in anemia.
    D. It may delay healing and interfere with cell growth.

12. The MOST common indication for cesarean delivery is   12.__
    A. jaundice
    B. vaginal atony
    C. cephalopelvic disproportion
    D. primary uterine inertia

13. Which of the following actions should be taken by a   13.__
    client on bed rest to prevent a pulmonary embolus?
    A. Periodically moving the legs
    B. Limiting fluid intake
    C. Keeping the head elevated
    D. Deep breathing

14. In chronic occlusive arterial disease, which of the   14.__
    following is MOST likely to be the cause of ulceration
    and gangrenous lesions?
    A. Trauma
    B. Emotional stress
    C. Stimulants such as caffeine
    D. Limited protein intake

15. Which of the following types of brain tumors occur MOST   15.___
    frequently?
    A. Glioma   B. Meningioma
    C. Neurofibroma   D. Pituitary adenoma

16. A 68-year-old client is admitted to the hospital with   16.___
    congestive heart failure and pulmonary edema. Her treat-
    ment includes digoxin, Lasix, oxygen by mask, and a low-
    sodium diet. She is restless and dyspneic.
    For the client's comfort, the oxygen should be set at
    _____ L.
    A. 1-3   B. 2-5   C. 5-7   D. 12-15

17. It is possible to follow the course of prostate cancer   17.___
    by monitoring the serum level of
    A. BUN (blood urea nitrogen)
    B. acid phosphatase
    C. albumin
    D. creatinine

18. Which of the following is a contraindication for an   18.___
    oxytocin challenge test (OCT)?
    A. Uterine activity   B. Hypertension
    C. Prematurity   D. Drug addiction

19. Which of the following is a guideline involved in suction- 19.___
    ing a client with a tracheostomy?
    A. Using a new sterile catheter with each insertion
    B. Removing the inner cannula before inserting the
       suction catheter
    C. Initiating suction as catheter is being withdrawn
    D. Inserting the catheter until stimulating the cough
       reflex

20. A client experiences hemostasis due to prolonged bed rest   20.___
    after surgery. Other than thrombus formation, which of
    the following pathological conditions is MOST likely to
    result from this hemostasis?
    A. Gangrene of a limb   B. Cerebral aneurysm
    C. Coronary occlusion   D. Pulmonary embolism

21. If a client undergoes a parotidectomy to remove a can-   21.___
    cerous lesion, which of the following postoperative
    complications may cause distress for the client?
    A. Chvostek's sign
    B. A tracheostomy
    C. Increased salivation
    D. Dysfunctional facial nerve

22. Which of the following BEST describes the normal amniotic   22.___
    fluid of a pregnant client?
    A. Clear, almost colorless, with small white specks
    B. Milky, greenish-yellow, with small white specks
    C. Clear, with a tint of dark amber
    D. Cloudy, greenish-yellow, with shreds of mucus

23. A client is admitted to the hospital with a diagnosis of   23.___
    acute pulmonary edema. She appears extremely anxious.
    Which of the following medications would MOST likely be
    used to reduce her anxiety?
        A. Sodium phenobarbital   B. Morphine sulfate
        C. Chloral hydrate   D. Atarax

24. After undergoing a submucosal resection, a client should   24.___
    be observed for
        A. vomiting or spitting up blood
        B. temporal headache
        C. tremors
        D. periorbital crepitus

25. In which of the following fetal blood vessels is oxygen   25.___
    content typically HIGHEST?
        A. Ductus venosus   B. Ductus arteriosus
        C. Umbilical artery   D. Pulmonary artery

―――

KEY (CORRECT ANSWERS)

1. A	11. D
2. C	12. C
3. D	13. A
4. B	14. A
5. B	15. A
6. A	16. C
7. B	17. B
8. C	18. C
9. B	19. C
10. B	20. D

21. D
22. A
23. B
24. A
25. A

―――

TEST 4

1. A client is admitted with an acute episode of right side   1.___
    heart failure, and is receiving Lasix. During the admis-
    sion history, the nurse should expect the client to
    complain of each of the following EXCEPT
       A. edema   B. nausea   C. fatigue   D. weakness

2. Which of the following drugs is contraindicated for   2.___
    clients who are receiving anticoagulants?
       A. Chloral hydrate   B. Thorazine
       C. Aspirin   D. Vasodilan

3. For Apgar scoring, the primary critical observation is   3.___
       A. the Moro reflex   B. heart rate
       C. presence of albumin   D. respiratory rate

4. Which of the following procedures would definitively   4.___
    differentiate between a gastric ulcer and gastric
    carcinoma?
       A. GI series   B. Gastroscopy
       C. Stool examination   D. Gastric analysis

5. Which of the following is suggested by laboratory results   5.___
    which show a bilirubin level above 2 mg/100 ml of blood
    volume?
       A. Pernicious anemia
       B. Decreased rate of red blood cell destruction
       C. Hemolytic anemia
       D. Increased cardiac output

6. Which of the following is a sign in muscle tissue of   6.___
    oxygen debt?
       A. Low lactic acid   B. High glycogen
       C. Low ATP   D. High calcium

7. Which of the following is included in the care of a   7.___
    client with placenta previa?
       A. Observing and recording the bleeding
       B. Vital signs at least twice per shift
       C. A high colonic enema after delivery
       D. Limiting ambulation until bleeding stops

8. Which of the following procedures is involved in preparing   8.__
a client for a sigmoidoscopy?
   A. Collecting a stool specimen
   B. Administering an enema the morning of the examination
   C. Explaining to the client that a chalky substance will
     have to be swallowed
   D. Withholding all fluids within 24 hours prior to the
     examination

9. Cardiac nitrates are administered to a client in order to   9.__
   A. improve cardiac output
   B. relieve anginal pain
   C. dilate superficial blood vessels
   D. decrease blood pressure

10. To obtain maximum benefits after postural drainage, a   10.__
patient should be encouraged to
   A. remain in a sitting position
   B. keep the legs elevated
   C. cough deeply
   D. rest for at least 30 minutes

11. A 23-year-old primigravida has missed two menstrual   11.__
periods. The patient works a desk job in a large office.
Which of the following recommendations would MOST likely
be made by a nurse caring for this client?
   A. Taking morning and afternoon breaks for extra
     nourishment
   B. Attempting to get up and walk every few hours of the
     work day
   C. Informing her employer that she cannot work past the
     second trimester
   D. Taking morning and afternoon breaks to stretch her
     legs

12. The MOST likely cause of a spontaneous pneumothorax is   12.__
   A. chest wall puncture   B. subpleural bleb rupture
   C. pleural friction rub   D. tracheoesophageal fistula

13. When advising a patient about orthostatic hypotension,   13.__
a nurse should inform the client that it can be adjusted
by
   A. wearing support hose
   B. sitting on the edge of the bed for a short time
     before rising
   C. lying down for thirty minutes after taking medication
   D. avoiding high-energy tasks

14. Which of the following radioisotopes would MOST likely   14.__
be used in brachytherapy of interstitial prostate cancer?
   A. Gold-198   B. Strontium-90
   C. Iodine-131   D. Phosphorus-32

15. Blood clotting requires the presence of which ion?   15.___
    A. Cl^- B. F^- C. Fe^{+++} D. Ca^{++}

16. Rotating tourniquets are used on a client suffering   16.___
from acute pulmonary edema in order to
    A. restrict visceral flow in the internal body cavities
    B. decrease the flow of venous blood to the heart
    C. increase the flow of blood through the capillaries
    D. decrease the flow of arterial blood to the body

17. After a client has undergone a mastectomy, the client's   17.___
arm on the affected side should be positioned
    A. with the hand higher than the arm
    B. lower than the level of the right atrium
    C. in abduction, supported by pillows
    D. in adduction, surrounded by pillows

18. Which of the following BEST describes the normal respira-   18.___
tions of a neonate?
    A. Regular, abdominal, 40-50 per minute, deep
    B. Irregular, thoracic, 30-60 per minute, deep
    C. Irregular, abdominal, 40-50 per minute, shallow
    D. Regular, thoracic, 40-60 per minute, shallow

19. Which of the following tests is MOST valuable in   19.___
assisting a physician in prescribing an effective antibiotic?
    A. Organ sensitivity   B. Susceptibility
    C. Serologic   D. Tissue culture

20. A 50-year-old patient is admitted to the hospital com-   20.___
plaining of chest pain and shortness of breath. The
diagnosis of myocardial infarction is made.
Each of the following laboratory tests will likely be
conducted to confirm this diagnosis EXCEPT
    A. LDH   B. AST   C. SGPT   D. CK-MB

21. Which of the following is a contraindication for breast-   21.___
feeding?
    A. Inverted nipples   B. Herpes genitalis
    C. Pregnancy   D. Mastitis

22. Which of the following is the primary nursing care objec-   22.___
tive for a client with acute lymphocytic leukemia who is
undergoing a chemotherapeutic protocol?
    A. Checking vital signs every 4 hours
    B. Avoiding contact with infected persons
    C. Preventing all physical activity
    D. Increasing fluid intake

23. Cervical polyps
    A. will only cause bleeding if they are malignant
    B. are usually benign, but curettage is always performed
       to rule out malignancy
    C. frequently signal the onset of cervical cancer
    D. are usually malignant, and curettage is always
       performed

24. Which of the following blood proteins is involved in
    impairment of a client's immune system?
    A. Globulin   B. Hemoglobin
    C. Thrombin   D. Albumin

25. An infant delivered at 29 weeks gestation, weighing
    3 pounds, 7 ounces, would be classified as
    A. nonviable   B. immature
    C. low birthweight   D. preterm

—

KEY (CORRECT ANSWERS)

1. B		11. B	
2. C		12. B	
3. B		13. B	
4. B		14. A	
5. C		15. D	
6. C		16. B	
7. A		17. A	
8. B		18. C	
9. B		19. A	
10. C		20. C	

21. C
22. B
23. B
24. A
25. D

—

EXAMINATION SECTION
TEST 1

DIRECTIONS: Each question or incomplete statement is followed by several suggested answers or completions. Select the one that BEST answers the question or completes the statement. *PRINT THE LETTER OF THE CORRECT ANSWER IN THE SPACE AT THE RIGHT.*

1. In the upper respiratory tract,   1.___
   A. air is filtered in the nasopharynx
   B. air is warmed to 37°C before reaching the lungs
   C. cilia sweep foreign matter towards the oropharynx
      where it may be expectorated or swallowed
   D. all of the above

2. The left lung consists of _____ lobe(s).   2.___
   A. two   B. three
   C. one   D. none of the above

3. Alveoli are NOT   3.___
   A. hollow sacs
   B. thick-walled
   C. the agents through which oxygenation occurs
   D. the most important functional unit of the respiratory
      system

4. By definition, normal ventilation is that which maintains   4.___
   the arterial PCO$_2$ at APPROXIMATELY _____ to _____ torr.
   A. 10; 15   B. 20; 30   C. 35; 40   D. 50; 60

5. If the arterial PO$_2$ falls below 80 torr., the patient   5.___
   is considered
   A. hypercapnic   B. hypocapnic
   C. hyoxemic   D. tachypnic

6. Elevated PCO$_2$ is commonly associated with all of the   6.___
   following conditions EXCEPT
   A. myasthenia gravis
   B. stroke
   C. hyperventilation syndrome
   D. head injury

7. Which of the following conditions is(are) associated   7.___
   with hypoxemia?
   A. Near drowning   B. Pulmonary edema
   C. Chest trauma   D. All of the above

8. The respiratory control center is located in the part   8.___
   of the brain known as the
   A. medulla   B. frontal lobe
   C. pineal gland   D. temporal lobe

9. The one of the following conditions which is NOT a cause   9.___
   of lower airway obstruction is
      A. epiglottitis   B. emphysema
      C. chronic bronchitis   D. asthma

10. Causes of respiratory center depression include all of   10.___
    the following EXCEPT
       A. a stroke   B. pulmonary edema
       C. depressant drugs   D. head trauma

11. _____ is NOT among the conditions which frequently affect   11.___
    alveoli.
       A. Flail chest   B. Pneumothorax
       C. Croup   D. Pulmonary edema

12. Regarding chronic obstructive pulmonary disease, it is   12.___
    FALSE that
       A. the condition is more common among men than women
       B. 82 percent of mortality is attributed to alcohol use
       C. the condition is more common among city dwellers than
          in rural populations
       D. it is seen primarily in individuals between the ages
          of 45 and 65

13. All of the following are considered classic features of   13.___
    pink puffers (emphysema) EXCEPT
       A. pain and wasted appearance
       B. barrel-shaped chest which is hyperresonant to per-
          cussion owing to air trapping within the lungs
       C. obvious shortness of breath and frequent pursing
          of the lips during exhalation
       D. none of the above

14. Symptoms and signs of decompensation in COPD include   14.___
       A. increasing dyspnea and sleep disturbance
       B. confusion, agitation, and combativeness resulting
          from hypoxemia
       C. lethargy and drowsiness resulting from hypercarbia
       D. all of the above

15. Of the following, _____ is(are) NOT helpful in the   15.___
    management of COPD.
       A. oxygen by nasal canvia or mask
       B. aminophylline
       C. sedatives and tranquilizers
       D. establishment of an IV lifeline with D5W

16. Among the common clinical features of the acute asthmatic   16.___
    attack is(are)
       A. wheezing that is audible without a stethoscope
       B. spasmodic coughing
       C. prominent use of accessor muscles of respiration
       D. all of the above

17. It is NOT a sign of a severe asthmatic attack when   17.___
    A. pulse rate is greater than 130 per minute
    B. respiratory rate is less than 20 per minute
    C. pulus paradoxus is greater than 15 mmhg
    D. chest is silent

18. Pre-hospital management of an acute asthmatic attack may   18.___
    employ all of the following EXCEPT
    A. albuterol   B. aminophylline
    C. cromolyn sodium   D. epinephrine

19. Of the following statements, which is(are) TRUE regarding   19.___
    bacterial pneumonia?
    A. Elderly patients with chronic illnesses and smokers
       are at greater risk to contract the illness.
    B. The most common form of bacterial pnemonia is
       pneumococcal pneumonia.
    C. The peak incidence occurs in winter and early spring.
    D. All of the above

20. The MOST effective treatment of pneumonia would be the   20.___
    use of
    A. antibiotics
    B. oxygen
    C. multiple doses of epinephrine
    D. all of the above

21. Specialized respiratory functions include   21.___
    A. coughing or sneezing   B. hiccupping
    C. sighing   D. all of the above

Questions 22-25.

DIRECTIONS: In Questions 22 through 25, match the numbered descrip-
              tion with the lettered symptomatic sound it describes
              listed in Column I. Place the letter of the CORRECT
              answer in the appropriate space at the right.

                        COLUMN I

                    A. Rales
                    B. Rhonchi
                    C. Wheezing
                    D. Stridor

22. Harsh, high-pitched sound upon inspiration indicating   22.___
    an upper airway obstruction.

23. Harsher sound indicating the presence of fluid in a   23.___
    larger airway.

24. High-pitched whistling sound of air moving through   24.___
    narrowed airways.

25. Fine, crackling sound indicating the presence of fluid   25.__
    in a small airway.

KEY (CORRECT ANSWERS)

1. D	11. C
2. A	12. B
3. B	13. D
4. C	14. D
5. C	15. C
6. C	16. D
7. D	17. B
8. A	18. C
9. A	19. D
10. B	20. B

21. D
22. D
23. B
24. C
25. A

TEST 2

DIRECTIONS: Each question or incomplete statement is followed by
              several suggested answers or completions. Select the
              one that BEST answers the question or completes the
              statement. *PRINT THE LETTER OF THE CORRECT ANSWER IN
              THE SPACE AT THE RIGHT.*

1. Physical factors influencing the respiratory center   1.___
    include all of the following EXCEPT _____ respiratory
    rate.
        A. high temperature increasing
        B. low temperature increasing
        C. low blood pressure increasing
        D. high blood pressure decreasing

2. Regarding the effect of carbon dioxide and oxygen on   2.___
    inspiratory activity, it is NOT true that
        A. high CO_2 concentration decreases respiratory activity
        B. high CO_2 concentration increases respiratory activity
        C. low CO_2 concentration decreases respiratory activity
        D. hypoxemia is the most profound stimulus to respiration
           in the normal individual

3. The single MOST common cause of airway obstruction in   3.___
    the unconscious victim is due to
        A. dentures   B. the tongue
        C. a foreign body   D. glottic edema

4. In order to eliminate airway obstruction due to the   4.___
    presence of a foreign body, you should NOT
        A. discourage the victim from coughing
        B. deliver four blows to the back of the victim
        C. apply abdominal thrust (Heimlich maneuver)
        D. do more than one but not all of the above

5. Among adults, the MOST common factor associated with   5.___
    drowning is
        A. alcohol intoxication   B. cocaine abuse
        C. heroin intoxication   D. none of the above

6. *A severe prolonged asthmatic attack that cannot be broken* 6.___
    with epinephrine is the definition of
        A. bronchitis   B. status asthmaticus
        C. asthmatic bronchitis   D. CO PD

7. All of the following are true statements regarding near-   7.___
    drowning EXCEPT:
        A. 10 percent of drowning victims do not aspirate any
           water at all
        B. The mortality rate from drowning is less than 5
           percent

C. In freshwater drowning, the hypotonic solution has been absorbed through the lungs

D. In saltwater drowning, pulmonary edema occurs as a result of aspiration

8. Management techniques for cases of near-drowning include   8.___
A. early performance of endotracheal intubation to prevent aspiration
B. determination of whether the victim has a pulse; if not, starting of external chest compression
C. insertion of a nasogastric tube to decompress the stomach (only after an endotracheal tube is in place)
D. all of the above

9. The treatment of choice for severe metabolic acidosis in drowning victims is   9.___
A. hyperventilation by ambu bag
B. sodium bicarbonate
C. calcium carbonate
D. 100% oxygen

10. The one of the following conditions that CANNOT produce pulmonary edema is   10.___
A. heroin overdose
B. left heart failure
C. ingestion of furosemide
D. inhalation of toxic fumes

11. The signs and symptoms of pulmonary edema include all of the following EXCEPT   11.___
A. presence of hypoxia, dyspnea, and cyanosis
B. patient laboring to breathe, often sitting bolt upright
C. low arterial CO_2 concentration and high oxygen concentration
D. rales heard when listening to the posterior bases of both lungs

12. In the management of pulmonary edema, it is NOT necessary to   12.___
A. manage and transport the patient in a sitting position
B. administer morphine if ordered by a physician
C. apply rotating tourniquets, if indicated
D. strictly avoid administering oxygen in high concentration

13. Among the common symptoms of acute mountain sickness is (are) included   13.___
A. throbbing bilateral frontal headache which is worse in the morning and in the supine position
B. sleep disturbance
C. dyspnea on exertion
D. all of the above

14. The MOST useful sign of progression from mild to moderate mountain sickness is
    A. ataxia   B. lassitude
    C. anorexia   D. dyspnea on exertion
14.___

15. If you anticipate a long delay in arranging rescue for a patient with acute mountain sickness, you should administer
    A. epinephrine   B. dexamethasone
    C. bronchodilator   D. none of the above
15.___

16. Common signs and symptoms of high altitude pulmonary edema include
    A. tachpnea, severe dysmnea, and chyne-stokes respirations
    B. cough, cyanosis, and tachycardia
    C. confusion and coma
    D. all of the above
16.___

17. The MOST important element in treating high altitude pulmonary edema is
    A. descent to lower altitude
    B. intravenous morphine
    C. intravenous diuretics
    D. all of the above
17.___

18. _____ are the MOST common scenarios of exposure to toxic gases.
    A. Municipal swimming pools
    B. Fires
    C. Transport accidents
    D. Industrial settings
18.___

19. The *dunglung* syndrome of pulmonary edema, metabolic acidosis, and cardiovascular collapse is produced by
    A. hydrogen sulfide   B. acrylics
    C. cotton   D. nitrogen dioxide
19.___

20. An IMPORTANT part of the treatment of suspected pulmonary embolism is to
    A. ensure an open airway and administer 100% oxygen
    B. monitor cardiac rhythm
    C. establish an IV lifeline with normal saline
    D. all of the above
20.___

Questions 21-25.

DIRECTIONS: In Questions 21 through 25, match the numbered characteristic with the lettered disorder listed in Column I
with which it is MOST closely associated. Place the
letter of the CORRECT answer in the appropriate space
at the right.

<u>COLUMN I</u>

A. Pickwickian syndrome
B. Hyperventilation syndrome
C. Chronic obstructive pulmonary disease
D. Pulmonary embolism
E. Spontaneous pneumothorax

21.   Birth control pill.   21._

22.   Patient is often young, thin, and tall.   22._

23.   Carpopedal spasms and low CO_2.   23._

24.   Extreme obesity, periods of apnea, and dysrhythmias   24._
      during sleep.

25.   Oxygen is the mainstay of treatment.   25._

——

KEY (CORRECT ANSWERS)

1. B		11. C	
2. A		12. D	
3. B		13. D	
4. A		14. A	
5. A		15. B	
6. B		16. D	
7. B		17. A	
8. D		18. B	
9. B		19. A	
10. C		20. D	

21. D
22. E
23. B
24. A
25. C

——

EXAMINATION SECTION
TEST 1

DIRECTIONS: Each question or incomplete statement is followed by several suggested answers or completions. Select the one that BEST answers the question or completes the statement. *PRINT THE LETTER OF THE CORRECT ANSWER IN THE SPACE AT THE RIGHT.*

1. All of the following are important actions to take in the management of a patient exposed to toxic fumes EXCEPT:
   A. Remove the patient from the environment of exposure
   B. Establish and maintain an open airway
   C. Cease constant supervision since it is not necessary for all victims of intense exposure to smoke or toxic fumes
   D. Assist breathing as required, with the demand value or bag value mask plus peep

   1.___

2. The MOST common source of pulmonary embolism is
   A. fat particles   B. blood clot
   C. amniotic fluid   D. air

   2.___

3. The typical pulmonary embolism patient is prone to sudden onsets of severe, unexplained
   A. dyspnea
   B. sharp chest pain made worse by coughing
   C. tachycardia and achpnea
   D. all of the above

   3.___

4. All of the following are immediate life-threatening chest injuries that must be detected and managed during the primary survey EXCEPT
   A. tension pneumothorax   B. pulmonary contusion
   C. cardiac tamponade   D. airway obstruction

   4.___

5. Regarding chest trauma, it is TRUE that
   A. 75 percent of those who die as a result of automobile accidents have suffered chest injuries
   B. simple rib fractures usually involve the fourth, fifth, sixth, and seventh ribs
   C. rib fractures are usually very painful, and they restrict respiratory activity
   D. all of the above

   5.___

6. Regarding simple pneumothorax, it is NOT true that
   A. it never requires any treatment
   B. it is often caused by blunt trauma
   C. small pneumothorax may absorb slowly
   D. subcutaneous emphysema may be present

   6.___

7. Which of the following statements is FALSE about tension   7.___
pneumothorax?
    A. The lung collapses and the mediastinum shifts to the
       opposite side.
    B. Venous return is compromised due to increased intra-
       thoracic pressure and distortion of the venae cavae.
    C. Tension should not be relieved.
    D. Mediastinal shift is augmented with every respira-
       tion.

8. The preferred site for chest decompression in tension   8.___
pneumothorax is the _____ intercostal space, _____ line.
    A. second; midclavicular   B. fifth; midclavicular
    C. third; mid axillary   D. fourth; mid axillary

9. A 25-year-old male has a puncture of the chest wall by a   9.___
knife. The result is a sucking chest wound.
The management of choice is
    A. immediate insertion of a chest tube
    B. application of a sterile occlusive dressing
    C. immediate endotracheal intubation
    D. all of the above

10. A 30-year-old male sustained a puncture wound on the   10.___
fifth intercostal space. The wound was caused by a
knife during a fight. Thirty minutes later, he developed
a distended neck vein and muffled heart sound.
The MOST likely diagnosis is
    A. tension pneumothorax   B. flail chest
    C. cardiac tamponade   D. none of the above

11. In pre-hospital treatment of flail chest, it is VITAL to   11.___
    A. assist ventilation with a bag valve mask if the
       patient is unable to take deep breaths on his own
    B. stabilize the flail segment by applying constant,
       firm, manual pressure, or buttressing the segment
       with sandbags or pillows
    C. start an IV en route, but restrict intravenous fluids
       unless there is a sign of shock
    D. all of the above

12. It is important to remember to do all of the following   12.___
when suctioning through an endotracheal tube EXCEPT
    A. carry out frequent endotracheal suction in the
       pre-hospital setting
    B. always pre-oxygenate the patient for 3 minutes
    C. observe strict sterile techniques
    D. re-oxygenate the patient the moment you finish
       suctioning

13. All of the following indicate endotracheal intubation   13.___
EXCEPT
    A. cardiac arrest
    B. deep coma with absent gag reflex
    C. simple pneumothorax
    D. airway obstruction due to burns

14. Advantages of endotracheal intubation do NOT include   15.___
   A. the cuffed endotracheal tube's protection of the
      airway from aspiration
   B. ventilation through the endotracheal tube causing
      severe gastric distention
   C. the allowance of intermittent positive pressure
      ventilation (IPPV) with 100% oxygen
   D. an endotracheal tubes enabling the delivery of
      aerosolized medication

15. The one of the following which is NOT an indication for   15.___
   blind nasotracheal intubation is
   A. suspected trauma to the cervical spine
   B. trauma to the mouth or mandible
   C. basilar skull fracture
   D. severe congestive heart failure

16. Contraindications to blind nasotracheal intubation   16.___
   include all of the following EXCEPT
   A. apnea
   B. respiratory depression from alcohol
   C. defect in blood clotting
   D. severe nasal polyps

17. The one of the following which is NOT a contraindication   17.___
   to esophageal obturator airway is
   A. a patient under 16 years of age
   B. cirrhosis of the liver
   C. a deeply unconscious patient
   D. the ingestion of caustic substances

18. The advantages of the esophageal obturator airway is(are)   18.___
   that it
   A. requires no visualization of the patient's airway
   B. may be inadvertently inserted in the trachea
   C. prevents gastric distension and aspiration
   D. A and C *only*

19. Common complications of cricothyrotomy include all of   19.___
   the following EXCEPT
   A. bleeding   B. subcutaneous emphysema
   C. cardiac tamponade   D. mediastinal emphysema

20. The MOST likely side effect of morphine sulphate on the   20.___
   respiratory system is
   A. bronchodilation   B. respiratory acidosis
   C. respiratory alkalosis   D. none of the above

Questions 21-25.

DIRECTIONS: In Questions 21 through 25, match the numbered function with the lettered piece of equipment it describes as listed in Column I. Place the letter of the CORRECT answer in the appropriate space at the right.

<u>COLUMN I</u>

    A. Nasal cannula
    B. Plastic face mask
    C. Partial rebreathing mask
    D. Nonrebreathing mask
    E. Venturi mask

21. Delivers 90% oxygen.   21.___

22. Delivers 50 to 60% oxygen.   22.___

23. Is useful in long-term treatment of a patient with COPD.   23.___

24. Delivers 25 to 40% oxygen.   24.___

25. Delivers 35 to 60% oxygen.   25.___

KEY (CORRECT ANSWERS)

1. C		11. D	
2. B		12. A	
3. D		13. C	
4. B		14. B	
5. D		15. C	
6. A		16. B	
7. C		17. C	
8. A		18. D	
9. B		19. C	
10. C		20. B	

21. D
22. B
23. E
24. A
25. D

TEST 2

DIRECTIONS: Each question or incomplete statement is followed by
several suggested answers or completions. Select the
one that BEST answers the question or completes the
statement. *PRINT THE LETTER OF THE CORRECT ANSWER IN
THE SPACE AT THE RIGHT.*

1. In a majority of pre-hospital settings, the airway can   1.___
   BEST be improved INITIALLY by
   A. proper positioning of the airway
   B. endotracheal intubation
   C. use of an esophageal obturator airway
   D. none of the above

2. Endotracheal intubation is a technique used to manage   2.___
   A. cardiac circulation   B. renal blood flow
   C. the unprotected airway   D. all of the above

3. A(n) _____ is to be expected when removing an esophageal   3.___
   obturator airway (EOA).
   A. esophageal rupture
   B. regurgitation of stomach contents
   C. spasm of the trachea
   D. all of the above

4. The MOST severe hazard of intubation using the esophageal   4.___
   obturator airway in an unconscious victim is
   A. severe abdominal distension
   B. failure to inflate the cuff
   C. undetected intubation of the trachea
   D. uncontrollable bleeding of the trachea

5. When a patient is suffering from poor ventilation, there   5.___
   is an obvious reduction in oxygen flow to all parts of
   the body.
   Poor ventilation quickly affects all of the following
   EXCEPT the
   A. anxiety level   B. pulse rate
   C. intravascular volume D. acid/base balance

6. Oxygen-powered mechanical breathing devices for use   6.___
   during CPR are
   A. satisfactory only if manually triggered
   B. satisfactory only if pressure cycled
   C. not capable of delivering high concentrations of
      oxygen to the patient
   D. all of the above

7. Tension pneumothorax   7.___
   A. can make CPR ineffective
   B. may be detectable by tracheal shift
   C. can be caused by a broken rib
   D. all of the above

8. Multiple attempts at tracheal intubation may cause   8.___
   A. esophageal intubation   B. laryngeal trauma
   C. anoxia   D. all of the above

9. Bag-valve-mask devices should be   9.___
   A. designed to deliver 100% oxygen for effective CPR
   B. used only by trained persons
   C. all of the above
   D. none of the above

10. Endotracheal suction   10.___
   A. should be limited to 5 seconds
   B. can produce hypoxemia
   C. can produce bradyarrythmia
   D. all of the above

11. To manage acute laryngeal edema due to an allergic   11.___
   reaction, one should
   A. establish an airway
   B. administer oxygen
   C. perform a cricothyrotomy (if the patient does not
      respond to medication)
   D. all of the above

12. The drug of choice for treating acute laryngeal edema   12.___
   due to allergic reaction is
   A. epinephrine   B. diphenhydramine
   C. oral prednisone   D. none of the above

13. Signs of choking include   13.___
   A. inability of the victim to speak or make any sound
   B. dusky or cyanotic skin
   C. exaggerated but ineffective breathing movements
   D. all of the above

14. Treatments of decompression sickness include all of the 14.___
   following EXCEPT
   A. steroids   B. nitronox for analgesia
   C. 100% oxygen   D. hyperbaric facility

Questions 15-18.

DIRECTIONS: Questions 15 through 18 refer to a diving injury.
              Match the numbered mechanisms and pathophysiologies
              with the lettered condition with which they are MOST
              closely related, as listed in Column I. Place the
              letter of the CORRECT answer in the appropriate space
              at the right.

COLUMN I

A. Barotitis externa and barotitis media
B. Bargdontalgia, aerogastralgia, and blindness
C. Bend, staggers, paraplegia, and the *chokes*
D. Symptoms similar to those of alcoholic intoxication

15. Barotrauma during ascent   15.___

16. Barotrauma during descent   16.___

17. Nitrogen narcosis   17.___

18. Decompression sickness   18.___

Questions 19-25.

DIRECTIONS: In Questions 19 through 25, match the numbered descrip-
              tions with the lettered parts of the respiratory system,
              as listed in Column I, which they describe MOST accurate-
              ly. Place the letter of the CORRECT answer in the
              appropriate space at the right.

COLUMN I

A. Alveoli
B. Bronchus
C. Glottis
D. Pharynx
E. Trachea
F. Vocal cords
G. Turbinates

19. One of the main branches of the trachea which carries   19.___
     air into various parts of the lung.

20. The saccular unit at the end of the terminal bronchiol   20.___
     where gas exchange takes place in the lung.

21. The portion of the airway between the nasal cavity and   21.___
     the larynx.

22. The opening to the trachea.   22.__

23. The cartilaginous tube extending from the larynx   23.__
    superiorly down to the carina.

24. It mixes up the air entering the nasopharynx.   24.__

25. The paired structures in the larynx whose vibrations   25.__
    produce sound.

———

KEY (CORRECT ANSWERS)

1. A	11. D
2. C	12. A
3. B	13. D
4. C	14. B
	15. B
6. A	
7. D	16. A
8. D	17. D
9. C	18. C
10. D	19. B

21. D
22. C
23. E
24. G
25. F

20. A

———

CARDIOVASCULAR SYSTEMS
EXAMINATION SECTION
TEST 1

DIRECTIONS: Each question or incomplete statement is followed by several suggested answers or completions. Select the one that BEST answers the question or completes the statement. *PRINT THE LETTER OF THE CORRECT ANSWER IN THE SPACE AT THE RIGHT.*

1. The wall of the heart is made up of all of the following 1.___
   EXCEPT the
   A. pericardium   B. epicardium
   C. myocardium   D. endocardium

2. Among the following statements, the one which is TRUE 2.___
   regarding the pericardium is:
   A. It contains about 30 ml of serous fluid
   B. It is tough and fibrous and does not readily stretch
   C. If more than 100 ml of fluid accumulates within the
      pericardium, it may compromise heart contractility
   D. All of the above

3. The MAIN function of the heart is to 3.___
   A. transport the waste products of metabolism to the
      cells
   B. deliver oxygenated blood and nutrients to every cell
      in the body
   C. deliver non-oxygenated blood to the cells in the body
   D. deliver chemical messages to the cells

4. Of the following, the structure which collects non- 4.___
   oxygenated blood returning from the body is the
   A. left atrium   B. right ventricle
   C. right atrium   D. left ventricle

5. The vessels that carry blood to the heart are 5.___
   A. arteries   B. arterioles
   C. capillaries   D. veins

6. It is NOT true that the heart 6.___
   A. weighs about 300 grams in males and 250 grams in
      females
   B. is usually 10-12 cm long
   C. is usually located in the right mediastinum
   D. is usually 9 cm wide and 6 cm thick

7. The MOST common location of atria is in the _____ portion 7.___
   of the heart.
   A. superior   B. inferior
   C. middle   D. all of the above

8. The MOST common location and function of the superior   8.___
   vena cava are that it is located _____ and drains _____.
   A. at the right side of the heart; unoxygenated blood
      from the upper body
   B. at the left side of the heart; oxygenated blood from
      the lower body
   C. on the right side; unoxygenated blood from the
      lower part of the body
   D. in the right atrium; blood from the heart itself

9. The high-pressure pump that drives blood OUT of the   9.___
   heart against the relatively high resistance of the
   systemic arteries is called the
   A. right atrium   B. left atrium
   C. left ventricle   D. right ventricle

10. Oxygenated blood is usually supplied to the heart via   10.___
    the _____ artery(arteries).
    A. carotid   B. coronary   C. pulmonary   D. subclavian

11. The MOST accurate definition of cardiac output is: 11.___
    A. The amount of blood pumped out by either ventricle,
       measured in liters per minute
    B. The amount of blood pumped out by either ventricle
       in a single contraction
    C. The number of cardiac contractions per minute
    D. None of the above

12. The MOST frequent location of the sino atrial node is   12.___
    the _____ near the _____.
    A. right atrium; inlet of the inferior vena cava
    B. right atrium; inlet of the superior vena cava
    C. left atrium; inlet of the pulmonary vein
    D. left ventricle; aortic valve

13. The sinoatrial (SA) node is the fastest pacemaker in the 13.___
    heart, normally firing at the rate of _____ to _____
    times per minute.
    A. 20; 40   B. 40; 60   C. 60; 100   D. 100; 300

14. _____ is the process by which muscle fibers are   14.___
    stimulated to contract.
    A. Depolarization   B. Repolarization
    C. Dyastole   D. Refractory period

15. The electrolyte that flows into the cell to initiate   15.___
    depolarization is
    A. magnesium B. potassium C. sodium   D. phosphate

16. Of the following electrolytes, the one which flows out 16.___
    of the cell to initiate repolarization is
    A. sodium   B. potassium C. calcium   D. magnesium

17. Depolarization of the atria produces which of the follow-   17.___
    ing waves on the ECG?
    A(n)
    A. P wave   B. T wave
    C. QRS complex   D. N wave

18. Of the following waves, repolarization of the atria and   18.___
    ventricles produces _____ on the ECG.
    A. QRS complex   B. P waves
    C. T waves   D. none of the above

19. The coronary arteries   19.___
    A. originate from the base of the ascending aorta
    B. are above the leaflets of the aortic valve
    C. provide blood supply to the cardiac muscles
    D. all of the above

20. All of the following are caused by the stimulation of   20.___
    beta receptors EXCEPT
    A. bronchoconstriction
    B. increased heart rate
    C. increased heart contractability
    D. vasodilation

21. Alpha receptor stimulation does NOT cause   21.___
    A. vasoconstriction   B. bronchoconstriction
    C. no effect on the heart   D. increased heart rate

22. Which of the following is pure beta agonist?   22.___
    A. Isoproterenol   B. Metaraminol
    C. Norepinephrine   D. Dopamine

23. The agent of choice to treat increased blood pressure   23.___
    when hypotension has been caused by neurogenic shock
    (vasodilation) is
    A. isoproterenol   B. atropin
    C. norepinephrine   D. propranolol

24. Of the following sympathetic agents, the one usually   24.___
    indicated for asystole and anaphylactic shock is
    A. dopamine   B. epinephrine
    C. metaraminol   D. isoproterenol

25. When used in low doses, this sympathetic agent increases   25.___
    the force of cardiac contraction and helps to maintain
    urine flow and good perfusion to abdominal organs.
    This is a description of
    A. dopamine   B. norepinephrine
    C. metaraminol   D. isoproterenol

KEY (CORRECT ANSWERS)

1. A
2. D
3. B
4. C
5. D

6. C
7. A
8. A
9. C
10. B

11. A
12. B
13. C
14. A
15. C

16. B
17. A
18. C
19. D
20. A

21. D
22. A
23. C
24. B
25. A

TEST 2

DIRECTIONS: Each question or incomplete statement is followed by several suggested answers or completions. Select the one that BEST answers the question or completes the statement. *PRINT THE LETTER OF THE CORRECT ANSWER IN THE SPACE AT THE RIGHT.*

1. Propranolol is used clinically to   1.___
   A. slow the heart rate in certain tachyarrythmias
   B. decrease the pain of chronic angina
   C. decrease irritability in the heart
   D. all of the above

2. All of the following are functions of the parasympathetic   2.___
   nervous system EXCEPT
   A. increasing salivation   B. constricting pupils
   C. slowing the gut   D. slowing the heart

3. Which of the following is NOT a function of the sympathetic 3.___
   nervous system?
   A. Dilate pupils   B. Increase gut motility
   C. Speed the heart   D. Constrict blood vessels

4. Chest pain is often the presenting sign of acute myocar-   4.___
   dial infarction.
   When treating a patient with chest pain, the MOST
   important question for you to ask him is:
   A. What provoked the pain?
   B. What is the quality and severity of the pain?
   C. Does the pain radiate?
   D. All of the above

5. Paroxymal nocturnal dyspnea is one of the classic signs   5.___
   of
   A. pericarditis   B. right heart failure
   C. left heart failure   D. asthmatic bronchitis

6. The MOST prevalent preventable cause of death in the   6.___
   United States is
   A. diabetes   B. hypertension
   C. cigarette smoking   D. high serum cholesterol

7. Common sources of risk to the coronary artery include   7.___
   A. birth control pills   B. lack of exercise
   C. male sex   D. all of the above

8. Among the MOST common symptoms of angina pectoris are   8.___
   included
   A. sensations of tightness or pressure
   B. pain induced by anything that increases oxygen
      requirements

   C. pain radiating to the lower jaw, upper neck, and
      left shoulder
   D. all of the above

9. The difference(s) between the pain of angina pectoris and   9.___
   the pain from acute myocardial infarction is(are) that
   the pain of acute myocardial infarction
   A. may occur at rest
   B. may last for hours
   C. is not relieved by rest
   D. all of the above

10. All of the following are characteristic of angina pectoris   10.___
    EXCEPT that the pain usually
    A. occurs after exercise, stress and/or cold weather
    B. is relieved by rest
    C. is unresponsive to nitroglycerine
    D. lasts 3 to 5 minutes

11. Among the following, the classic symptoms of acute   11.___
    myocardial infarction include
    A. squeezing or crushing chest pain which is not
       relieved by rest
    B. a feeling of impending death
    C. diaphoresis, dyspnea, and dizziness
    D. all of the above

12. An elderly patient suffers a sudden onset of dyspnea,   12.___
    hypotension, and confusion.
    The MOST likely diagnosis is
    A. acute myocardial infarction
    B. angina pectoris
    C. pericarditis
    D. congestive heart failure

13. What is the treatment of choice for angina pectoris?   13.___
    A. Propranolol   B. Nitroglycerin
    C. Epinephrine   D. Metaraminol

14. The MAIN goal of treatment for acute myocardial infarction   14.___
    is to
    A. alleviate the patient's fear and pain
    B. prevent the development of serious cardiac dysrhyth-
       mias
    C. limit the size of the infarct
    D. all of the above

15. Cardiac work is minimal in the _____ position.   15.___
    A. standing   B. sitting
    C. semi-recumbent   D. none of the above

16. _____ therapy is the mainstay of emergency cardiac care.   16.___
    A. Epinephrine   B. Oxygen
    C. Propranolol   D. Norepinephrine

17. The proper treatment of uncomplicated acute myocardial   17.___
    infarction en route to the hospital should include all
    of the following EXCEPT
    A. administering oxygen by mask or nasal cannula
    B. D5W using a 250 ml bag and the infusion rate should
       be just enough to keep the vein open
    C. giving normal saline bolus
    D. taking blood pressure and repeating at least every
       5 minutes

18. In which of the following conditions should the patient   18.___
    be transported before he is stabilized?
    Cardiac
    A. arrest due to uncontrollable hemorrhaging
    B. arrest secondary to cold exposure
    C. rhythms that require immediate pacemaker insertion
    D. all of the above

19. The preferred pain medication for treating a hypotensive   19.___
    patient with acute myocardial infarction is
    A. morphine sulphate   B. nitrous oxide
    C. codeine   D. acetominophen

20. Of the following medications, the one you should draw   20.___
    BEFORE administering morphine to a patient with an
    acute myocardial infarction is
    A. atropine sulphate   B. nitroglycerine
    C. propranolol   D. digoxin

21. It would be acceptable to administer morphine to a   21.___
    patient suffering from
    A. low blood pressure
    B. bronchial asthma
    C. AMI involving the inferior wall of the heart
    D. hypertension and pulmonary edema

22. Criteria for thrombolytic therapy for acute myocardial   22.___
    infarction includes all of the following EXCEPT
    A. recent CPR
    B. alert patient who is able to give informed consent
    C. age between 30 and 75 years
    D. chest pain lasting more than 20 minutes but less
       than 6 hours

23. Common signs and symptoms of left heart failure include   23.___
    A. extreme restlessness and agitation
    B. severe dyspnea and tachypnea
    C. frothy pink sputum
    D. all of the above

24. Which of the following heart chambers is MOST commonly   24.___
    damaged by acute myocardial infarction?
    A. Right ventricle   B. Left ventricle
    C. Left atrium   D. Right atrium

25. Of the following medications, the one(s) which should be   25.___
    drawn up ready, pending the physician's order for
    administration, for the treatment of left heart failure
    is(are)
        A. morphine sulphate   B. furosemide
        C. digoxin   D. all of the above

Questions 26-30.

DIRECTIONS: In Questions 26 through 30, match the numbered descrip-
             tion with the lettered part of the circulatory system,
             as listed in Column I, to which it is most closely
             related. Place the letter of the CORRECT answer in the
             appropriate space at the right.

                            COLUMN I

                    A. Epicardium
                    B. Endocardium
                    C. Myocardium
                    D. Pericardium
                    E. Coronary sinus

26. The tough fibrous sac which surrounds the heart.   26.___

27. The outermost layer of the heart wall.   27.___

28. The innermost layer of the heart wall.   28.___

29. The middle layer of the heart wall.   29.___

30. A large vessel in the posterior part of the coronary   30.___
    sulcus into which venous blood empties.

KEY (CORRECT ANSWERS)

1. D	11. D	21. D
2. C	12. A	22. A
3. B	13. B	23. D
4. D	14. D	24. B
5. C	15. C	25. D
6. C	16. B	26. D
7. D	17. C	27. A
8. D	18. D	28. B
9. D	19. B	29. C
10. C	20. A	30. E

TEST 3

DIRECTIONS: Each question or incomplete statement is followed by several suggested answers or completions. Select the one that BEST answers the question or completes the statement. *PRINT THE LETTER OF THE CORRECT ANSWER IN THE SPACE AT THE RIGHT.*

1. Pre-hospital treatment of left heart failure would NOT include   1.___
   A. administration of beta blocker
   B. administration of 100% oxygen
   C. seating the patient with his feet dangling
   D. starting an intravenous line with D5W

2. The MOST common cause of right heart failure is   2.___
   A. cor pulmonale   B. tricuspid stenosis
   C. left heart failure   D. cardiac tamponade

3. All of the following can occur as a result of ventricle failure EXCEPT   3.___
   A. blood backs up into the vein
   B. back-up increases the venous pressure
   C. back-up decreases the venous pressure
   D. blood serum escapes into the tissue and produces edema

4. Signs and symptoms of right heart failure do NOT include   4.___
   A. collapsed jugular vein   B. hepatosplenomegaly
   C. peripheral edema   D. tachycardia

5. Common signs and symptoms of cardiogenic shock include all of the following EXCEPT   5.___
   A. pulse racing and thready
   B. severe hypertension
   C. respiration rapid and shallow
   D. confused or comatose state

6. The differentiating factor(s) between the pain of a dissecting aneurysm and an acute myocardial infarction is(are) that the pain of a dissecting aneurysm   6.___
   A. is maximal from the outset
   B. is often included in the back between the shoulder blades
   C. does not abate once it has started
   D. all of the above

7. A 60-year-old male has sudden back pain and a pulsatile abdominal mass. Ten minutes later, his blood pressure starts dropping.
   Pre-hospital management for this patient would include all of the following EXCEPT   7.___

A. administering oxygen
B. stabilizing the patient before transport
C. applying (but not inflating) the mast
D. starting an IV en route with normal saline or lactated ringer's

8. A 35-year-old comatose male has cold and clammy skin, shallow breathing, and thready pulse.
   The FIRST thing you should do to treat this patient is
   A. start an IV D5W
   B. apply monitoring electrodes
   C. secure an open airway
   D. administer epinephrine

   8.___

9. The MOST common complications of hypertension include
   A. renal damage   B. stroke
   C. heart failure   D. all of the above

   9.___

10. Acute hypertensive crisis is usually signaled by a sudden marked rise in blood pressure to a level greater than
    _____ mmHg.
    A. 120/80   B. 140/80
    C. 200/130   D. none of the above

    10.___

11. Which of the following is the drug of choice for treatment of hypertensive encephalopathy?
    A. Propranolol   B. Diazoxide
    C. Furosemide   D. Reserpin

    11.___

12. The P wave represents depolarization of the atria. When examining the ECG, you should look for the presence of
    A. P waves in general
    B. a P wave before every QRS complex
    C. a QRS complex before every P wave
    D. all of the above

    12.___

13. A P-R interval exceeding 0.2 second is called _____ degree AV block.
    A. first   B. second
    C. third   D. none of the above

    13.___

14. Potential causes of sinus tachycardia include
    A. pain and fever
    B. shock and hypoxia
    C. hypotension and congestive heart failure
    D. all of the above

    14.___

15. The treatment of choice for sinus tachycardia is
    A. atropin sulphate
    B. treatment of the underlying cause
    C. propranolol
    D. all of the above

    15.___

16. You should NOT treat patients with sinus bradycardia if   16.___
    they have
    A. unconsciousness
    B. a good or strong pulse
    C. cold and clammy skin
    D. systolic blood pressure of 80 mmHg or less

17. Which of the following drugs can be used to treat sinus   17.___
    bradycardia?
    A. Atropin sulphate   B. Propranolol
    C. Isoproterenol   D. A and C *only*

18. For premature atrial contraction,   18.___
    A. epinephrine is the best treatment
    B. dopamine is the best treatment
    C. no satisfactory treatment exists
    D. all of the above

19. A 40-year-old male has paroxymal supraventricular tachy-   19.___
    cardia and stable vital signs. The physician tells you
    to apply vagal maneuvers but, at the same time, the
    patient develops hypotension.
    The treatment of choice is
    A. to continue valsalva maneuver
    B. cardioversion
    C. verapamil
    D. digoxin

20. Some maneuvers that stimulate the vagus nerve will slow   20.___
    the heart rate and may convert some PSVT's back to normal
    sinus rhythm.
    These maneuvers include all of the following EXCEPT
    A. valsalva maneuver   B. ice water
    C. carotid sinus massage   D. hot water

21. You are taking a patient with PSVT to the hospital, which   21.___
    is 30 minutes away.
    The physician may tell you to administer
    A. verapamil   B. digoxin
    C. dopamine   D. all of the above

22. You are looking at the ECG of a patient who has regular   22.___
    rhythm, a rate of 50 per minute, absent P wave, and
    normal QRS complexes.
    The MOST likely diagnosis is
    A. sinus bradycardia
    B. junctional bradycardia
    C. third degree heart block
    D. none of the above

23. If the patient in the above question develops signs of   23.___
    poor perfusion, you should administer
    A. atropin sulphate   B. digoxin
    C. procainamide   D. all of the above

24. Propranolol is known by the trade name(s)   24.__
    A. pronestyle   B. inderal
    C. procardia   D. all of the above

Questions 25-30.

DIRECTIONS: In Questions 25 through 30, match the numbered descrip-
               tion or function with the appropriate lettered part of
               the cardiovascular system, as listed in Column I. Place
               the letter of the CORRECT answer in the space at the
               right.

                          COLUMN I

                    A. Tricuspid valve
                    B. Mitral valve
                    C. Coronary sulcus
                    D. Systole
                    E. Diastole
                    F. SA node

25. The groove which separates the atria and the ventricle, in   25.__
    which the arteries and the main coronary vein cross the
    heart.

26. Separates the right atrium from the right ventricle.   26.__

27. Separates the left atrium from the left ventricle.   27.__

28. Atrial and ventricular relaxation.   28.__

29. Atrial and ventricular contraction.   29.__

30. Located in the right atrium near the inlet of the   30.__
    superior vena cava.

                          _____

KEY (CORRECT ANSWERS)

1. A	11. B	21. A
2. C	12. D	22. B
3. C	13. A	23. A
4. A	14. D	24. B
5. B	15. B	25. C
6. D	16. B	26. A
7. B	17. D	27. B
8. C	18. C	28. E
9. D	19. B	29. D
10. C	20. D	30. F

                          _____

EXAMINATION SECTION
TEST 1

DIRECTIONS: Each question or incomplete statement is followed by several suggested answers or completions. Select the one that BEST answers the question or completes the statement. *PRINT THE LETTER OF THE CORRECT ANSWER IN THE SPACE AT THE RIGHT.*

1. The MOST common primary malignant neoplasm of the lung is   1.___
   A. adenocarcinoma
   B. bronchial adenoma
   C. alveolar cell carcinoma
   D. squamous cell carcinoma
   E. undifferentiated carcinoma

2. A candidate virus for the induction of cervical carcinoma is   2.___
   A. adenovirus
   B. C-type virus
   C. varicella zoster
   D. Epstein-Barr virus
   E. herpes virus hominis Type 2

3. In MOST slow viruses, tissue damage occurs in the   3.___
   A. lung   B. heart
   C. brain   D. spleen
   E. kidney

4. The MOST common causative organism in gram-negative sepsis is   4.___
   A. pneumococcus   B. virus organism
   C. escherichia coli   D. streptococcus viridans
   E. streptococcus pyogenes

5. Fluoride is MOST effective and safe as a prophylactic measure when it is   5.___
   A. in the F_2 state
   B. applied topically
   C. taken intravenously
   D. supplied in sucrose
   E. added to the water supply

6. The MOST common etiologic agent of septic arthritis in adults is   6.___
   A. neisseria gonorrhoeae
   B. hemophilus influenzae
   C. streptococcus pyogenes
   D. streptococcus pneumoniae
   E. herpes hominis

7. The delayed type of hypersensitivity can be transferred by   7.___
   A. lysozyme   B. antibodies
   C. mast cells   D. plasma cells
   E. sensitized lymphocytes

8. The BASIC effect of x-radiation upon living tissues is   8.___
   A. ionization   B. denaturation
   C. agglutination   D. precipitation
   E. cauterization

9. The PRINCIPAL antibody-producing cell is the   9.___
   A. mast cell   B. lymphocyte
   C. macrophage   D. eosinophil
   E. plasma cell

10. The histologic pattern in a renal ischemic infarct is   10.___
    ____ necrosis.
       A. caseous   B. gummatous
       C. gangrenous   D. coagulation
       E. liquefaction

11. Dextrans are extracellular polysaccharides readily   11.___
    produced by streptococcus
       A. mitis   B. mutans
       C. pyogenes   D. salivarius
       E. acidogenic

12. A bacterial mutation leading to the requirement for a   12.___
    single amino acid is due to
       A. lack of mRNA
       B. loss of ability to utilize glucose
       C. absence of a single enzyme activity
       D. absence of cell wall polysaccharide
       E. absence of several enzyme activities

13. Transmission of the hepatitis B virus may be through   13.___
      I. parental administration of blood or blood products
     II. use of contaminated instruments or injection equipment
    III. microabrasions in skin and mucous membranes by contact
         with infected materials (blood, saliva, feces)

    The CORRECT answer is:
       A. I only   B. II only
       C. I, III   D. II, III
       E. I, II, III

14. Rickettsiae are similar to bacteria in that they   14.___
      I. multiply by binary fission
     II. can be cultured on enriched blood agar
    III. are capable of producing heat-resistant endospores
     IV. possess an energy-yielding, autonomous enzyme
         metabolism
      V. are susceptible to the lethal effects of certain
         antibiotics

The CORRECT answer is:
A. I, II, III
B. I, III, IV
C. I, IV, V
D. II, III, V
E. II, IV, V

15. Significant functions of polymorphonuclear leukocytes 15.___
    in inflammation are
    I. replication of new cells
    II. phagocytosis of bacteria
    III. elaboration of proteolytic enzymes
    IV. elaboration of antibodies

    The CORRECT answer is:
    A. I, II
    B. I, III
    C. II, III
    D. II, IV
    E. III, IV

16. Neonatally thymectomized mice and nude mice exhibit 16.___
    I. reduced numbers of T-lymphocytes
    II. inability to reject allografts
    III. reduced antibody production to most antigens

    The CORRECT answer is:
    A. I *only*
    B. II *only*
    C. I, II
    D. II, III
    E. I, II, III

17. The choice that *correctly* shows the following types of 17.___
    cells or tissues in DECREASING order of radiosensitivity
    from MOST sensitive to LEAST sensitive is:
    I. Osteocyte
    II. Endothelium
    III. Smooth muscle
    IV. Spermatogonium
    V. Intestinal mucosa

    The CORRECT answer is:
    A. II, III, I, V, IV
    B. III, I, II, IV, V
    C. IV, II, III, I, V
    D. IV, V, II, III, I
    E. V, IV, III, I, II

18. Cells of which of the following retain a latent capacity 18.___
    for mitotic division?
    I. Liver
    II. Bone marrow
    III. Cardiac muscle
    IV. Salivary glands
    V. Neurons

    The CORRECT answer is:
    A. I, II, III
    B. I, II, IV
    C. I, III, IV
    D. II, III, V
    E. II, IV, V

19. Which of the following statements explain the advantageous 19.___
    effects of fibrin formation? Fibrin
    I. transforms into fibroblasts serving in repair
    II. generates hyaluronidase to dissolve exudates
    III. serves as scaffolding for fibroblasts to proliferate
        in repair
    IV. serves to wall off attacking agents to prevent further
        spread

The CORRECT answer is:
   A. I, II   B. I, III
   C. I, IV   D. II, III
   E. III, IV

20. Which of the following are possible sequelae to acute appendicitis?   20.___
   I. Generalized peritonitis
  II. Periappendiceal abscess formation
 III. Pylephlebitis
  IV. Hepatic abscess

The CORRECT answer is:
   A. I, II, III   B. I, II, IV
   C. I, III, IV   D. II, III, IV
   E. I, II, III, IV

21. Which of the following are related to streptococcal cross-antigenicity?   21.___
   I. Sympathetic opthalmia
  II. Milroy's disease
 III. Systemic lupus erythematosus
  IV. Rheumatic fever
   V. Acute glomerulonephritis

The CORRECT answer is:
   A. I, III   B. II, III
   C. II, V   D. III, V
   E. IV, V

22. Which of the following hormones has the GREATEST effect on granulation tissue in healing wounds?   22.___
   A. Thyroxin   B. Estrogen
   C. Cortisone   D. Parathormone
   E. Antidiuretic hormone

23. When horse serum is injected intravenously into a rabbit and again into the skin two or three weeks later, what is the necrotizing reaction that occurs at the site of the second injection?   23.___
   A. Atopy
   B. Anaphylaxis
   C. Serum sickness
   D. Arthus phenomenon
   E. Prausnitz-Kustner reaction

24. Recurring attacks of bronchial asthma may predispose to   24.___
   A. empyema   B. emphysema
   C. tuberculosis   D. cor pulmonale
   E. none of the above

25. The one of the following that is classified as a
    hemolytic anemia is ____ anemia.
       A. aplastic   B. pernicious
       C. sickle-cell   D. iron deficiency
       E. none of the above

                  25.____

KEY (CORRECT ANSWERS)

1. D		11. B	
2. E		12. C	
3. C		13. E	
4. C		14. C	
5. E		15. C	
6. A		16. D	
7. E		17. D	
8. A		18. B	
9. E		19. E	
10. D		20. E	

21. E
22. C
23. D
24. B
25. C

TEST 2

DIRECTIONS: Each question or incomplete statement is followed by several suggested answers or completions. Select the one that BEST answers the question or completes the statement. *PRINT THE LETTER OF THE CORRECT ANSWER IN THE SPACE AT THE RIGHT.*

1. Increased functional demand on the heart produces increased size of the myocardium by
   A. hyperplasia
   B. hypertrophy
   C. calcification
   D. fatty infiltration
   E. increased amounts of fibrous connective tissue

   1.___

2. An infectious disease with low morbidity and which is constantly present in a given community is considered to be
   A. endemic   B. epidemic
   C. pandemic   D. epizootic
   E. polyzygotic

   2.___

3. A tumor composed of multiple tissues in which there may be representatives of all three embryonal layers is a(n)
   A. teratoma   B. adenoma
   C. carcinoma   D. sarcoma
   E. hamartoma

   3.___

4. Shock is a circulatory disturbance characterized by
   A. *increased* blood pressure
   B. *elevated* body temperature
   C. *increased* atmospheric pressure
   D. *decreased* volume of circulating blood
   E. *decreased* volume of interstitial fluid

   4.___

5. Diphtheria, pertussis, smallpox, poliomyelitis and tetanus have in common the fact that all are
   A. air-borne diseases
   B. vector-borne diseases
   C. characterized by toxemia
   D. primarily diseases of infants
   E. prevented by active immunization

   5.___

6. The three general classes of vaccines are
   A. killed organisms, virulent bacteria and attenuated viruses
   B. toxoids, antitoxins and attenuated organisms
   C. killed organisms, toxoids and attenuated organisms
   D. killed organisms, antitoxins and gamma globulins
   E. none of the above

   6.___

7. Adjuvants are nonspecific, mildly irritating substances   7.___
   which are used to
      A. enhance antibody response
      B. depress antibody response
      C. desensitize to a given antigen
      D. remove antibodies from circulation
      E. none of the above

8. Hemorrhage might be difficult to curb in patients with   8.___
   liver disorders because of
      A. anemia which invariably accompanies liver dysfunction
      B. vitamin C shortage caused by impaired fat absorption
      C. deficiency of vitamin B_{12}
      D. hypoprothrombinemia
      E. lack of bile pigments

9. The MOST common complication of chronic peptic ulcer is   9.___
      A. hemorrhage
      B. malabsorption syndrome
      C. development of carcinoma
      D. development of hypoacidity
      E. development of obstruction during healing

10. Acute glomerulonephritis is *most commonly* a sequela of   10.___
       A. measles
       B. diphtheria
       C. upper respiratory infections due to hemolytic
         streptococci
       D. upper respiratory infections due to nonhemolytic
         streptococci
       E. mumps

11. When a thrombotic embolus originates in a femoral vein,   11.___
    it *usually* becomes arrested in the
       A. right heart   B. renal circulation
       C. portal circulation   D. hepatic circulation
       E. pulmonary circulation

12. Ribonucleic acid is considered to be the chemical basis   12.___
    for heredity in poliomyelitis virus because
       A. it is the only nucleic acid present
       B. ultraviolet light induces mutations
       C. DNA is infective under appropriate conditions
       D. viral infectivity is destroyed by deoxyribonuclease
       E. none of the above

13. Transfer of inheritable characteristics among bacteria is   13.___
    dependent on
       A. ATP   B. DPT   C. DNA   D. RNA   E. FDS

14. Enzymes responsible for suppuration in an abscess are   14.___
    derived *mainly* from
       A. serum
       B. lymph
       C. lymphocytes
       D. polymorphonuclear leukocytes
       E. hemoglobin

15. Heat sensitive materials may be sterilized without   15.___
    destruction by means of
        A. dry heat
        B. boiling water
        C. ethylene oxide
        D. quaternary ammonium compounds
        E. laser sterilization

16. Orchitis is a serious complication in adults with   16.___
        A. mumps
        B. measles
        C. nongonococcal urethritis
        D. ECHO virus meningoencephalitis
        E. parainfluenza virus nasopharyngitis

17. Rickettsia are distinguishable from viruses because   17.___
    viruses contain
        A. DNA; rickettsia contain RNA
        B. RNA; rickettsia contain DNA
        C. either RNA or DNA; rickettsia contain both RNA and DNA
        D. both RNA and DNA; rickettsia contain either RNA or DNA
        E. either RNA or DNA; rickettsia contain neither RNA
           nor DNA

18. Organisms which exhibit dimorphism, are gram-positive, and   18.___
    grow on Sabouraud's medium are
        A. fungi   B. bacteria
        C. mycoplasma   D. rickettsia
        E. spirochetes

19. The genus bacillus is distinguished from the genus   19.___
    clostridium chiefly in that the strains of bacillus are
        A. aerobic   B. anaerobic
        C. parasitic   D. sporebearers
        E. none of the above

20. Striated muscle, smooth muscle and cardiac muscle have in   20.___
    common the fact that
        A. hyperplasia of these elements is common
        B. hypertrophy is a common response to injury
        C. they have a limited capacity to regenerate
        D. they need a constant high O_2 concentration to function
        E. none of the above

21. The cell MOST important in the production of antibody is   21.___
    the
        A. mast cell
        B. histiocyte
        C. lymphocyte
        D. plasma cell
        E. polymorphonuclear leukocyte

22. Osteomyelitis is MOST commonly caused by
    A. nocardia asteroides
    B. borrelia vincentii
    C. actinomyces bovis
    D. staphylococcus aureus
    E. mycobacterium tuberculosis

    22.___

23. Histamine released by mast cells is responsible for the principal symptoms of
    A. anaphylaxis
    B. serum sickness
    C. macroglobulinemia
    D. immune-complex diseases
    E. delayed hypersensitivity

    23.___

24. The BASIC difference between gram-positive and gram-negative bacteria is
    A. cell wall structure
    B. chromosome structure
    C. that gram-negative bacteria are motile
    D. that gram-positive bacteria have capsules
    E. there is no basic difference

    24.___

25. A benign mushroom-like neoplasm of bone showing a peripheral cartilage cap in the metaphyseal area of a young person is *most likely* a(n)
    A. exostosis   B. osteosarcoma
    C. chondrosarcoma   D. osteochondroma
    E. metaphyseal defect

    25.___

———

KEY (CORRECT ANSWERS)

1. B		11. E	
2. A		12. A	
3. A		13. C	
4. D		14. D	
5. E		15. C	
6. C		16. A	
7. A		17. C	
8. D		18. A	
9. A		19. A	
10. C		20. C	

21. D
22. D
23. A
24. A
25. D

———

EXAMINATION SECTION
TEST 1

DIRECTIONS: Each question or incomplete statement is followed by several suggested answers or completions. Select the one that BEST answers the question or completes the statement. *PRINT THE LETTER OF THE CORRECT ANSWER IN THE SPACE AT THE RIGHT.*

Questions 1-10.

DIRECTIONS: Questions 1 through 10 are to be answered on the basis of the following information.

Rosa Dawson, a primigravida, comes to the antepartal clinic accompanied by her husband. This is Rosa's first prenatal visit.

1. Presumptive signs and symptoms (subjective) for pregnancy do not include   1.___
   A. amenorrhea   B. urinary frequency
   C. weight change   D. irritability

2. All of the following are known as probable signs and symptoms (objective) for pregnancy EXCEPT   2.___
   A. uterine enlargement
   B. ballottement
   C. quickening
   D. Braxton Hicks' contractions

3. Positive signs and symptoms of pregnancy include   3.___
   A. presence of chorionic gonadotrophin hormone
   B. fetal heartbeat detection as early as eight weeks with an electronic device
   C. demonstration of fetal outline by ultrasound after third week
   D. all of the above

4. Rosa now needs to consume an extra amount of iron in her meals.   4.___
   The BEST source for Rosa to meet her increased daily iron requirement is
   A. adding at least two extra pounds of beef to her daily diet
   B. consuming at least six glasses of milk daily
   C. taking ferrous sulphate preparations with a vitamin C source
   D. including extra fruits in her daily diet

5. Rosa informs the health care staff that she has noticed   5.__
   her husband's gaining weight and suffering from fatigue
   and nausea throughout her pregnancy.
   This phenomenon is known as
       A. motivation   B. identification
       C. mitleiden   D. bondage

6. Rosa comes to the antepartal unit for a nonstress test   6.__
   after experiencing pregnancy-induced hypertension at
   34 weeks' gestation.
   Of the following, the MOST accurate statement about this
   test is that it
       A. determines fetal-maternal placental function
       B. is considered positive if there are no decelerations
       C. is considered positive if there are no fetal heart-
          beats
       D. is non-invasive and observes the response of fetal
          heart rate to the stress of activity

7. Rosa's doctor orders an L/S ratio for her.   7.__
   The nurse knows that this test is an assessment of
       A. fetal renal maturity and function
       B. fetal lung maturity through measurement of lung
          surfactants, using amniotic fluid
       C. bilirubin level, using amniotic fluid
       D. the level of maternal-fetal estriol production

8. An oxytocin challenge test is done to determine fetal   8.__
   well-being.
   The results of this test are considered
       A. *positive* if persistent late decelerations occur in
          more than 50 percent of contractions
       B. *positive* if persistent late decelerations occur in
          more than 75 percent of contractions
       C. *negative* if there are three contractions in ten
          minutes, lasting two minutes without late decelera-
          tion
       D. *negative* if there are six contractions in ten minutes,
          lasting forty seconds without late deceleration

9. Rosa comes to the clinic for evaluation after experiencing 9.__
   contractions throughout the night.
   If Rosa is experiencing Braxton Hicks contractions, the
   nursing assessment will reveal that the contractions
       A. are confined to the upper back
       B. are intensified by excessive rest
       C. are intensified by walking about
       D. do not increase in frequency or intensity

10. Rosa delivers a healthy eight pound boy and wants to   10.__
    breastfeed.
    In teaching Rosa about breastfeeding, all of the following
    information provided by the nurse would be helpful EXCEPT:
        A. Breastfeeding provides the exact type and distribution
           of nutrients needed by a human newborn in the amounts
           required

B. Breastfeeding is initiated by prolactin, which
stimulates milk production
C. Ovulation is suppressed and pregnancy is impossible
while breastfeeding
D. Oxytocin causes *let-down* or delivery of milk to
the nursing baby

11. A pregnant woman notices enlargement of her breast,   11.___
darkening of nipple, and widening of areola. Veins also
become visible in the breast.
All of the following are conditions besides normal
pregnancy that can produce this breast picture EXCEPT
   A. hyperprolactinemia
   B. calcitonin-producing tumors
   C. pseudocyesis
   D. pre-menstrual syndrome

12. Pregnancy-induced causes of skin changes, such as linea   12.___
nigra, chloasma, and vascular marking, do NOT include
   A. increased melanocyte-stimulating hormone
   B. increased estrogen
   C. decreased melanocyte-stimulating hormone
   D. stretching and atrophy of connective tissue

13. Constipation is a common complaint during the first and   13.___
last trimesters of pregnancy.
To relieve constipation, the nurse should advise the
patient to make all of the following dietary changes
EXCEPT
   A. increase daily intake of fruit and vegetables
   B. choose unrefined grains, which contain more fiber
   C. decrease daily fluid intake
   D. include prunes or prune juice, which have a natural
      laxative effect

14. The FALSE statement regarding changes in the cardio-   14.___
vascular system as a result of pregnancy is:
   A. The heart is displaced to the left and upward
   B. Diastolic murmurs are common in pregnancy
   C. There is an exaggerated splitting of the first heart
      sound
   D. There is a loud, easily heard third heart sound

15. Height of fundus roughly measures the fetal growth or   15.___
duration of pregnancy.
Of the following measurements of uterine growth and
estimated fetal growth, it is INCORRECT that fundus at
_____ is equal to _____ weeks of gestation.
   A. symphasis pubis; 6
   B. umbilicus; 20
   C. 28 cm. from top of symphasis pubis; 28
   D. lower border of rib cage; 36

16. A nurse should advise the pregnant woman to report at   16.__
    once to the clinic with any unusual signs.
    NOT included among these unusual signs requiring a visit
    to the clinic is
       A. abnormal or severe abdominal pain
       B. chilling fever or burning on urination
       C. ankle edema
       D. vaginal bleeding, new or old blood

17. A fundal height greater than expected period of gestation   17.__
    suggests all of the following EXCEPT
       A. oligohydramnios   B. miscalculated due date
       C. multiple pregnancy   D. hydatiform mole

18. Amniocentesis is a procedure in which amniotic fluid is   18.__
    removed from the uterine cavity by insertion of a needle
    through the abdominal and uterine walls and into the
    amniotic sac.
    During amniocentesis, it is NOT the nurse's responsibility
    to
       A. reduce the anxiety related to the procedure
       B. reduce the pain and discomfort related to the proce-
          dure
       C. start with the prophylactic antibiotic after the
          procedure
       D. reduce the potential for traumatic injury to the
          fetus, placenta, or maternal structure

19. To minimize the chances of traumatic injury, either to   19.__
    the mother or fetus during amniocentesis, it is TRUE
    that
       A. if the fetus is more than 20 weeks of gestation,
          the woman should empty her bladder before the
          procedure
       B. the nurse should obtain maternal vital signs and a
          20-minute fetal heart tracing to serve as a baseline
          to evaluate possible complications
       C. the nurse should monitor the woman during and follow-
          ing the procedure for signs of premature labor or
          bleeding
       D. all of the above

20. The *non-stress test* (NST) is used to evaluate fetal   20.__
    heart rate accelerations that normally occur in response
    to fetal activity in a fetus in good condition.
    Indications for NST include all of the following EXCEPT
       A. 30th week of gestation
       B. RH sensitization
       C. suspected intrauterine growth retardation
       D. sickle cell disease, maternal diabetes, and hyper-
          thyroidism

21. During non-stress testing, the nurse should   21.___
    A. place the woman in semi-Fowler's position to monitor
       fetal and uterine activity externally
    B. evaluate the response of fetal heart rate immediately
       following fetal activity
    C. monitor the mother's blood pressure and uterine
       activity for deviations during the procedure
    D. all of the above

22. A *contraction stress test* is used to evaluate the ability   22.___
    of a fetus to withstand the stress of uterine contractions
    as would occur during labor.
    All of the following are indications for a contraction
    stress test EXCEPT
    A. evidence of potential fetal distress
    B. woman with a reactive non-stress test
    C. history of previous stillbirth
    D. abnormal estriol values

23. Contraindications to a contraction stress test do NOT   23.___
    include
    A. prolonged pregnancy
    B. woman with previous cesarean birth
    C. third trimester bleeding
    D. premature rupture of membranes

24. A nurse attending during contraction stress testing   24.___
    should do all of the following EXCEPT
    A. obtain a 30-minute strip of fetal heart rate and
       uterine activity for baseline data
    B. place the woman in a sitting position
    C. have the woman void
    D. administer diluted oxytocin via an infusion pump and
       keep increasing oxytocin every 20-30 minutes, until
       three contractions occur within 10 minutes

25. To avoid constipation, a pregnant woman should   25.___
    A. perform adequate daily exercise
    B. establish regular patterns of elimination
    C. take in additional fluids and dietary roughage
    D. all of the above

26. By the 10th lunar month, the fetus is supposed to have   26.___
    reached all of the following developmental milestones
    EXCEPT
    A. lanugo almost absent
    B. testes begins descent to scrotal sac
    C. vernix caseosa mainly on back
    D. ample subcutaneous fat

27. Regarding sexual activity during pregnancy, it is NOT   27.__
    true that
    A. there is no contraindication to intercourse during
       pregnancy
    B. women may experience heightened sexual activity
       during the second trimester
    C. the female inferior position is more comfortable
       in the latter half of pregnancy
    D. women may find deep penile penetration uncomfortable

28. Nursing intervention to help the pregnant woman in her   28.__
    employment planning would provide the advice that
    A. there is no reason to stop working unless complica-
       tions arise
    B. exposure to toxic substances, such as chlorinated
       hydrocarbons, lead, benzene, toluene, mercury, and
       radioactive substances, should be avoided
    C. it is desirable to avoid severe physical strain and
       get adequate periods of rest
    D. all of the above

29. In the health teaching of a pregnant woman, the nurse   29.__
    should advise cessation of smoking because of the
    increased risk of complications.
    NOT among these risked complications is
    A. spontaneous abortion
    B. neonatal death increasing directly with increasing
       level of maternal smoking during pregnancy
    C. birth of a high birth weight infant
    D. fetal death

30. Nursing intervention to set a good daily nutrition plan   30.__
    must contain iron because iron performs all of the
    following functions EXCEPT
    A. providing iron for fetal development
    B. enhancing the light and dark adaptation of vision
    C. maintaining mother's stores of iron
    D. maintaining hemoglobin level of mother

KEY (CORRECT ANSWERS)

1. D	11. B	21. D
2. C	12. C	22. B
3. B	13. C	23. A
4. C	14. B	24. B
5. C	15. A	25. D
6. D	16. C	26. B
7. B	17. A	27. C
8. A	18. C	28. D
9. D	19. D	29. C
10. C	20. A	30. B

TEST 2

DIRECTIONS: Each question or incomplete statement is followed by several suggested answers or completions. Select the one that BEST answers the question or completes the statement. *PRINT THE LETTER OF THE CORRECT ANSWER IN THE SPACE AT THE RIGHT.*

1. Nursing advice to relieve respiratory discomfort associated with pressure of the enlarged uterus on the diaphragm include providing relief by
    A. assuming semi-Fowler's position arranged with pillow
    B. good posture and standing tall
    C. eating small, frequent meals, preventing increased pressure from full stomach
    D. all of the above

    1.___

2. Calcium should be an important dietary constituent of the nutrition plan of a pregnant woman because it provides all of the following important functions EXCEPT
    A. skeletal structures of the fetus
    B. maintenance of healthy skin
    C. production of breast milk
    D. blood coagulation, neuro-muscular irritability, and muscle contractility

    2.___

3. *Fetoscopy* is the insertion of a fiberoptic instrument into the uterine cavity to examine the fetus visually or to obtain blood, placental or tissue samples for identification, and diagnosis of
    A. congenital anomalies or teratogenic-induced malformations
    B. hemoglobinopathies such as sickle cell anemia and beta-thalassemia
    C. sex-linked autosomal abnormalities or neural tube disorders
    D. all of the above

    3.___

4. Percutaneous umbilical cord blood sampling is used to identify fetal blood dyscrasias and also for fetal karyotyping.
    Complications of this procedure involve all of the following EXCEPT
    A. prematurity   B. infections
    C. postmaturity   D. fetal loss

    4.___

5. The one of the following that is NOT a possible complication of chorionic villous biopsy is
    A. rupture of membranes
    B. incidence of fetal loss of about 55%
    C. maternal tissue contamination
    D. spontaneous abortion

    5.___

6. By the 9th lunar month, the fetus is supposed to reach   6.__
   all of the following developmental milestones EXCEPT
      A. 320 mm. crown-rump length and 2500 gms weight
      B. fingernails reach fingertips
      C. testes in inguinal canal
      D. skin is pink and smooth

7. If a couple at risk for passing along a genetic defect   7.__
   chooses to begin a pregnancy, chorionic villi sampling
   may be performed as early as the fifth week of pregnancy.
   Chorionic villi sampling is indicated if
      A. the woman is a carrier of an x-linked disorder
      B. both parents are carriers of a metabolic disease
      C. either partner is a known balanced translocation
         carrier
      D. all of the above

8. After chorionic villi sampling, a woman is found to have   8.__
   a fetus with Down's syndrome.
   All of the following are signs of Down's syndrome EXCEPT
      A. webbing of neck   B. protruding tongue
      C. epicanthal folds   D. hypotonia

9. A nurse should have all of the legal guidelines for   9.__
   genetic screening in her mind before performing the
   procedure.
   The one of the following statements NOT in keeping with
   these guidelines is:
      A. People desiring genetic counseling should sign an
         informed consent form before the procedure
      B. Results may be given to persons other than those
         directly involved
      C. Participation in a genetic screening program must
         be elective, not mandatory
      D. Results must not be withheld from individuals

10. After genetic counseling, a fetus is found to have   10.__
    Klinefelter's syndrome.
    Klinefelter's syndrome manifests itself by all of the
    following clinical signs EXCEPT
       A. small testes   B. gynecomastia
       C. cat-like cry   D. infertility

11. It is INCORRECT that after the 4th lunar month of gesta- 11.__
    tion the fetus'
       A. rudimentary kidneys secrete urine
       B. sex is not differentiated
       C. heartbeat is present
       D. nasal septum and palate close

12. Which of the following is a basic principle that guides   12.___
    nursing practices in the care of women?
    A. Health promotion and disease prevention are more
       satisfying for the consumer and more cost effective
       for society
    B. Nursing services are targeted towards helping women
       develop a sense of mastery of their bodies and their
       roles in culture
    C. The health of one individual within a social system,
       such as a family, influences all the other members
    D. All of the above

13. Any maternal condition that impairs the blood flow to the   13.___
    placenta causes impairment of oxygen suppy to the fetus,
    resulting in fetal distress and increased level of
    corticosteroids, which triggers the elaboration of
    surfactant in alveolar cells, causing accelerated maturity.
    All of the following maternal conditions lead to
    accelerated maturity EXCEPT
    A. chronic glomerulonephritis
    B. hyperthyroidism
    C. sickle cell disease
    D. narcotic addiction

14. Specific physiologic alteration resulting from pregnancy   14.___
    may cause neurologic or neuromuscular symptomatology,
    such as
    A. compression of pelvic nerves or vascular stasis
    B. edema involving the peripheral nerves which may result
       in carpal tunnel syndrome during the last trimester
    C. acroesthesia, i.e., numbness and tingling of the
       hands
    D. all of the above

15. The mother-child relationship progresses through preg-   15.___
    nancy as a developmental process.
    Which of the following developmental tasks are identified
    in the evolution of this relationship?
    To
    A. accept the biologic fact of pregnancy
    B. accept the growing fetus as distinct from the self
       and as a person to nurture
    C. prepare realistically for the birth and parenting
       of the child
    D. all of the above

16. Nursing interventions to prevent potential intrauterine   16.___
    infection and reduce anxiety of injury to fetus after
    sexual intercourse during pregnancy include all of the
    following EXCEPT
    A. inform woman that intercourse is safe as long as the
       membranes are intact
    B. caution against use of hot tub

C. advise that intercourse is strongly contraindicated
   during the end of the second trimester and onwards
D. review signs of ruptured membranes

17. To determine the expected date of delivery, the nurse   17._
    should use
    A. information from the patient's history and then
       apply Naegle's Rule
    B. ultrasound
    C. fundal height measurements
    D. all of the above

18. To reduce nausea in a pregnant woman, a nurse should   18._
    advise her to
    A. eat small, frequent meals instead of three large ones
    B. avoid eating fried or greasy foods, especially before
       bed
    C. keep crackers or other dry carbohydrates at the bed-
       side
    D. all of the above

19. *Varicose veins* are large, distended, tortuous superficial   19._
    veins that may occur during pregnancy.
    To help prevent varicose veins, _____ should be avoided.
    A. obesity
    B. wearing loose clothing
    C. lengthy standing or sitting
    D. constipation and bearing down with bowel movements

20. For the prevention and treatment of joint pain, backache,   20._
    and pelvic pressure in a pregnant woman, nursing sugges-
    tions would include
    A. maintaining good posture and body mechanics
    B. wearing low-heeled shoes
    C. pelvic floor exercises, rest, and reassurance
    D. all of the above

21. Heartburn is a frequent complication occurring in the   21._
    first trimester of pregnancy.
    Nursing advice to prevent and treat heartburn would
    include all of the following EXCEPT
    A. avoid fatty foods and large meals
    B. take sips of milk for temporary relief
    C. use baking soda to reduce symptoms
    D. maintain good posture

22. GI tract motility is slowed down because of the effect   22._
    of progesterone, leading to constipation.
    In the prevention and treatment of constipation, a nurse
    would NOT suggest that a patient
    A. ingest mineral oil
    B. drink six glasses of water per day
    C. use relaxation techniques and deep breathing
    D. avoid taking stool softeners, laxatives, or other
       drugs without first consulting a physician

23. Nursing care of a pregnant woman with headaches would include
    A. emotional support
    B. prenatal teaching
    C. conscious relaxation
    D. all of the above

23.___

24. In the general nursing care plan for a pregnant woman, a nurse should educate the woman about
    A. good nutrition, eating habits, and favorable weight gain
    B. the importance of maintaining an exercise program
    C. safety hazards relevant to work and travel
    D. all of the above

24.___

25. A nurse caring for a woman experiencing anxiety and negative feelings towards her body should
    A. discuss with her the normal physiologic processes responsible for changes in body shape and pigmentation
    B. assess the relationship of the couple
    C. discuss with her maternity clothing that will enhance the woman's professional image and self-concept
    D. all of the above

25.___

26. To help a woman with the problem of leukorrea, the nurse should talk with her, discussing
    A. what leukorrea is and what causes it
    B. signs to watch for impending leukorrhea
    C. types of undergarments that aid in controlling problems with leukorrhea
    D. all of the above

26.___

27. All of the following are signs and symptoms of preterm labor EXCEPT
    A. uterine contractions that occur every 10 minutes or more often
    B. decrease in vaginal discharge
    C. abdominal cramping with or without diarrhea
    D. pelvic pressure that feels like the baby is pushing down constantly or intermittently

27.___

28. Hospital, not home, birth is indicated for women
    A. who cannot be transferred easily to a hospital should the need arise unexpectedly
    B. who are opposed to home birth
    C. with inadequate home facilities
    D. all of the above

28.___

29. General goals regarding maternal and fetal nutrition include
    A. involving the woman as a participant in her own care
    B. ensuring optimum nutrition for the gravida and her fetus
    C. ensuring optimum nutrition for women of childbearing age
    D. all of the above

29.___

30. To prepare a woman for amniocentesis, it is NOT necessary   30.__
    to
    A. place the woman in a sitting position with her hands
       under her head or across her chest
    B. take baseline vital signs and fetal heart rate
    C. prepare the abdomen with a shave and a scrub with
       povidone-iodine
    D. pre-medicate if ordered by physician

——————

KEY (CORRECT ANSWERS)

1. D	11. B	21. C
2. B	12. D	22. A
3. D	13. A	23. D
4. C	14. D	24. D
5. B	15. D	25. D
6. C	16. C	26. D
7. D	17. D	27. B
8. A	18. D	28. D
9. B	19. B	29. D
10. C	20. D	30. A

——————

EXAMINATION SECTION
TEST 1

DIRECTIONS: Each question or incomplete statement is followed by several suggested answers or completions. Select the one that BEST answers the question or completes the statement. *PRINT THE LETTER OF THE CORRECT ANSWER IN THE SPACE AT THE RIGHT.*

1. All of the following features usually favor the diagnosis of preeclampsia over essential hypertension EXCEPT
    A. family history negative
    B. onset of hypertension during the first 20 weeks of pregnancy
    C. primigravida
    D. proteinuria

1.___

2. The one of the following that is NOT considered a danger sign for pregnancy-induced hypertension is
    A. weight gain
    B. marked hyperreflexia, especially transient or sustained ankle clonus
    C. severe headache
    D. rapid rise of blood pressure and generalized edema

2.___

3. To teach a woman how to assess for pregnancy-induced hypertension, teach her to
    A. make a weight assessment every day and watch for an increase of 2 or more pounds per week
    B. observe for pitting edema of lower extremities, tight rings, shoes, and facial puffiness
    C. use a dipstick for assessment of proteinuria
    D. all of the above

3.___

4. The general health care plan of a woman with pregnancy-induced hypertension advises that she remain in bed.
In order to aid in enforcing this suggestion, a nurse should
    A. explain to her the importance of remaining in bed
    B. teach her relaxation techniques
    C. assess her family and internal support systems
    D. all of the above

4.___

5. Magnesium sulphate is given for the prevention of eclampsia in a pre-eclamptic woman.
Danger signs for both the fetus and mother associated with magnesium sulphate toxicity include all of the following EXCEPT
    A. urinary output less than 25 ml/hr
    B. respiratory rate of more than 22/min.
    C. sudden hypotension
    D. sudden decrease in fetal heart rate

5.___

6. The antidote for toxicity of magnesium sulphate is   6.___
    A. sodium bicarbonate   B. calcium carbonate
    C. calcium gluconate   D. potassium chloride

7. The immediate care during a convulsion in an eclamptic   7.___
    woman is to ensure a patent airway.
    Nursing care of a woman with convulsions does NOT
    include
    A. keeping the woman supine to prevent aspiration of
       vomitus and hypotension
    B. inserting folded towel, plastic airway, or padded
       tongue blade into side of mouth to prevent biting
       of lips or tongue and to maintain airway
    C. suctioning food and fluid from glottis or trachea
    D. administering oxygen by means of face mask or tent
       after convulsion ceases

8. To monitor and minimize the severity of disease and effects 8.___
    of edema, proteinuria and hypertension in a woman with
    severe preeclampsia, the nurse should
    A. keep the woman on absolute bedrest with side rails up
    B. start IV and maintain rate to keep line open
    C. have the woman select people she wishes to stay with
       her and limit other visitors
    D. all of the above

9. To prevent adverse sequelae to severe PIH, the nurse   9.___
    should
    A. control the amount of external stimuli
    B. monitor symptoms and access level of consciousness
       and reflexes
    C. record findings of fundoscopic examination
    D. all of the above

10. To check urinary elimination in a patient with severe   10.___
    preeclampsia, the nurse should do all of the following
    EXCEPT
    A. keep accurate intake and output records
    B. check urine for glucose every 4 hours
    C. report output of less than 100 ml/4 hours
    D. send blood specimen to laboratory for measurement
       of creatinine

11. To monitor the severity of maternal response to PIH, the   11.___
    nurse should make assessments twice a week to note changes.
    She would NOT be assessing changes in
    A. glycosuria
    B. vital signs and blood pressure
    C. proteinuria
    D. edema and weight gain

12. To prevent further seizure in a woman with severe pre-   12.___
    eclampsia, the nurse should
        A. assess CNS status periodically and look for level
           of consciousness, fundoscopic changes, etc.
        B. assess for impending seizures and look for ankle
           clonus, epigastric pain, oliguria, etc.
        C. decrease environmental stimuli
        D. all of the above

13. All of the following are diseases spread by bodily   13.___
    contact but not necessarily by coitus EXCEPT
        A. pediculosis   B. molluscum contagiosum
        C. giardiasis   D. scabies

14. To treat an infected mother and newborn, the nurse should 14.___
        A. obtain specimen ordered for laboratory testing
        B. ensure adequate rest and nutrition
        C. provide high risk care to infant
        D. all of the above

15. Toxic shock syndrome is a potentially life-threatening   15.___
    systemic disorder MOST probably caused by
        A. toxin secreted by strains of S. aureus
        B. endotoxin secreted by E. coli
        C. enterococci
        D. salmonella toxin

16. Commonly associated conditions that may predispose a   16.___
    person to toxic shock syndrome by providing a portal of
    entry into systemic circulation include
        A. use of high-absorbency tampons or barrier contra-
           ceptives
        B. skin infection following a bee sting
        C. intravenous injection of heroin
        D. all of the above

17. Among the danger signs of toxic shock is   17.___
        A. fever of sudden onset, over 102°F
        B. hypotension, systolic pressure less than 90 mmHg
        C. rash, diffuse macular erythrodema
        D. all of the above

18. α-fetoprotein levels are measured at 16 weeks.   18.___
    All of the following conditions lead to elevated α-feto-
    protein level EXCEPT
        A. omphalocele   B. Down's syndrome
        C. multiple gestation   D. duodenal atresia

19. All of the following are routinely done in the third   19.___
    trimester of pregnancy EXCEPT
        A. repeat hemoglobin or hematocrit level
        B. α-fetoprotein measurement
        C. repeat antibody testing in unsensitized RH-negative
           patients at 28-32 weeks
        D. prophylactic RH_0 (anti-D) immune globulin administra-
           tion, to reduce incidence of RH isoimmunization in an
           RH negative woman with a negative antibody screen and
           an RH positive husband

20. In an uncomplicated pregnancy, office visits of the   20.___
    pregnant woman do NOT need to be scheduled
    A. every four weeks for the first 28-30 weeks of
       pregnancy
    B. every 2 weeks from 30-36 weeks of pregnancy
    C. weekly from 36th week until delivery
    D. daily from 36th week until delivery

21. With real-time ultrasonography, fetal heart activity   21.___
    can be seen as early as _____ after the first missed
    menses.
    A. 2-3 weeks   B. 4-5 days
    C. 1 week   D. 5-6 weeks

22. During a routine office visit, a pregnant woman should   22.___
    be examined to gather information about the fetus,
    including
    A. fetal heart rate
    B. size of fetus and amount of amniotic fluid
    C. presenting part and station
    D. all of the above

23. It is unreasonable to advise rigid caloric restriction   23.___
    during pregnancy.
    The recommended weight gain during pregnancy is _____ lbs.
    A. 5-10   B. 10-15   C. 20-30   D. 35-45

24. It was advocated in the past that sodium intake should   24.___
    be restricted in a pregnant woman.
    This concept has been overruled because of the
    A. use of diuretics
    B. natriuretic effect of progesterone
    C. effect of prolactin
    D. reduction in dietary intake as general awareness
       develops in pregnant women

25. Folic acid is required in the formation of heme, the iron   25.___
    containing protein of hemoglobin.
    Folate deficiency in the pregnant woman may cause all of
    the following EXCEPT
    A. intrauterine growth retardation
    B. abruptio placentae
    C. pregnancy-induced hypertension
    D. anencephaly

KEY (CORRECT ANSWERS)

1. B	6. C	11. A	16. D	21. A
2. A	7. A	12. D	17. D	22. D
3. D	8. D	13. C	18. B	23. C
4. D	9. D	14. D	19. B	24. B
5. B	10. B	15. A	20. D	25. A

TEST 2

DIRECTIONS: Each question or incomplete statement is followed by several suggested answers or completions. Select the one that BEST answers the question or completes the statement. *PRINT THE LETTER OF THE CORRECT ANSWER IN THE SPACE AT THE RIGHT.*

1. Nursing intervention to teach women about diabetes mellitus, its management, and its effects on pregnancy would NOT include
   A. reviewing the pathophysiology of the disease and clarifying any misconceptions
   B. teaching home monitoring tests, demonstrating techniques of interpretation, and recording of results
   C. reviewing effects of diabetes on pregnant woman and fetus and stressing weekly prenatal visits during the second half of pregnancy
   D. injection techniques

1.____

2. To assist a woman in verbalizing her concerns and adjusting to the strict management of diabetes, a nurse should NOT
   A. discuss the issues quickly in a hurried way
   B. provide consistency in caregivers and encourage verbalization of concerns and feelings
   C. compliment the woman on successful learning, problem solving, and coping
   D. refer her to a community diabetes support group

2.____

3. When teaching a diabetic woman about insulin, its effects on the body, and its proper administration, a nurse should do all of the following EXCEPT
   A. review the actions of insulin on the body and signs of hypoglycemia
   B. explain the importance of fixation to a particular site, which is always supposed to be used for insulin injection
   C. monitor the woman's self-administration of insulin until techniques are learned and understood
   D. teach proper techniques of insulin storage

3.____

4. To teach a diabetic woman about hyperglycemia, a nurse would NOT
   A. explain that any other illness, infection, vomiting, and diarrhea can precipitate keto-acidosis
   B. encourage the woman to call a physician when illness occurs and continue to administer insulin
   C. teach the danger signs of keto-acidosis
   D. instruct the patient to avoid fruit juice

4.____

5. To teach a diabetic woman on insulin therapy about hypo-   5.____
glycemia, a nurse should NOT
   A. teach the signs and symptoms of hypoglycemia and
      review the causes and dangers of insulin reaction
   B. stress the importance of carrying fast-acting
      sugar when traveling and of having milk on hand at
      home
   C. review the relationship of exercise and diet
   D. tell the patient to read books to learn about it

6. Nursing intervention to teach a diabetic woman about   6.____
diabetes diet management during pregnancy should do
all of the following EXCEPT
   A. consider cultural and financial implications when
      planning teaching
   B. stress the importance of losing weight during
      pregnancy
   C. explain the importance of a balanced diet and refer
      the woman to a registered dietician
   D. encourage the woman to design sample menus

7. To identify and treat infection in a pregnant woman with   7.____
gestational diabetes, the one of the following that the
nurse would NOT do is
   A. teach the woman to understand the signs and symptoms
      of infection, either locally or systemically
   B. obtain specimens for culture
   C. explain that infection decreases insulin resistance
      and keto-acidosis
   D. administer prophylactic antibiotic as ordered

8. Certain factors may place a woman and fetus at risk for   8.____
problems during pregnancy.
When obtaining preconception health history, the nurse
should be expecially alert for all of the following
demographic factors so she can help prevent potential
problems EXCEPT
   A. age 15 or below and 35 or above
   B. high socio-economic status
   C. location in rural or isolated area and lack of
      transportation
   D. non-white and unmarried

9. Which of the following factors in the obstetric history   9.____
places the woman and fetus at risk for problems during
pregnancy?
   A. Previous spontaneous or elective abortion
   B. Previous premature neonate or neonate with a
      congenital anomaly
   C. Maternal anatomic difficulty, such as severe retro-
      flexed uterus or pelvis too small for normal delivery
   D. All of the above

10. Oral contraceptives inhibit ovulation by blocking the actions of the hypothalamus and anterior pituitary on the uterus.
Although oral contraceptives do have some disadvantages, they do NOT increase the risk of
    A. endometrial and ovarian cancer, ovarian cysts, and noncancerous breast tumors
    B. thromboembolic disorders, cerebrovascular accidents, and sub-arachnoid hemorrhage, especially if the woman is a smoker or has hypertension
    C. monilia vaginitis
    D. hepatic lesions, including hepatic adenomas

10.___

11. All of the following are advantages of vaginal spermicide EXCEPT
    A. easy to insert
    B. must be inserted before each act of intercourse
    C. decreases risk of PID
    D. requires no prescription

11.___

12. All the steps of the nursing process should be documented. When caring for a couple who request help with pre-conception planning, documentation should include
    A. significant health history and physical assessment findings
    B. results of diagnostic studies performed
    C. instructions given to the couple
    D. all of the above

12.___

13. History can reveal the risk of genetic disorders and may aid in diagnosing genetic disorders.
Risk factors include all of the following EXCEPT
    A. previous birth of an affected child
    B. woman under 35 years of age and history of one abortion or stillbirth
    C. family history of genetic defects
    D. intrauterine exposure to known teratogens

13.___

14. The woman at increased risk for bearing a child with a genetic defect may need assistance in deciding on reproductive alternatives.
Before becoming pregnant, she may need to choose among different options, but it is NOT necessary for her to
    A. accept the risk and attempt pregnancy or avoid the risk and refrain from pregnancy
    B. minimize the risk by considering such alternatives as artificial insemination
    C. refrain from sex
    D. monitor the risk by undergoing prenatal diagnostic tests to identify an affected fetus

14.___

15. Genetic disorders or associated birth defects may place   15.___
    severe physical, psychological, and economic strains on
    a woman and her family.
    The nursing role in assisting a woman and her family in
    care management, referrals, and successful adjustments
    include
    A. identifying physical or developmental abnormalities
    B. assessing the need for referrals to specialty
       services for genetic evaluations, genetic counseling,
       or prenatal diagnostic studies
    C. demonstrating sensitivity to the attitudes of a
       woman with a genetic disorder, especially regarding
       reproduction
    D. all of the above

16. The fetal period involves growth and further development   16.___
    of organ systems established in the embryonic period.
    The fetal period extends from week ____ to week ____.
    A. 8; 40   B. 12; 20   C. 18; 36   D. 12; 30

17. Fetal circulation differs from neonatal circulation in   17.___
    that three shunts bypass the liver and lungs and separate
    the systemic and pulmonary circulations.
    NOT included among these shunts is the
    A. foramen of Monro   B. ductus venosus
    C. foramen ovale   D. ductus arteriosus

18. All of the following are possible causes of nausea and   18.___
    vomiting in a suspected pregnant woman EXCEPT
    A. anorexia nervosa
    B. gastric disorders
    C. rising levels of HCG
    D. pseudocyesis

19. In a pregnant woman, the vaginal pH turns acidic, which   19.___
    helps prevent bacterial infection. This change in pH
    arises with increased production of lactic acid from
    glycogen in the vaginal epithelium.
    Increased lactic acid results from the action of
    A. E. coli   B. lactobacillus acidophilus
    C. nessaria gonorrhea   D. trichomonas vaginalis

20. All of the following are functional changes in the   20.___
    urinary system as a result of pregnancy EXCEPT
    A. renal plasma flow rises to 40-50% above prepregnant
       level by the third trimester
    B. GFR starts declining by the beginning of the second
       trimester and remains low until term
    C. renal tubular resorption increases as much as 50%
       during pregnancy
    D. loss of increased amount of some nutrients, such as
       amino acids, water soluble vitamins, folic acid, and
       iodine

21. Which of the following is NOT a sign of fetal distress
    in a pregnant woman with insulin-dependent diabetes
    mellitus?
    A. A non-reactive NST
    B. Decreased insulin requirement
    C. Negative CST
    D. Poor biophysical profile

21.___

22. In a multiparous woman, pre-eclampsia may be associated
    with
    A. multiple gestation
    B. chronic hypertension
    C. diabetes and coexisting renal disease
    D. all of the above

22.___

23. Severe pregnancy-induced hypertension is manifested by
    all of the following EXCEPT
    A. diastolic blood pressure of 110 mmHg or more
    B. elevated creatinine
    C. 1+ proteinuria
    D. presence of thrombocytopenia and fetal growth
       retardation

23.___

24. Indications for delivery in a pregnant woman with
    pregnancy-induced hypertension include
    A. a compromise in fetal well-being, as manifested by
       poor biophysical profile, etc.
    B. worsening hypertension
    C. increasing proteinuria
    D. all of the above

24.___

25. Sickle cell anemia occurs when an individual receives
    the gene for the production of hemoglobin 5 from each
    parent.
    Pregnancy is a serious burden in women with SS disease
    because of the likelihood of all of the following EXCEPT
    A. anemia becoming more intense
    B. infection and pulmonary dysfunction
    C. pain crises becoming more infrequent
    D. death of the woman and child

25.___

KEY (CORRECT ANSWERS)

1. D	6. B	11. B	16. A	21. C
2. A	7. C	12. D	17. A	22. D
3. B	8. B	13. B	18. C	23. C
4. D	9. D	14. C	19. B	24. D
5. D	10. A	15. D	20. B	25. C

TEST 3

DIRECTIONS: Each question or incomplete statement is followed by several suggested answers or completions. Select the one that BEST answers the question or completes the statement. *PRINT THE LETTER OF THE CORRECT ANSWER IN THE SPACE AT THE RIGHT.*

1. A 28 year-old primipara with a hemoglobin of 9.2 before becoming pregnant has a hemoglobin of 8 during her pregnancy, despite oral iron and folic acid supplementation. Her infant is born with a normal hemoglobin. This woman was suffering from
   A. hemoglobin SC disease B. megaloblastic anemia
   C. iron deficiency anemia D. sickle cell anemia

   1.___

2. All of the following factors increase a pregnant woman's risk of contracting HIV infection and acquired immuno-deficiency syndrome EXCEPT
   A. using illicit IV drugs or having a sexual partner who uses such drugs
   B. having frequent sex with the same partner
   C. receiving, or having a sexual partner who received, blood or blood products
   D. having a bisexual male partner

   2.___

3. The one of the following changes that does NOT appear in a pregnant woman around the 23rd to 27th week is
   A. umbilicus appears level with abdominal skin
   B. Braxton Hicks contractions stop
   C. shape of uterus changes from globular to ovoid
   D. striae gravidarum usually become apparent

   3.___

4. Most pregnant women can travel without undue risk to the fetus. However, risk of accident increases with the amount of traveling.
   Recommended precautions include
   A. in moving vehicle, wear shoulder lap belts to reduce injury in case of accident
   B. do not remain seated for longer than 2 hours
   C. as term approaches, determine the availability of medical care at destination
   D. all of the above

   4.___

5. Whether childbirth education occurs in client-teaching sessions with individuals or in classrooms with groups of clients and their parents, it should include education about the
   A. physiologic aspects of pregnancy and childbirth
   B. proper relaxation and breathing techniques
   C. transition to parenthood
   D. all of the above

   5.___

6. For the normal antepartal initial visit, it is NOT   6.___
   necessary to document
       A. patient's vital signs, height, weight, age, occupa-
          tion, and social history, including smoking, drugs,
          and alcohol
       B. the number of previous pregnancies and complications
       C. how often sex is performed
       D. any danger sign encountered, fetal activity, aller-
          gies to medication, and date of next visit

7. There are various risk factors during pregnancy that   7.___
   can affect nutrition.
   These factors include
       A. pregnancy-induced hypertension
       B. multiple gestation
       C. inadequate or excessive weight gain
       D. all of the above

8. A few nutritionally related blood tests typically are   8.___
   performed during pregnancy.
   These include all of the following EXCEPT
       A. serum ceruloplasmin level
       B. hemoglobin levels, hematocrit, mean corpuscular
          volume, and mean corpuscular hemoglobin concentration
       C. a fasting 1 hour glucose tolerance test at 24-28
          weeks gestation to screen for gestational diabetes
       D. serum albumin levels

9. Basic goals for nutrition throughout pregnancy include   9.___
       A. adjusting dietary intake to promote appropriate
          weight gain
       B. increasing nutrient intake to meet the RDA's for
          pregnancy
       C. establishing an appropriate food intake pattern for
          nutritionally-related problems such as anemia and
          nausea
       D. all of the above

10. In the general teaching plan of a pregnant woman, which   10.___
    of the following dietary plans will NOT be recommended
    to maximize iron uptake from food?
        A. Drink tea or coffee as they increase iron absorption
        B. Eat poultry, fish, and meat often to provide easily
           absorbable iron
        C. Cook with iron pots and pans
        D. Eat iron-rich vegetables, such as spinach, broccoli,
           asparagus, and other dark green vegetables

11. The hyperglycemia and insulin deficiency associated with   11.___
    diabetes mellitus produce all of the following classical
    signs and symptoms of diabetes EXCEPT
        A. polyuria   B. polydipsia and polyphagia
        C. dysphagia   D. weight loss

12. Iron deficiency anemia in a pregnant woman will NOT   12.___
    produce
    A. spontaneous abortion and stillbirth
    B. decreased fetal iron stores
    C. fetal distress from hypoxia during later pregnancy
       and labor
    D. neonate small for gestational age

13. Sickle cell anemia is diagnosed in a pregnant woman.   13.___
    She can expect all of the following complications EXCEPT
    A. pulmonary emboli
    B. excessive bleeding after delivery
    C. urinary tract infection
    D. pregnancy-induced hypertension

14. Sickle cell anemia in a pregnant woman will NOT lead to   14.___
    A. abruptio placentae complications
    B. prematurity
    C. large for gestational age neonate
    D. intrauterine growth retardation

15. As a result of folic acid deficiency, _____ can be   15.___
    expected in a pregnant woman.
    A. urinary tract infection
    B. bleeding complications during delivery
    C. pancytopenia
    D. all of the above

16. _____ is NOT expected in a pregnant woman as a result of   16.___
    iron deficiency anemia.
    A. Poor tissue integrity
    B. Pulmonary emboli
    C. Excessive bleeding after delivery
    D. Antepartal or postpartal infection with impaired
       healing

17. All of the following fetal and neonate complications are   17.___
    expected as a result of maternal toxoplasmosis EXCEPT
    A. premature and/or stillbirth
    B. hypertonia
    C. blindness, deafness, or chorioretinitis
    D. mental retardation, seizures, and coma

18. Nursing intervention in the prevention of maternal toxo-   18.___
    plasmosis includes advising the woman to
    A. cook meat thoroughly to kill bacteria
    B. avoid contact with cat box filler, especially if the
       cats roam outside
    C. wear gloves while gardening
    D. all of the above

19. All of the following fetal and neonatal complications are 19.___
    expected in a pregnant woman with cytomegalovirus infec-
    tion EXCEPT
    A. macrocephaly
    B. neonatal jaundice and hepatosplenomegaly
    C. hearing loss and blindness
    D. mental retardation, cerebral palsy, and epilepsy

20. A nurse treating a pregnant woman with cytomegalovirus 20.___
    infection should
    A. be aware that CMV can be transmitted by any close
       contact, including kissing and sexual intercourse
    B. advise the infected woman not to breastfeed her
       neonate because the virus can be transmitted through
       breast milk
    C. expect to isolate the mother and neonate after birth
    D. all of the above

21. Spontaneous abortion may occur as a result of rubella 21.___
    infection in a pregnant woman.
    The fetal and neonatal complications expected as a
    result of rubella infection include
    A. cardiac defects, such as pulmonary artery stenosis
       and patent ductus arteriosus
    B. intrauterine growth retardation
    C. deafness, cataracts, glaucoma, and mental retardation
    D. all of the above

22. For the prevention of rubella infection, it is CORRECT 22.___
    that
    A. it is alright for a pregnant woman to have contact
       with people known to have rubella
    B. a negative antibody titer indicates that the woman
       is immune to rubella
    C. it is alright for the woman to become pregnant within
       1 year after receiving the vaccine
    D. it is not necessary for her to obtain rubella vaccina-
       tion after delivery

23. Nursing intervention while dealing with a woman having 23.___
    vaginal candidiasis includes
    A. telling the patient to practice thorough perineal
       hygiene
    B. teaching the patient about candidiasis and supporting
       her during occurrences
    C. assessing the neonate after delivery for signs of
       thrush, such as creamy, white, slightly elevated
       plaque inside the mouth
    D. all of the above

24. All of the following are fetal and neonatal complications   24.___
    of ethanol consumption in a pregnant woman EXCEPT
        A. intrauterine growth retardation
        B. long palpebral fissures and macrocephaly
        C. irritability and poor coordination
        D. mild to moderate mental retardation

25. Complications expected in a pregnant woman as a result   25.___
    of cocaine abuse include
        A. dilated pupils and muscle twitching
        B. cardiac and respiratory arrest
        C. increased spontaneous abortion, abruptio placentae,
           and pre-term labor
        D. all of the above

KEY (CORRECT ANSWERS)

1. C		11. C	
2. B		12. B	
3. B		13. B	
4. D		14. C	
5. D		15. D	
6. C		16. B	
7. D		17. B	
8. A		18. D	
9. D		19. A	
10. A		20. D	

21. D
22. C
23. D
24. B
25. D

EXAMINATION SECTION

TEST 1

DIRECTIONS: Each question or incomplete statement is followed by several suggested answers or completions. Select the one that BEST answers the question or completes the statement. *PRINT THE LETTER OF THE CORRECT ANSWER IN THE SPACE AT THE RIGHT.*

1. Which of these occurrences in a postpartal woman would be MOST indicative of an abnormality?
   A. A chill shortly after delivery
   B. A pulse rate of 60 the morning after delivery
   C. Urinary output of 3,000 ml. on the second day after delivery
   D. An oral temperature of 101°F. (38.3°C.) on the third day after delivery

   1.___

2. While discussing nutrition with the nurse, a woman who is a primigravida says that she eats an egg for breakfast every day.
   The woman should be informed that the absorption of iron from the egg would be BEST facilitated by the woman's also eating _____ at the same meal.
   A. toast
   B. butter
   C. orange juice
   D. bacon

   2.___

Questions 3-8.

DIRECTIONS: Questions 3 through 8 are to be answered on the basis of the following information.

   Ms. Judy Lee, 28 years old and gravida I, is attending the antepartal clinic regularly. Ms. Lee is carrying twins. In the 38th week of gestation, she is admitted to the hospital in labor. Her membranes have ruptured.

3. Since Ms. Lee's admission, the nurse has been able to hear and count the heartbeats of both twins. Suppose that at a later time during Ms. Lee's labor, the nurse can hear only one heartbeat, even after several attempts. Which of these interpretations of this finding would be ACCURATE?
   A. Inaudibility of one of the heartbeats can result from a change in the position of the twins, but it could also be due to fetal distress; prompt evaluation of the situation by the physician is mandatory.
   B. Muffled fetal heartbeats are common when uterine contractions are strong and frequent, as they are in a multiple pregnancy; more frequent evaluation of the fetal heartbeats is advisable.

   3.___

C. Inability to hear one heartbeat in a twin pregnancy can normally be expected at intervals throughout labor; no action is indicated.

D. Inability to hear fetal heartbeats in a twin pregnancy does not indicate fetal difficulty unless accompanied by additional symptoms; amniotic fluid should be examined for meconium staining.

4. Ms. Lee's labor progresses, and she delivers spontaneously two girls - one weighs 4 lbs. (1,814 gm.) and the other weighs 4 lb. 8 oz. (2,041 gm.). The twins are transferred to the premature nursery, and Ms. Lee is transferred to the postpartum unit.
Which of these concepts should be MOST basic to planning care for the Lee twins?
   A. Circulatory function is enhanced by frequent change of position.
   B. A well-lubricated skin is resistant to excoriation and damage.
   C. A premature infant's rectal temperature reflects the infant's ability to conserve heat.
   D. Optimal environmental temperature results in minimal oxygen consumption in the premature infant.

4.__

5. The method used for a premature infant's first formula feeding and the time at which it is begun will be based CHIEFLY upon the infant's
   A. birth weight
   B. degree of hydration
   C. level of physiologic maturity
   D. total body surface

5.__

6. The smaller of the Lee twins is to be gavaged.
In determining the location of the catheter after its insertion into the infant, it would be MOST desirable to insert
   A. the tip of a large syringe into the catheter and withdraw an amount of air equal to the amount of feeding
   B. a few drops of sterile water into the catheter, hold the end of the catheter below the level of the infant's stomach, and observe it for drainage of gastric contents
   C. about 0.5 to 1 ml. of air into the catheter and listen to the infant's abdomen with a stethoscope
   D. about 5 ml. of sterile water into the catheter and observe the infant's respirations

6.__

7. On her second postpartum day, Ms. Lee says to the nurse, *I've been to the bathroom four times in the past hour to urinate. The funny thing about it is that I only pass a small amount of urine each time.* Which of these initial actions by the nurse would demonstrate the BEST judgment?
   A. Palpate Ms. Lee's abdomen for bladder distention.
   B. Explain to Ms. Lee that frequent voiding is expected during the first few days after delivery.

7.__

    C. Advise Ms. Lee to use a bedpan for her next voiding.

    D. Discuss with Ms. Lee the relationship between trauma during delivery and signs of bladder irritation during the postpartum period.

8. On the third postpartum day, Ms. Lee is discharged. The twins are to remain until they have reached an appropriate weight. When the twins are to be discharged, Mr. and Ms. Lee come to the hospital to take them home.
Which of these statements, if made by Ms. Lee, would indicate the BEST understanding of her babies' needs?   8.___

    A. Our babies' needs are different from those of full-term infants, and we will do all we can to protect them.

    B. We are going to try very hard to counteract the effects of our babies' having been born prematurely.

    C. For a while the smaller baby will need special attention, and then we will be able to treat both of our babies similarly.

    D. We expect to enjoy our babies and will give them the kind of care babies need.

Questions 9-18.

DIRECTIONS: Questions 9 through 18 are to be answered on the basis of the following information.

Ms. Angela Dobbs, 32 years old and gravida I, is now in her third trimester of pregnancy. She has had diabetes mellitus since the age of 16 and has been attending the antepartal clinic regularly for the past 5 months.

9. Compared with Ms. Dobbs' insulin requirements when she was not pregnant, it can be expected that the insulin dosage during her third trimester will   9.___

    A. remain the same

    B. be increased

    C. be decreased

    D. be increased or decreased, depending upon fetal activity

10. At 30 weeks' gestation, Ms. Dobbs has an ultrasonic examination.
The results of this examination disclose information about the fetus'   10.___

    A. circulatory function

    B. gestational age

    C. presence of surfactant

    D. presence of congenital defects

11. Because the incidence of fetal death is higher in women who have diabetes mellitus, indications of placental insufficiency should be suspected if Ms. Dobbs has a(n)   11.___

    A. sustained drop in her blood glucose level

    B. urinary output of more than 1500 ml. a day

    C. increase in the secretion of gonadotropin

    D. albumin content in her urine of +1

12. At 35 weeks' gestation, Ms. Dobbs is admitted to the   12.__
    hospital for evaluation of her pregnancy and diabetic
    status. Ms. Dobbs is to have a urinary estriol level
    determination.
    Which of these instructions should be among those given
    to her about collecting the urine for this procedure?
    Collect
       A. the first morning specimen before eating breakfast
       B. a specimen about an hour after the evening meal
       C. a twenty-four hour specimen
       D. a clean-voided specimen

13. Ms. Dobbs is to have an amniocentesis done to determine   13.__
    the lecithin/sphingomyelin (L/S) ratio.
    The purpose of this study is to
       A. assess placental functioning
       B. assess the amount of fetal body fat
       C. determine fetal kidney functioning
       D. determine fetal pulmonary maturity

14. Ms. Dobbs has a cesarean section and is delivered of a   14.__
    boy who weighs 8 lb. 4 oz. (3,742 gm.). He is trans-
    ferred to the intensive care nursery. Ms. Dobbs is
    transferred to the postpartum unit from the recovery
    room.
    Postpartum orders for Ms. Dobbs include an estrogen
    preparation to
       A. promote sodium excretion
       B. suppress the production of chorionic gonadotropin
       C. inhibit secretion of the lactogenic hormone
       D. diminish lochial flow

15. Two hours after delivery, the nurse observes that Baby   15.__
    Boy Dobbs is lethargic and has developed mild generalized
    cyanosis and twitching.
    In view of the fact that his mother has diabetes
    mellitus, the infant is PROBABLY exhibiting symptoms of a
       A. low blood sugar level   B. high CO_2 level
       C. subnormal temperature   D. withdrawal from insulin

16. Because Ms. Dobbs has diabetes mellitus, her infant   16.__
    should be assessed for the presence of
       A. a blood group incompatibility
       B. meconium ileus
       C. phenylketonuria
       D. a congenital abnormality

17. Ms. Dobbs is bottle-feeding her baby. Ms. Dobbs, who   17.__
    has previously observed a demonstration of diapering,
    is changing her baby's diaper for the first time, under
    the supervision of the registered nurse. Ms. Dobbs is
    holding the baby's feet correctly, but when she starts to
    raise his legs to remove the diaper, the feet slip from
    her grasp, and the baby's legs drop back onto the
    mattress of the bassinet. The baby whimpers briefly, and
    Ms. Dobbs looks dismayed.

Which of these responses by the nurse would be BEST?
   A. I'll show you again how to change the baby's diaper,
      Ms. Dobbs.
   B. I'll diaper the baby for you this time, Ms. Dobbs.
   C. You've almost got it, Ms. Dobbs. Try again?
   D. Why are you so nervous, Ms. Dobbs?

18. Some time after discharge, Ms. Dobbs calls the hospital   18.___
    to report the loss of her baby's birth certificate.
    Where would it be BEST for her to apply for a duplicate?
    The
       A. record room of the hospital where the baby was born
       B. agency that records vital statistics for the commu-
          nity in which the baby was born
       C. Census Bureau
       D. National Office of Vital Statistics

Questions 19-25.

DIRECTIONS: Questions 19 through 25 are to be answered on the
             basis of the following information.

    Ms. Linda Young, a 17-year-old high school student, attends
the antepartal clinic on a regular basis. This is Linda's first
pregnancy.

19. Linda is now 7 months pregnant.   19.___
    In assessing whether Linda is retaining abnormal amounts
    of fluid, it would be ESPECIALLY significant that she
    has gained
       A. 3 lb. (1,361 gm.) during the past week
       B. 4½ lb. (2,041 gm.) since her last clinic visit a
          month ago
       C. 11 lb. (4,990 gm.) in the second trimester of
          pregnancy
       D. 14 lb. (6,350 gm.) since the onset of pregnancy

20. Which of these measures will contribute MOST to the   20.___
    prevention of postpartal uterine infections?
       A. Routine use of serologic tests for syphilis early
          in the antepartal period
       B. Limitation of sexual intercourse during the last six
          weeks of pregnancy
       C. Maintenance of cleanliness of the perineal area
          during labor
       D. Taking showers or sponge baths exclusively during
          the last six weeks of pregnancy

21. At term, Linda is admitted to the hospital in active   21.___
    labor. Linda's cervix is 2 cm. dilated and 80% effaced.
    Which of these interpretations of these findings is
    CORRECT?
    The
       A. cervix is 2 cm. short of complete dilatation, and
          it is 80% thinner than it was before labor started

    B. cervix is still 2 cm. long, and 80% of the thinning
       of the cervix is completed
    C. walls of the cervix are 2 cm. thick, and 80% of the
       widening of the cervical opening has been achieved
    D. opening of the cervix is 2 cm. wide, and the cervical
       canal is 80% shorter than normal

22. Linda has an episiotomy and delivers a 7 lb. (3,175 gm.)   22.__
boy. Baby Boy Young is transferred to the nursery and
Linda is transferred to the postpartum unit. Linda plans
to bottle-feed her baby. The nurse is assessing Baby Boy
Young.
Which of these observations, if made, would be considered
characteristics of a newborn?
    A. Branlike desquamation of the hands and fee; alternat-
      ing limpness and stiffness of the body; and pink,
      moist skin
    B. Cool, mottled hands and feet; quivering lower jaw;
      and flexion of body parts
    C. Clenched fists; arching of the back when recumbent;
      and frequent crying
    D. Butterfly-shaped area of pigmentation at the base of
      the spine; extension of the arms and legs when the
      head is turned to the side; and diaphragmatic
      breathing

23. When Linda has been admitted to the postpartum unit,   23.__
she says to the nurse, *I'm so glad my baby is a boy.
Maybe Jack will marry me now because he'll be so proud
to have a son.*
It is probably MOST justifiable to say that Linda
    A. wants to get married in order to gain her independence
      from her family
    B. is capable of subordinating her personal needs to the
      needs of others
    C. is showing a beginning awareness of the problems
      associated with having a baby out of wedlock
    D. lacks insight into the factors that contribute to a
      successful marriage

24. When Baby Boy Young is brought to his mother for the   24.__
first time to be fed, Linda asks the nurse, *What's wrong
with my baby's eyes? He looks cross-eyed.*
Which of these initial responses by the nurse would
probably be MOST helpful?
    A. Babies seem to be cross-eyed for a while after birth
      because the muscles in their eyes aren't able to
      work together.
    B. You feel that your baby's eyes are abnormal?
    C. I can see that you're upset about this. It would be
      advisable for you to talk with the doctor about it.
    D. Your baby will appear cross-eyed for some time
      because his eyes won't be completely developed until
      he is about six months old.

25. When Linda is talking with the nurse about feeding her   25.___
baby, she says, *I've heard that if I breastfed him, he'd
develop a close feeling toward me more quickly. I had
planned to bottle-feed him.*
The nurse's initial reply should convey which of these
understandings about the development of a mother-child
relationship?
   A. A satisfactory mother-child relationship will
      develop more readily through breastfeeding than
      bottle-feeding.
   B. Holding the baby during bottle-feeding will help to
      promote a good mother-child relationship.
   C. The times at which the baby is fed by the mother
      will affect the quality of the mother-child relation-
      ship more than the feeding method.
   D. Since bottle-feeding is less complicated than breast-
      feeding, the mother will be able to focus more
      attention on mothering functions such as cuddling
      and talking while the baby is eating.

KEY (CORRECT ANSWERS)

1. D			11. A	
2. C			12. C	
3. A			13. D	
4. D			14. C	
5. C			15. A	
6. C			16. D	
7. A			17. C	
8. D			18. B	
9. B			19. A	
10. B			20. C	

21. D
22. B
23. D
24. A
25. B

TEST 2

DIRECTIONS: Each question or incomplete statement is followed by several suggested answers or completions. Select the one that BEST answers the question or completes the statement. *PRINT THE LETTER OF THE CORRECT ANSWER IN THE SPACE AT THE RIGHT.*

1. The instructions that are ESPECIALLY important to give to a pregnant woman who has heart disease are:
   A. Increase protein intake
   B. Take no drugs unless they have been prescribed
   C. Limit high-calorie foods
   D. Avoid fatigue

1.__

Questions 2-9.

DIRECTIONS: Questions 2 through 9 are to be answered on the basis of the following information.

Ms. Mary White, 35 years old, is pregnant for the third time. She is receiving antepartal care from a private physician. Ms. White is in the seventh month of pregnancy and has symptoms of preeclampsia.

2. The physician instructs Ms. White not to eat foods which have a high sodium content. The nurse tells Ms. White about foods containing sodium and then asks her to identify foods lowest in sodium.
   Which of these foods, if selected by Ms. White, would be CORRECT?
   A. Creamed chipped beef on dry toast
   B. Cheese sandwich on whole wheat toast
   C. Frankfurter on a roll
   D. Tomato stuffed with diced chicken

2.__

3. In Ms. White's 39th week of gestation, her physician recommends that she be hospitalized. When the physician leaves after examining Ms. White, Ms. White says to the nurse, *It's easy for you people to say, "Go to the hospital," but it's not so easy for me to do it. I can't go just like that!*
   After acknowledging her feeling, which of these approaches by the nurse would probably be BEST?
   A. Stress to Ms. White that her husband would want her to do what is best for her health.
   B. Explore with Ms. White ways that immediate hospitalization could be arranged.
   C. Repeat the physician's reasons for advising immediate hospitalization for Ms. White.
   D. Explain to Ms. White that she is ultimately responsible for her own welfare and that of her baby.

3.__

4. Ms. White is admitted to the hospital.   4.___
    Because of the possibility of convulsive seizures, which
    of these articles should be readily available for Ms.
    White's care?
        A. Oxygen and suction machine
        B. Suction machine and mouth care tray
        C. Mouth care tray and venous cutdown set
        D. Venous cutdown set and oxygen

5. The next morning, Ms. White tells the nurse that she   5.___
    thinks she is beginning to have contractions.
    For the timing of uterine contractions, it is recommended
    that she place
        A. her hands on the upper part of the abdomen, on oppo-
           site sides, and curve them somewhat around the
           uterine fundus
        B. the heel of the hand on the abdomen, just above the
           umbilicus, and press firmly
        C. her hand flat on the abdomen over the uterine fundus,
           with the fingers apart, and press lightly
        D. her hand in the middle of the upper part of the
           abdomen and then move the hand several times to
           different parts of the upper abdomen during each
           contraction

6. Ms. White goes into labor.   6.___
    If Ms. White were to complain of a severe headache while
    she is in labor, the nurse should INITIALLY
        A. put Ms. White flat in bed with one pillow under her
           head
        B. take Ms. White's blood pressure
        C. check Ms. White's chart to determine whether she has
           recently received an analgesic
        D. count the fetal heart rate

7. Ms. White delivers a girl. Baby White's Apgar score at   7.___
    1 minute is 8.
    The CHIEF purpose of the first Apgar scoring of a newborn
    is to
        A. obtain a baseline for comparison with the infant's
           future development
        B. evaluate the efficiency of the infant's vital func-
           tions
        C. assess the effectiveness of the initial care given to
           the infant
        D. determine the presence of gross malformations in
           the infant

8. Ms. White is transferred to the postpartum unit, and   8.___
    Baby Girl White is transferred to the newborn nursery.
    Ms. White had a normal vaginal delivery, but is having
    difficulty voiding in the early postpartum.
    The cause of her difficulty is MOST likely due to
        A. decreased abdominal pressure and trauma to the trigone
           of the bladder

    B. decreased blood volume and increased production of
       estrogen and progesterone
    C. increased bladder tone and emotional stress
    D. constriction of the kidney pelves and ureters

9. Ms. White is bottle-feeding her baby.   9.__
   Which of these manifestations developing in her nipples
   or breasts on the third day after delivery would be NORMAL?
    A. Decrease in secretion from the breasts
    B. Engorgement of the breasts
    C. Inversion of the nipples
    D. Tenderness and redness of the nipples

Questions 10-11.

DIRECTIONS: Questions 10 and 11 are to be answered on the basis
               of the following information.

   Ms. Ellen Stone, an 18-year-old primigravida, is brought to the
hospital in early active labor. She has received no antepartal care
during her pregnancy.

10. Which of these observations of Ms. Stone would be the   10.__
   MOST reliable indication that she is in true labor?
    A. Strong, intermittent uterine contractions
    B. Progressive cervical effacement and dilatation
    C. Rupture of the membranes
    D. Engagement of the presenting part

11. During the first stage of Ms. Stone's labor, which of   11.__
   these measures by the nurse would be MOST supportive of
   her?
    A. Administering sufficient analgesia to minimize pain
       from uterine contractions and encouraging her to
       remain on her back
    B. Keeping her informed about the progress of her labor
       and helping her to relax between contractions
    C. Having her hold on to the nurse's hand during the
       height of contractions and reminding her to breathe
       rapidly with her mouth open
    D. Telling her to bear down with her contractions and
       instructing her to sleep between contractions

Questions 12-21.

DIRECTIONS: Questions 12 through 21 are to be answered on the
               basis of the following information.

   Ms. Karen Newman, a 26-year-old multipara, is pregnant. Her
obstetric history includes 2 full-term pregnancies terminating in
normal deliveries and, prior to her present pregnancy, a spontaneous abortion at 14 weeks' gestation. She is receiving antepartal
care from a private physician.

12. On the basis of Ms. Newman's obstetric history, she is   12.___
    designated as a gravida _____, para _____.
    A. III; II   B. III; IV   C. IV; II   D. IV; III

13. Ms. Newman weighs 152 lb. (68.95 kg.) at the end of the   13.___
    fourth month of gestation. Her weight before she became
    pregnant was 135 lb. (61.23 kg.), which was normal for
    her age and body build.
    It is justifiable to say that Ms. Newman's 17-lb.
    (7.72 kg.) weight gain for her stage of pregnancy is
    A. below average   B. average
    C. somewhat above average D. excessive

14. Ms. Newman tells the nurse that her 2½-year-old son,   14.___
    Danny, tends to be jealous and that she is worried about
    how he may react to the new baby.
    The nurse's reply should indicate that jealousy in a
    2½-year-old
    A. can be lessened by providing a mother-substitute for
       the child when the mother first returns home from
       the hospital
    B. can be suppressed if the child's contact with the
       new baby is restricted
    C. cannot be handled by reasoning with the child
    D. cannot be dealt with therapeutically

15. Ms. Newman is 2 weeks past term. She is admitted to the   15.___
    hospital for induction of labor with an oxytocic drug.
    Upon admission, Ms. Newman is permitted to have liquids
    by mouth.
    Which of these foods would probably be CONTRAINDICATED
    for her?
    A. Tea with lemon   B. Ginger ale
    C. Milk   D. Gelatin dessert

16. Which of these findings, if present in Ms. Newman, would   16.___
    it be ESSENTIAL for the registered nurse to report to
    the physician before the oxytocic infusion is started?
    A. Low backache
    B. A rise in blood pressure from 122/80 to 130/84
    C. An increase in pulse rate from 88 to 98
    D. Regular contractions of 60 seconds' duration

17. Ms. Newman has an intravenous infusion running, to which   17.___
    oxytocin injection (Pitocin) has been added.
    Which of these conditions would warrant IMMEDIATE dis-
    continuation of Ms. Newman's intravenous infusion of
    Pitocin?
    A. Increase in show
    B. Rupture of the membranes
    C. A sustained uterine contraction
    D. A fetal heart rate of 120 during a contraction

18. Ms. Newman has an order for 100 mg. of meperidine   18.__
    (Demerol) hydrochloride.
    Which of these groups of signs in Ms. Newman would MOST
    clearly indicate that a dose of Demerol could be given
    to her with safety?
    Cervical dilatation, _____ cm.; presenting part at _____
    station; uterine contractions q. _____ minutes, lasting
    _____ seconds; fetal heart rate, _____ beats per minute.
    A. 3; 0; 10; 45; 100   B. 4; 0; 3; 50; 172
    C. 5; -1; 5; 40; 144   D. 7; -1; 2; 60; 120

19. In view of the fact that Ms. Newman had general anes-   19.__
    thesia, it would be safe to start giving her oral fluids
    A. after she voids for the first time
    B. after she has coughed voluntarily
    C. when her pulse rate is 70 beats per minute
    D. when she has rested for about an hour after admission
       to the postpartum unit

20. Penicillin ointment rather than silver nitrate is used   20.__
    in the prophylactic eye care of Baby Boy Newman to
    A. promote a more lasting bacteriostatic effect
    B. gain a more rapid systemic effect
    C. administer therapeutic amounts with greater ease
    D. cause less irritation of the conjunctivae

21. Six weeks after the birth of her baby, Ms. Newman returns 21.__
    to the clinic for a routine follow-up visit. At the
    clinic, Ms. Newman says to the nurse, *Having so many
    children makes it very hard for us to manage, but my
    husband won't do anything to prevent me from getting
    pregnant. He gets angry when I even mention the idea.*
    Which of these approaches by the nurse is LIKELY to be
    MOST useful?
    A. Give Ms. Newman a pamphlet for her husband that
       describes various contraceptive methods.
    B. Ask Ms. Newman to have her husband accompany her to
       the clinic to talk with the nurse about contracep-
       tion.
    C. Refer Ms. Newman to an agency that provides family
       planning services.
    D. Find out from Ms. Newman if her husband would be
       willing to accept a method of contraception that
       would not involve him directly.

Questions 22-30.

DIRECTIONS: Questions 22 through 30 are to be answered on the
            basis of the following information.

    Ms. Barbara Wing, 21 years old, attends the antepartal clinic
for the first time when she has missed two menstrual periods. The
physician determines that she is pregnant and finds her to be in
good health. This is her first pregnancy.

22. During Ms. Wing's initial conference with the registered   22.___
    nurse, she mentions that although she usually feels well,
    there are times when she feels tired.
    Which of these responses by the nurse would be BEST?
    A. Fatigue is normal when the body is adjusting to the
       pregnant state. Let's talk about your daily schedule
       so we can plan extra rest for you.
    B. It will be necessary for you to cut down on your
       usual activities and try to get more rest. About
       how many hours of sleep do you get at night?
    C. Your fatigue is probably due to hormonal changes
       that occur in early pregnancy. As your body adapts
       to the demands of your developing baby, this feeling
       will pass.
    D. Your fatigue at this time indicates that you probably
       will have to give special consideration to rest, and
       possibly even to diet, throughout your pregnancy.

23. Ms. Wing is to include extra amounts of vitamin C in her   23.___
    diet.
    She should be instructed that the juice that has the
    LEAST vitamin C per average serving is
    A. canned apple   B. canned tomato
    C. fresh grapefruit   D. frozen orange

24. Ms. Wing's pregnancy progresses normally.   24.___
    In the latter part of the third trimester, Ms. Wing
    should be advised to take which of these precautions
    relative to bathing?
    A. Take sponge baths exclusively
    B. Avoid using bath salts
    C. Bathe only in tepid water
    D. Place nonskid material at the bottom of the bathtub

25. Ms. Wing is at term and in early active labor when she   25.___
    is brought to the hospital by her husband. Mr. and Ms.
    Wing attended a series of preparation for childbirth
    classes.
    Such a program is MOST likely to be successful if the
    A. parents and the medical and nursing staff have
       accepted the philosophy, principles, and techniques
       of the classes
    B. physician is present during labor and gives support
       to the mother
    C. nurse who is to stay with the mother during labor
       and delivery is prepared to assist the father in
       coaching his wife
    D. mother and father are truly prepared for their roles
       during labor and delivery

26. The nurse makes all of the following observations of Ms.   26.___
    Wing during the second stage of her labor.
    Which one would be of GREATEST significance in terms of
    her welfare and that of her baby?
    A(n)
    A. sudden increase in blood-tinged show
    B. change in the baseline blood pressure from 110/80
       to 90/60

C. fetal heart rate of 152 to 160 beats per minute between contractions

D. increase in maternal pulse rate from 90 to 95 beats per minute during contractions

27. Ms. Wing has an episiotomy and delivers a girl weighing 7 lb. 5 oz. (3,317 gm.).
Which of these observations of Ms. Wing would indicate that normal placental separation is occurring?
She has

    A. hardening and thickening of the exposed portion of the umbilical cord, softening of the uterine fundus, and a steady stream of blood from the vagina

    B. strong uterine contractions, recession of the uterine fundus below the symphysis pubis, and temporary absence of vaginal bleeding

    C. gaping of the vulva in conjunction with strong uterine contractions, rapid enlargement of the uterus, and oozing of blood from the vagina

    D. increased protrusion of the umbilical cord from the vagina, the uterus' becoming globular-shaped, and a sudden spurting of blood from the vagina

    27.__

28. Ms. Wing is transferred to the postpartum unit, and Baby Girl Wing is transferred to the newborn nursery.
In examining Ms. Wing's episiotomy incision, which of these positions would be appropriate for the patient and would BEST help to minimize strain on the sutures?

    A. Prone   B. Knee-chest

    C. Sim's   D. Trendelenburg

    28.__

29. Which of these measures, if carried out before Baby Girl Wing's discharge, will PROBABLY contribute to Ms. Wing's confidence in her ability to care for her baby?

    A. Having Ms. Wing observe demonstrations of infant care in which equipment commonly found in the home is used

    B. Having Ms. Wing take care of the baby in the hospital under the guidance of the registered nurse

    C. Arranging for Mr. Wing to learn how to assist Ms. Wing with caring for the baby

    D. Arranging to have the community health nurse visit with Ms. Wing and discuss areas that are of concern to Ms. Wing

    29.__

30. Mr. and Ms. Wing discuss birth control with the nurse.
In selecting a method of birth control, the Wings should give priority to

    A. Ms. Wing's age

    B. the length of their marriage

    C. the technique they find most acceptable

    D. the success rate of a particular method

    30.__

KEY (CORRECT ANSWERS)

1. D	11. B	21. D
2. D	12. C	22. A
3. B	13. D	23. A
4. A	14. C	24. D
5. C	15. C	25. A
6. B	16. D	26. B
7. B	17. C	27. D
8. A	18. C	28. C
9. B	19. B	29. B
10. B	20. D	30. C

GLOSSARY OF MEDICAL TERMS (EYE, EAR, NOSE AND THROAT)

CONTENTS

GLOSSARY OF MEDICAL TERMS (EYE, EAR, NOSE AND THROAT)

<u>A</u>

ABDUCT
  To draw away from the median line. When the vocal cords abduct, they separate.

ACCELERATION
  A quickening or speeding up.

ACOUSTIC
  As pertaining to sound or to the sense of hearing.

ACUTE
  Having a short and relatively severe course.

ADDUCT
  To move towards the median. When the vocal cords adduct, they come together.

ADENOIDITIS
  Inflammation of the adenoid tissue in the nasopharynx.

ALLERGEN
  The material responsible for an allergic reaction.

AMPLIFY
  The process of making larger or louder, as the increase of an auditory stimulus.

ANATOMY
  The science of the structure of the body and the relation of its parts.

ANGINA
  A severe pain.

ANGULAR
  Sharply bent; having corners or angles.

ANTIBIOTIC
  A chemical substance which has the capacity to inhibit the growth of or destroy bacteria and other microorganisms.

ANTIHISTAMINE
  Any of several drugs used to minimize an allergic reaction.

ANTISEPTIC
  A substance that will inhibit the growth and development of micro-organisms.

ASCENT
  A rising up. The amount of upward slope or elevation.

ASEPTIC
  Not septic. Free from infectious material.

ASPIRATION
  The removal of fluids or debris from a cavity by means of an aspirator.

ASTHMA
  A disease marked by recurrent attacks of difficult breathing.

ATMOSPHERIC PRESSURE
  The pressure due to the weight of the earth's atmosphere, equal at sea level to about 14.7 pounds per square inch.

AUDIOMETER
  Device for testing the power of hearing.

AUDITORY CORTEX
   The sensory area of hearing located in the temporal lobe of the
   brain.
AURICLE
   That portion of the external ear not contained within the head.
AUTOCLAVE
   An apparatus for effecting sterilization by steam under pressure.

<u>B</u>

BACTERIA
   A loosely used generic name for any microorganism of the order
   Eubacteriales.
BACTERIAL
   Pertaining to or caused by bacteria.
BAROTRAUMA
   Injury caused by pressure, such as injury to the middle ear or
   sinus cavity due to difference in pressure between the atmosphere
   and the inside of the cavity.
BENIGN
   Not malignant.
BIFID
   Clefts into two parts or branches.
BILATERAL
   Having two sides or pertaining to two layers.

<u>C</u>

CANNULATION
   The insertion of a cannula into a hollow organ or body cavity.
CAUTERIZE
   To burn with a hot instrument or with a caustic substance so as
   to destroy tissue or prevent the spread of infection.
CELLULITIS
   Infection or inflammation of the loose subcutaneous tissue.
CENTIMETER
   A unit of measurement in the metric system. Being equal to
   0.3937 inch.
CEREBRAL SPINAL FLUID
   A clear fluid contained within the cavities of and surrounding the
   brain and spinal cord.
CERUMEN
   The wax-like secretion found within the external auditory canal.
CHONDROMA
   A benign tumor of cartilage.
CHRONIC
   Persisting over a long period of time.
COMMINUTION
   Broken into small fragments.
COMPLAINT
   The symptom or group of symptoms about which the patient consults
   the physician.

COMPRESSION
  The act of pressing together to diminish volume and increase
  density.
CONCOMITANT
  Accompanying or joined with another.
CONGENITAL
  Existing at or before birth.
CULTURE
  The propagation of microorganisms in a special media.
CURRETAGE
  To remove by scraping.
CYCLES PER SECOND
  In audiology, the number of sound waves passing a point per second.
CYST
  A sac which contains a liquid or semisolid material.

D

DECAY
  The process of stage of decline. The decomposition of dead organic
  matter.
DECONGESTANT
  A drug which reduces congestion or swelling.
DEMARKATION
  Any dividing line apparent on the surface of the body, such as the
  boundary between normal and infected tissue.
DERMATITIS
  Inflammation of the skin.
DESCENT
  A coming down, going down, or downward motion.
DIPLOPIA
  Double vision.
DISCRIMINATION
  The ability to make or to perceive distinctions.

E

EDEMA
  The presence of abnormally large amounts of fluid in the inter-
  cellular tissue spaces of the body.
ENDOLYMPH
  The fluid contained in the membranous labyrinth of the ear.
ENOPHTHALMUS
  Abnormal retraction of the eye into the orbit.
ENTITY
  An independently existing thing; a reality.
EPISTAXIS
  Nose bleed or hemorrhage from the nose.
EPITHELIUM
  The covering of the internal and external surfaces of the body.

EQUILIBRIUM
A state of balance. A condition in which opposing forces exactly counteract each other.

ERYTHEMA
A name applied to redness of the skin produced by congestion of the capillaries. This may result in a variety of causes such as infection and trauma.

EUSTACHIAN TUBE
A slender tube between the middle ear and the pharynx which serves to equalize air pressure on both sides of the ear drum. Named after Bartolommeo Eustachio, an Italian anatomist.

EVACUATE
To make empty; to remove the contents.

EXACERBATION
An increase or recurrence in the severity of any symptom or disease.

EXCISION
An act of removing by cutting away.

EXOSTOSIS
An abnormal bony protuberance.

EXTRINSIC
Coming from or originating outside the organ or limb where found.

EXUDATE
Material such as fluid, cells, or cellular debris which has been deposited in or on tissue surfaces. This usually is the result of inflammation.

F

FIBROUS
Composed of or containing fibers.

FILAMENTOUS
Long, thread-like structures.

FIXATION
The act of holding, suturing, or fastening in a fixed position. Direction of a gaze so that the image of the object looked at falls on the fovea centralis.

FORAMEN
A natural opening or passage, especially a passage into or through a bone.

FREQUENCY
The number of vibrations made by a particle or ray per unit of time.

FUNCTIONAL HEARING LOSS
Hearing loss without an organic basis, such as malingering or psychological.

FUNGUS
A class of vegetable organisms of a low order of development which includes molds, mushrooms, and toadstools.

FURUNCLE
A painful nodule formed in the skin by bacteria which enter into the hair follicles causing a localized infection.

G

GUSTATORY
  Pertaining to the sense of taste.

H

HEMATOMA
  A swelling containing blood.
HERTZ
  The international unit of frequency, equal to one cycle per second.
HIVES
  An allergic skin condition characterized by itching, burning, and
  stinging during the formation of a red papular rash.
HYPERACTIVE
  Abnormally increased activity.
HYPEREMIA
  Redness of a part due to engorgement of blood vessels.
HYPERTENSION
  Abnormally high blood pressure.
HYPERTROPHIC
  The enlargement or overgrowth of an organ due to an increase in
  size of its cells.
HYPERVENTILATION
  Abnormally rapid and deep breathing.
HYPOACTIVE
  Abnormally diminished activity.
HYSTERIA
  A psychoneurosis characterized by lack of control of emotions.

I

IMPREGNATE
  To saturate one material with another, such as to saturate gauze
  with an ointment.
INBIBITION
  The absorption of a liquid.
INCISION
  A cut or a wound produced by cutting.
INFECTION
  Invasion of the body by pathogenic microorganisms and the reaction
  of the tissue to their presence and to the toxins generated by
  the microorganisms.
INFLAMMATION
  The condition into which tissues enter as a reaction to injury or
  infection. It is characterized by pain, heat, redness, and
  swelling of the area.
INTRINSIC
  Situated entirely within or pertaining exclusively to a part.

L

LACERATION
   A wound made by tearing.

LARYNGITIS
   Inflammation of the larynx.

LARYNGOPHARYNX
   That portion of the pharynx lying between the upper edge of the epiglottis and the vocal cords.

LATENT
   Concealed or not yet manifest.

LATERAL
   The position of a part further from midline than another part of the same side.

LESION
   A pathologic or traumatic lack of continuity of tissue or loss of function of a part.

LEUKEMIA
   A fatal disease of the blood-forming organs characterized by a marked increase in the number of white blood cells.

LINEAR
   Pertaining to or resembling a line. Linear acceleration means acceleration in a straight line.

M

MALAISE
   A vague feeling of discomfort.

MALIGNANT
   As applied to tumors, malignant means the tendency to invade surrounding structures and the ability to spread to other parts of the body by way of the bloodstream or lymphatic channels.

MALINGERING
   The faking or exaggeration of symptoms of an illness or injury.

MALOCCLUSION
   The lack of occlusion between the maxillary and mandibular teeth which interferes with mastication.

MANIFEST
   Something which is readily evident or clear to the sight or mind.

MARSUPIALIZATION
   An operation which removes a portion of a cyst, abscess, or tumor, empties its contents, and sutures its edges to the line of incision.

MASTICATION
   The chewing of food.

MEMBRANE
   A layer of tissue which covers the surface or divides a space or organ.

MENINGITIS
   An inflammation or infection of the meningeal covering of the brain.

MICRON
   A unit of measurement equal to 1/1000th of a millimeter.

MILLIMETER
   A unit of measurement equaling 1/1000th of a meter or 0.03937 inch.

MOLECULAR
  Pertaining to molecules or a chemical combination of two or more
  atoms.
MORBIDITY
  The condition of being diseased or sick.
MORTALITY
  Death.
MUCOSA
  The mucous membrane covering a surface such as the membrane cover-
  ing the surface of the palate or tongue.
MYRINGITIS
  Inflammation of the tympanic membrane.
MYRINGOTOMY
  An incision through the tympanic membrane.
MYRINGOPLASTY
  The surgical repair of a perforation in the tympanic membrane.

<u>N</u>

NECROSIS
  The death of a tissue or a part.
NEOPLASM
  Any new growth or tumor. It may be either a benign or malignant
  process.
NYSTAGMUS
  An involuntary rapid movement of the eyeball which may be horizon-
  tal, vertical, or rotary.

<u>O</u>

OBJECTIVE
  Pertaining to things which are perceptible to the senses.
OCCLUSION
  The relationship of the maxillary and mandibular teeth when in
  functional contact.
OINTMENT
  A semisolid preparation for external application to the body.
OLFACTION
  The sense of smell or the act of smelling.
OMINOUS
  Serving as an omen, or having a character of an evil omen.
OPEN REDUCTION
  Reduction of a fracture after exposing the fracture by an incision.
ORGANISM
  A body of living material. It may be a single cell, plant, or
  animal.
ORIFICE
  The entrance or outlet of any body cavity.
OSSEOUS
  Bone or bony.
OSTEOMYELITIS
  Inflammation or infection of bone.

OTOLARYNGOLOGIST
A physician who has specialized in the surgical and medical treatment of diseases of the ear, nose, and throat.

OTORRHEA
A discharge from the ear.

OTOTOXIC
Pertaining to something which is toxic to the ear. Specifically, certain drugs destroy the minute sensory cells of the inner ear.

P

PARENTERAL
Refers to medicine given by the subcutaneous, intramuscular, or intravenous route.

PARESIS
Slight or incomplete paralysis.

PATENT
Open, unobstructed.

PATHOGENIC
Refers to an organism or substance capable of causing disease.

PEDIATRIC
That branch of medicine which treats children.

PERCEPTION
The awareness of objects or other data through the medium of the senses.

PERFORATE
To pierce with holes.

PERIPHERY
Away from center. Example: The finger is peripheral to the elbow.

PETROUS
Resembling a rock. The petrous bone is so-called because of its hardness.

PHARYNGITIS
Inflammation of the pharynx.

PHARYNX
The tube between the posterior portion of the mouth and nose above, and the trachea and esophagus below.

PRACTITIONER
An authorized practitioner of medicine.

PHYSIOLOGY
The science or study of the function of living organisms.

PITCH
The quality of sound dependent upon the frequency of vibration.

PNEUMATIZATION
The formation of air-filled cells or cavities in tissues. Especially such formation in the temporal bone.

PROPAGATE
To reproduce, multiply, or spread.

PROPHYLACTIC
An agent that tends to ward off disease.

PSYCHIATRIC
That branch of medicine which deals with disorders of the human mind.

PULMONARY
  Pertaining to the lungs.
PURULENT
  Consists of or contains pus.

Q

QUALITATIVE
  Having to do with the quality of something.
QUANTITATIVE
  Having to do with the quantity of something, capable of being
  measured.

R

RAPPORT
  A close or sympathetic relationship.
RAREFACTION
  The condition of being or becoming less dense.
REVOLUTION
  A turning or spinning motion of a body or thing around a center
  axis.
RHINORRHEA
  The discharge of material from the nose.
RHINOSCOPY
  The examination of the nasal passages.
ROENTGENOGRAM
  The film produced by x-ray.

S

SALINE
  A solution of salt and water.
SALPINGITIS
  Inflammation of a tube. For example: eustachian salpingitis.
SAPROPHYTE
  An organism that lives on dead or decaying organic matter.
SEBACEOUS GLANDS
  Glands which secrete a greasy lubricating substance.
SEPTOPLASTY
  An operation to straighten the nasoseptum.
SEROUS
  Material which resembles blood serum.
SIMPLE FRACTURE
  A fracture of bone in which the bone does not protrude through
  the skin.
SPECULUM
  An appliance used to view a passage or cavity in the body.
  Examples include nasal and ear speculums.

SPHINCTER
A ring-like band of muscle fibers that constrict a passage or close a natural orifice.

SPONDEE
Two heavily accented syllables.

SPONTANEOUS
Occurring without external influence. Such as the spontaneous recovery from an illness.

STAPEDECTOMY
An operation which includes the removal of the stapes and its footplate, and placement of some form of prosthesis, such as wire, to take the place of the stapes.

STEROID
A group of compounds that resemble cholesterol. For the most part, these drugs are used for their anti-inflammatory effect. Cortisone is the best known example of this group of medications.

STIMULUS
Any agent, act, or influence that produces a reaction in the receptor.

STOMATITIS
Inflammation of the oral mucosa.

STRIDOR
The wheezing noise present on inspiration or expiration when partial obstruction of the larynx is present.

SUBCUTANEOUS
Situated or occurring beneath the skin.

SUBEPITHELIAL
Situated beneath the epithelium.

SUBJECTIVE
Pertaining to or perceived only by the affected individual.

SUBMUCOUS RESECTION
Excision of the cartilage of the nasoseptum.

SUPINE
The position assumed when lying on the back.

SYMPTOM
Any change in a patient's condition indicative of some bodily or mental state.

SYSTEMIC
Pertaining to or affecting the body as a whole.

T

THERMAL
Pertaining to, characterized by heat.

THRESHOLD
That value at which a stimulus minimally produces a sensation.

TINNITUS
A buzzing or ringing noise in the ears.

TRANSUDATE
A fluid substance which has passed through a membrane or has been extruded from a tissue as a result of inflammation.

TRAUMA
A wound or injury.

TRISMUS
Difficulty in opening the mouth due to mascular spasms, pain, or disturbance of the 5th cranial nerve.

TUMOR
Any swelling. It may indicate either inflammation, infection, or neoplasm.

TYMPANOPLASTY
Surgical reconstruction of the hearing mechanism of the middle ear.

U

UNILATERAL
Affecting one side only.

V

VENEREAL
Due to or propagated by sexual intercourse.

VERTIGO
A hallucination of movement. A sensation as if the external environment is revolving around the patient, or as if the patient were revolving in space.

VESICULATION
Small circumscribed elevations of epithelium containing a serous liquid.

VIRUS
One of a group of minute infectious agents which are too small to be seen under a microscope.

VOCALIZATION
The act of making a sound through the mouth.

ANSWER SHEET

TEST NO. _____ PART _____ TITLE OF POSITION _____

(AS GIVEN IN EXAMINATION ANNOUNCEMENT - INCLUDE OPTION, IF ANY)

PLACE OF EXAMINATION _____ DATE _____

(CITY OR TOWN)　　　　　　　　　　　(STATE)

RATING

USE THE SPECIAL PENCIL.　MAKE GLOSSY BLACK MARKS.

	A B C D E		A B C D E		A B C D E		A B C D E		A B C D E
1		26		51		76		101	
2		27		52		77		102	
3		28		53		78		103	
4		29		54		79		104	
5		30		55		80		105	
6		31		56		81		106	
7		32		57		82		107	
8		33		58		83		108	
9		34		59		84		109	
10		35		60		85		110	

Make only ONE mark for each answer.　Additional and stray marks may be
counted as mistakes.　In making corrections, erase errors COMPLETELY.

	A B C D E		A B C D E		A B C D E		A B C D E		A B C D E
11		36		61		86		111	
12		37		62		87		112	
13		38		63		88		113	
14		39		64		89		114	
15		40		65		90		115	
16		41		66		91		116	
17		42		67		92		117	
18		43		68		93		118	
19		44		69		94		119	
20		45		70		95		120	
21		46		71		96		121	
22		47		72		97		122	
23		48		73		98		123	
24		49		74		99		124	
25		50		75		100		125	

ANSWER SHEET

USE THE SPECIAL PENCIL. MAKE GLOSSY BLACK MARKS.

Make only ONE mark for each answer. Additional and stray marks may be counted as mistakes. In making corrections, erase errors COMPLETELY.